# GAMES OF DISCONTENT

## McGill-Queen's Studies in Protest, Power, and Resistance

Series editor: Sarah Marsden

Protest, civil resistance, and political violence have rarely been more visible. Nor have they ever involved such a complex web of identities, geographies, and ideologies. This series expands the theoretical and empirical boundaries of research on political conflict to examine the origins, cultures, and practices of resistance. From grassroots activists and those engaged in everyday forms of resistance to social movements to violent militant networks, it considers the full range of actors and the strategies they use to provoke change. The series provides a forum for interdisciplinary work that engages with politics, sociology, anthropology, history, psychology, religious studies, and philosophy. Its ambition is to deepen understanding of the systems of power people encounter and the creative, violent, peaceful, extraordinary, and everyday ways they try to resist, subvert, and overthrow them.

# Games of Discontent

Protests, Boycotts, and Politics at the
1968 Mexico Olympics

HARRY BLUTSTEIN

McGill-Queen's University Press
Montreal & Kingston • London • Chicago

© Harry Blutstein 2021

ISBN 978-0-2280-0675-6 (cloth)
ISBN 978-0-2280-0693-0 (ePDF)
ISBN 978-0-2280-0694-7 (ePUB)

Legal deposit second quarter 2021
Bibliothèque nationale du Québec

Printed in Canada on acid-free paper that is 100% ancient forest free
(100% post-consumer recycled), processed chlorine free

---

Library and Archives Canada Cataloguing in Publication

Title: Games of discontent : protests, boycotts, and politics at the 1968
    Mexico Olympics / Harry Blutstein.
Names: Blutstein, Harry, author.
Description: Includes bibliographical references and index.
Identifiers: Canadiana (print) 20200412973 | Canadiana (ebook)
    20200412981 | ISBN 9780228006756 (hardcover) | ISBN
    9780228006930 (PDF) | ISBN 9780228006947 (EPUB)
Subjects: LCSH: Olympic Games (19th : 1968 : Mexico City, Mexico)
    | LCSH: Olympics—Political aspects.
Classification: LCC GV722.1968 B58 2021 | DDC 796.48—dc23

---

This book was typeset in 10.5/13 New Baskerville ITC Pro.

To Carol Lawson

# Contents

# Figures

# Acknowledgments

While writing is a solitary profession, during the gestation of this book I did not lack human contact: I conducted more than a hundred interviews. I would therefore like to start by thanking the many former athletes, journalists, and officials who were in Mexico City for the 1968 Olympic Games who so generously gave up their time to speak with me about their memories and share some delightful stories. I have kept in touch with a few of them, and I would like to particularly thank Marjorie Margolies, Paul Hoffman, Art Simburg, Dick Bank, and Linda Evans, all of whom have taken my calls when I wanted to check a detail or when I've asked them to add to anecdotes they had shared with me.

Tracking down athletes I wanted to interview was at times difficult, so many thanks to the people who put me in touch with athletes and officials: Tom Lough, John Bell, Maria Cabeliza, and Leon Wiegard. Urla Hill also helped with contacts, and I appreciated her insights into what it was – and still is – like to be an African American female athlete. Even after we've known one another for over six months, she still insists on calling me 'Dr Blutstein', much to my chagrin.

I would like to acknowledge the kindness of the strangers, both academics and individuals, who helped me ferret out hard-to-find books, documents, unpublished dissertations, photographs, and newspapers from archives and libraries. They include Allyson Houlihan (Worcester State University), Anthea Nadalet (Zimbabwe), Enrique Labadie (Tucson, Arizona), Claudia Pinto and her daughter Elizabeth (who tracked down a difficult-to-find book, the only copy of which was in Brazil), Svetlana Chervonnaya (Moscow), Carlien Scholtz (University of the Free State), Chris de Broglio, David Austin (Quebec), David Goldberg (Wayne State University), Estevão

Mabjaia (Mozambique), Evelyn Floret (New York), Francois Cleo-
phas (Stellenbosch University), Hermine Roby Klinger (Ann Arbor,
Michigan), Jan C. Rode (Hamburg), John B. Gilmour (College of
William & Mary), Kai Mishuris (Detroit, Michigan), Katherine Diane
Majewski (University of Illinois at Urbana-Champaign), Horta Van
Hoye (Belgium), Noel Cary (Worcester, Massachusetts), Noor Nief-
tagodien (Wits University), Patrick Bond (University of the Western
Cape), Sheelagh Halstead (Zimbabwe), Thomas Sekelez (Czech Re-
public), Tina Klauž (Institute for the Study of Totalitarian Regimes,
Prague), Vic Mackenzie (Zimbabwe), and Yoav Veichselfish (Israel).

I'm particularly grateful to Stewart Russell, who provided me with
a copy of the audio of a rare interview he conducted with Peter Norman; to Anthea Nadalet for sending me a large cache of cuttings
from Zimbabwe; and to Margaret Cheffers for sending through
photographs of sport in Rhodesia.

Access to a good academic library is essential to an independent
researcher and I would like to extend my appreciation to the University of Melbourne for appointing me a Research Fellow. Without
this support, the book would simply not have happened.

While they were anonymous, I was lucky to have three excellent
reviewers, whose perceptive comments led me to improve the book.
I thank Richard Baggaley from McGill-Queen's University Press for
helping shepherd me through the publication process, and Sam
Clark at T&T Productions Ltd for his eagle-eye and empathetic editing of the manuscript.

I was very lucky to have generous friends read drafts, and I appreciate the feedback they gave me. They are Sally Bouvier, Heather
Dunn, Peter Duras, Larry Shore, Jim Wilson, and Pamela Elligate.
I am particularly indebted to Jean Roberts, whose attention to the
finer points of grammar was invaluable, as was her knowledge of
both athletics and the Mexico Olympics, which she attended as a
competitor. I owe her a bottle of fine champagne when we meet.

Having little talent for foreign languages, I appreciated the assistance of Lenka Nemeckova, who translated great swathes of Czech,
and I also thank Valeria Xochiatzin Tapia, Charles Gireth, and Mel-
anie Cobham for their help on Spanish texts.

Writing a book is a marathon, and I appreciate the encouragement
and support of friends – too many to mention – and, importantly,
many hugs from Charlotte and Millie. I hope they never get too old
to lavish affection on their Uncle Harry.

Finally, to my favourite wife, Carol Lawson, thank you for being there. No words I can say will tell you how much I have appreciated your love, support, and encouragement all the way through. Thanks for the cups of tea and the raisin toast when I was flagging after a long morning; for the long walks during which I bounced ideas off you; and for allaying my doubts when it seemed the book would never get done. Not only have you patiently reviewed draft after draft, (thankfully) with brutal honesty, but you've also kept an eye on me to ensure that I didn't get distracted by too many cat videos on YouTube. You've had to endure my obsession with all things Olympics for the last five years – not your favourite topic – and I know you dearly hope that I move on to something different. I will. I promise.

# Author's Note

This book addresses racism in the 1960s, and the words used to describe racial groups are charged with meaning that is different from how we understand racial terms today.

During the 1960s, the term 'African American' was not in common usage,[1] and various terms were used, including ones that today, as they were then, are considered vile and unacceptable.

In South Africa, race was legally defined under apartheid laws: specifically the Population Registration Act of 1950. All South Africans were classified as either 'Bantu' (black Africans), 'Coloured' (those of mixed race), or 'White'. For a while, Asians were classified as Coloured, but they were later given their own category. Particular opprobrium was cast on Coloureds because, according to the philosophic underpinning of apartheid, 'racial mixing was an evil thing, bringing biological, moral, and social pollution'.[2]

During the 1960s, then, the South Africans mentioned in this book would have generally used the words 'Coloured', 'Black', and 'White' to describe themselves, and therefore so have I.

I've chosen not to impose twenty-first-century sensibilities on the language used when referring to ethnicity, as my intention is to provide a feel for the times, including the language used.

Direct quotes have not been censored. I respect my reader too much to abridge words, such as using 'n—', when quoting. Also, when presenting the point of view of characters, I will use terms they would have used at the time.

GAMES OF DISCONTENT

# Introduction

The whole world is watching.

Protest chant at the 1968 US Democratic Convention

Oh! I have slipped the surly bonds of Earth
And danced the skies on laughter-silvered wings

John Gillespie Magee, *High Flight*

The sixties receded into haze and myth: lingering images of nobility and violence.

Todd Gitlin, *The Sixties*

On 16 October 1968, after a busy day of athletics in the Estadio Olímpico Universitario, evening had fallen and not much was happening.

The last race, the final of the men's 200 metres, had just been run. Taking the gold and bronze medals were two African Americans: Tommie 'Jet Gear' Smith and John Carlos. Peter Norman, an Australian, won the silver medal. After the race the three medallists had retired to the Athletes' Lounge under the stadium and would reappear 50 minutes later to receive their medals.

Roone Arledge, president of ABC Sports, was sitting in the control room and had watched the race with even greater intensity than usual. Before the Games, Smith and Carlos had been identified by the media as being among the discontents who threatened to protest during the Olympics. There was no protest immediately after the race, which allowed Arledge to relax a little.

Arledge had been the driving force at ABC to win the North American television rights to the Mexico Olympic Games and he was determined to put on a sporting spectacle to be remembered. He knew that sports fans would not welcome the intrusion of politics.

With little happening in the main stadium, Arledge's eyes flicked across the twenty-five screens receiving feeds from the Olympic venues. Highly strung, a maestro of the medium, he barked out instructions: 'Punch up one, dammit!', 'My god, we've blown a commercial', or he called for a 'honey shot' in which the camera zoomed in for a close-up of an attractive young woman in the stands.[1] He was determined to deliver a programme of compelling images, excitement, and drama that would do justice to the majesty of the Olympics.

Arledge had persuaded ABC to bid high for the North American rights, US$4.5 million (equivalent to US$33 million in 2020), so there was a lot at stake. ABC was keen to outshine the coverage of the Tokyo Olympics four years earlier by NBC. Because of the time difference, Americans only saw live feeds of those Games in 15-minute snatches, late at night. By comparison, even where the time difference was not a problem, live coverage elsewhere in the world was patchy.

In 1967, for the first time, an array of geostationary satellites allowed all parts of the Earth to be covered. As a result, ABC was able to show 44 hours live, much of it in prime time. And it wasn't just ABC: the Australian Broadcasting Commission, the European Broadcasting Union, the Japanese Broadcasting Corporation (NHK), and Intervision (Eastern Europe and Soviet Union) were now able to televise the Games live too. ABC was by far the largest network present in Mexico and its footage was distributed to other networks that lacked its coverage. Through this technology, the Mexico Olympics were seen by an estimated audience of around 600 million,[2] the largest TV audience for any event, not just sport, up to that date.[3]

The Olympics attracts such a large viewership because, as a sporting event, it 'crosses language barriers and slices through national boundaries, attracting both spectators and participants to a common lingua franca of passions, obsessions and desires,' explained social scientist, Toby Miller.[4] And so, for sixteen days in October, Mexico City was turned into a truly global media space; a first.

The 200 metres sprint was popular because the media liked to hail the winner as one of the fastest men on Earth, and therefore it was well covered. Instead of waiting to watch the medal ceremony, which usually doesn't make for compelling viewing, almost all the television crews headed to the Magdalena Mixhuca Sports City complex where the basketball and fencing events were being held. ABC, being the largest network, left one crew at the Estadio Olímpico Universitario.

As dusk fell and the lights were turned on, the three place-getters returned to the stadium to receive their medals. Smith and Carlos approached the victory podium in stocking feet. Each wore a single black glove and on their warm-up jackets they had pinned white and green protest buttons, 'Olympic Project for Human Rights', as had Peter Norman. 'Get in there. This is Black Power!', yelled Arledge to his camera crew that was still in the stadium.[5]

As his crew rushed over, four photographers were already at work. They were John Dominis from *Life* magazine, Neil Leifer from *Sports Illustrated*, Angelo Cozzi from the Italian agency Moroldo Portfolio, and a photographer from Associated Press, whose name we do not know.

As each athlete's name was called, he stepped onto the podium and bent his head down so that the Marquess of Exeter could drape a medal around his neck before shaking his hand. Next, there was an announcement over the public address system that the American national anthem was about to play to honour the gold medallist. The three men turned to their right and stood to attention, facing the flags of their countries.

As the first bars of 'The Star-Spangled Banner' reverberated around the stadium, Tommie Smith raised his right fist into the air, the one on which he was wearing a black glove. An instant later, John Carlos raised his left fist; it too was gloved. They stayed in that position, heads bowed, for 72 seconds, until the music stopped.[6]

For Smith and Carlos, the presence of cameras was important. They had carefully choreographed a performance calculated to be photographed, filmed, and reported on by the international media. As far as they knew, no athlete had ever protested on the playing field, so Smith and Carlos had no idea what impact their protest would have. It was very much a leap into the dark.

The photographers witnessing the ceremony used motorised cameras to capture the protest, and the ABC's cameraman shot a few minutes of invaluable footage. Over the next 24 hours a global audience watched the protest live, on replay, or saw a photograph of the salute in their newspapers. With 4,377 representatives of the media in Mexico,[7] it soon became a global story.

Such was the success of their protest in attracting international attention, that the photograph of Smith and Carlos on the victory podium is the best remembered moment of the XIX Olympiad. With a few notable exceptions, the records broken and the sporting heroics have been forgotten.

Nor are the Games remembered as a festival of peace, despite the best efforts of the Mexican organisers who, on every main thoroughfare, displayed pastel-coloured banners featuring a white dove. Instead, news that soldiers had massacred students at a rally in Tlatelolco, twenty kilometres north of the Estadio Olímpico Universitario, ten days before the opening ceremony, left a dark shadow over the Olympics, as did other protests and political campaigns associated with them. *Games of Discontent* describes these events as well as the grievances that led activists to target the Olympics.

The demonstration by Smith and Carlos was undoubtedly one of the quietest moments in 1968, which writer Paul Auster described as 'the year of craziness, the year of fire, blood and death'.[8] Such was the power of the salute that Rod Ackermann, writing for the *Neue Zürcher Zeitung*, described it as 'emblematic of the revolutionary mood at the time'.[9]

Smith and Carlos's salute was part of a spate of protests for which 1968 is remembered, and activists who came of age during the 1960s are known as ''68ers',[10] named for the year in which global activism peaked.

Certainly 1968 was a busy year. There were noisy protest rallies, mass marches, sit-ins, and pitched battles between activists, police, and national guards around the world. In May 1968 street protests in Paris almost overthrew the De Gaulle government; in the US women demonstrated in Atlantic City, where the Miss America pageant was held; rallies were held in front of the Malacañang Palace in Manila; across Turkey students occupied university buildings; Australian high school kids circulated underground newspapers; and on every continent, and on both sides of the Iron Curtain, young people were taking to the streets.

According to John Saul, a former activist and now a political economist, '68ers possessed 'a distinctive and novel kind of radical and global consciousness'.[11] What drew them together was their shared mission of overturning the existing order, although in particulars they differed. While there were few tangible connections between

'68ers in different countries, historian Timothy Scott Brown concluded that they formed transnational 'communities of affinity' that were connected indirectly through their consumption of the same books, the same music, and the same images.[12] So, possessing this global consciousness, it should not have come as a surprise that '68ers at the Olympics saw it as an opportunity to appeal to a global audience through their unprecedented access to the media.

However, as much as they would like to think otherwise, '68ers were defined by geography, and their activism was shaped by their local political, social, and cultural experiences. For this reason, almost all academic and popular historians describe the protests and political demonstrations of 1968 as a series of geographically contained narratives. The protest by Smith and Carlos, the Tlatelolco massacre, and other protests staged during the Olympics are included as episodes in those seperate narrative streams. However, they have more in common than most historians credit.

Olympic protests deserve special attention because, for the first time, activists had the opportunity to address a global audience directly through the mass media, as Mexico City had truly become a 'global village'.[13] There is another reason. Since its inception, the International Olympic Committee (IOC) had harboured a humanistic mission and aspired to be a moral movement with global reach. Up until 1968, the world's glimpses of the Olympics had been somewhat remote and static. The presence of television allowed the IOC to realise this ambition. Now it could promote its moral mission to the world.

What, then, are the global ambitions of the Olympic movement? The modern Olympic Games were inspired by humanistic internationalism that flowered in the late nineteenth century, which some have called the 'first wave of globalisation'.[14] According to sociologist Maurice Roche, the Olympics 'promote "one world" awareness, and the impacts of the globalising features of the Olympics on international society as a world of participating nations'.[15]

To organise the Games, Baron Pierre de Coubertin convened a meeting in 1894 at Sorbonne University in Paris. The participants decided to create the IOC, which was charged with reviving the Olympic Games.

The IOC was one of a number of non-governmental organisations that were intent on creating a secular global moral order. Examples of others are the Red Cross (1863), the Universala Esperanto-Asocio

(1908), the International Council of Women (1888), the Permanent International Peace Bureau (1891), the Nobel Prize (1895), and the Boy Scouts (1908).

As for its moral mandate, de Coubertin posited that the Games would be 'peculiar celebrations during which people of all religions, all tribes, all nations and all ranks can be unified with the others, during which it is revealed to them the deep sense of community above every kind of difference and border'.[16] The Olympic movement would provide a sanctuary in which internationalism would thrive when, during the Games, 'national sentiments must be ... suspended, so to speak sent on a temporary holiday'.[17] De Coubertin called his ideology 'Olympism', which he claimed would be 'a potent, if indirect, factor securing universal peace'.[18] Indirect, because it lacked political power. Instead, the movement promoted its ideology through education and moral suasion.

Olympism is showcased through friendly competition at sporting festivals held every four years in different host cities. For sixteen days, the stadiums, swimming pools, gymnasia, and playing fields of the host city are symbolically and ritually excised from their geographic locality and become a global commons.

Of the humanistic bodies that have been created since the late nineteenth century, the Olympic movement is singular in the way it has promoted internationalism. The characteristics that have made it remarkably unique are difficult to describe, although some have tried.

Clarence Bush, who attended the 1936 Berlin Olympics, claims that at those Games he witnessed 'a new sovereign state', whose boundaries extended 'to the limits of the arena, the Stadium, the Olympic Village and all the accessory fields and buildings' where contests are held. Within these boundaries was 'an international state, ruled over by the International Olympic Committee', whose supreme law was the Olympic statutes. According to Bush, it was not a 'make-believe or cardboard domain' but was 'actual and real, in effect superseding the regular civil, police and military power'.[19]

Less prosaically, Avery Brundage, the president of the IOC during the Mexico Olympic Games, described the Olympics as, 'a friendly oasis where correct human relations and concepts of moral order still prevail'.[20] Willi Daume, another member of the IOC, described the Olympic Games lyrically as the 'isle of the blessed'.[21] De Coubertin saw the Olympic Games as a 'sacred Fortress'.[22]

The dominant imagery that comes through in these descriptions is of a verdant patch of land in a barren landscape, or, in the case of de Coubertin, a consecrated sanctuary protected against a venal world.

It is in this global commons that spectators, whether in the stadium or watching on television, vicariously experience the emotion of the Olympic Games. They can delight in sublime athletic performances, revel in the heroics on the sporting field, and watch its spectacular ceremonies. Above all, spectators are transported to the global Olympic space – an oasis, an island (but not a cardboard domain), a 'sacred Fortress' – which leaves memories that stay with them until the next Olympiad, four years later. It provides a visceral engagement with globalisation, allowing the humanistic values of Olympism to percolate into the consciousness of spectators – or at least that is what de Coubertin and the other high priests of the Olympic movement hoped.

Olympic protests were therefore quite different, in that they were staged in an international space, one that was part of the 'global moral order',[23] making them worthy of study. There is no better example than the protest by Smith and Carlos. There is little in images of their protest to indicate where in the world they were. They were in a global commons, with the stadium surrounded by the flags of the participating countries: 112 in total. The symbol that dominated was the five Olympic rings, for the five continents, on flags and on the podium where Smith, Norman, and Carlos received their medals. The medal ceremony was the same as had been seen in the previous Olympics and those before, and its symbolism was replete with meaning. The only nod to the personality of the host nation was the three Mexican women in colourful national dress who brought out the medals on yellow pillows. The important task of handing out the medals was in the hands of Olympic officials.

*Games of Discontent* examines how '68ers used the Olympics to escape the tenacious bonds of geography and address a global audience by exploiting the confluence of the global media space carved out by television and the moral space created by the Olympic movement.

The book also tells the stories of the women who were among the discontents in Mexico, as their parts in the protests have largely been written out of the history of the Olympics. Their treatment was not unusual for the times, and female '68ers around the world had also been sidelined by their male confederates. While male '68ers railed against oppression, they were oblivious to the way they exploited women, whose 'roles ended up concentrating on food-making, typing, mimeographing, general assistance work and as a sexual supply for their male comrades after hours,' according to US feminist Anne Koedt.[24] Female '68ers who tried to speak up were frequently belittled, so it is not surprising that most kept quiet.

Women athletes also had good reason to complain about the institutional sexism they faced within the Olympic movement. From the very beginning of the modern Olympics, de Coubertin opposed the participation of female athletes. At the first Olympiad, held in Athens in 1896, only males competed. While women were allowed to compete in subsequent Olympiads, de Coubertin remained firmly against their participation, which he described as 'monstrous'.[25] Instead, the role of women should be to 'crown the [male] victors, as was the case in the ancient tournaments,' he argued.[26]

While such prejudices within the Olympic movement were less acute by 1968, women still faced significant discrimination and sexism. There were no women on the IOC and few on national Olympic committees, and in Mexico only 14 per cent of competitors were women. It would not be until 1981 that former athletes Flor Isava Fonseca of Venezuela and Pirjo Häggman of Finland became the first women elected to the IOC.

There were insults suffered by women at the Games too. The Australian Olympic Committee stoutly refused to appoint female coaches. As a result, triple gold medallist Shirley Strickland, who was amply qualified, attended the Mexico Olympics as an 'Assistant Manager'. The position had been called 'Chaperone' at the previous Olympics, so there was some cosmetic improvement in Strickland's job title, but not in her duties. These included 'preserving the girls' public image at all times', 'maintaining a code of behaviour', and 'organizing domestic facilities and arrangements'.[27]

Female '68ers at the Olympics were also passionate about issues such as racism, injustice, and inequality. However, it was the early days of feminism, and only a few female activists were sufficiently courageous to put their heads above the parapet to call out sexism and assert their role in protests. Their stories are told in *Games of Discontent*.

Finally, the epilogue looks at how Olympic protests evolved in the years that followed 1968, and, in the face of these challenges, how the Olympic movement struggled to maintain its commitment to the global moral order. This was further complicated by the demands of television networks and their advertisers, who had little time for the sacred mission of the Olympics: they just wanted a show that drew ratings. They were, after all, paying a lot of money for that show.

# 1

# Bidding for Olympic Glory

Perhaps some day the people of the world will conclude that the politicians have made a mess of it and will turn over their affairs to sportsmen to manage.

Avery Brundage

## PAX OLIMPICA

In December 1962 the IOC winnowed the field of cities allowed to bid to host the 1968 Olympic Games to four contenders: Detroit, Lyon, Mexico City, and Buenos Aires. Bids from Cairo, Lausanne, Manila, and Vienna were dismissed as being fatally flawed. Yet in early 1963, nine months before the vote, IOC president Avery Brundage was told about a fifth city that was thinking of submitting a late bid, one that was much more problematic, if not hopelessly impractical – yet it excited him.

More often remembered as a loud, bombastic, and uncompromising defender of the faith against athletes who dared defy the rules of the IOC, Brundage much preferred to be thought of as the propagator of the faith: Olympism. Among its important tenets was that the Olympic movement was an agent for peace. And should this fifth city win, it would be a glorious example of Pax Olimpica.

Brundage had been introduced to the term 'Pax Olimpica' by Reverend Robert de Courcy Laffan in 1912, during the opening ceremony for the Stockholm Olympics. In those Games, Brundage represented the US in the pentathlon and decathlon. A classical scholar, Laffan's inspiring sermon alluded to the ancient Greek origins of Pax Olimpica and contended that its traditions bequeathed to modern Olympism the splendid precepts of tolerance, mutual respect, and harmony.[1]

The Greek origins of Pax Olimpica are elusive. During Hellenic times there are references to *Ekecheiria*, a truce that operated for the period of the Olympic Games, during which armed conflict would cease, although historians have cast doubt on whether this actually took place.[2] Having had the Olympics interrupted by two world wars, the truce certainly had no currency in the twentieth century.

Since becoming IOC president, Brundage had found another way to promote Pax Olimpica. In what he described as 'my biggest Olympic success',[3] Brundage brought together the fierce Cold War enemies East Germany and West Germany. Between 1956 and 1964, athletes from these countries competed as one team. Their athletes marched as one behind a neutral flag, wore the same uniform, and had their victories marked by a rendition of Beethoven's *Ode to Joy* rather than by either country's national anthem. 'I must admit that we are pleased with ourselves with having reunited Germany at least in sport, a thing the politicians have been unable to do,' Brundage boasted.[4]

Behind the facade, in qualifiers between athletes to see who would be selected onto the united German team, relations were anything but cordial. For example, West German gymnast Kurt Friedrich was abused by spectators when he competed in East Germany, and East German gymnasts were pelted with eggs in West Germany.[5]

The future of the all-German team looked doomed when, on 13 August 1961, East Germany commenced construction of a barbed wire and concrete wall between the two halves of Berlin, sharply escalating Cold War tensions.

In retaliation, among other measures, West Germany severed sporting ties with the East.[6] In response, the head of Das Nationale Olympische Komitee (the East German Olympic Committee), Heinz Schöbel, told Brundage that the ban marked a 'unilateral disregard of IOC regulations'.[7] He was right; a core value of Olympism was that politics should not intrude into sport. Unconvincing in his defence of his government's policy, Willi Daume, the president of the West Germany Olympic committee, assured Brundage that it was a 'transitory measure'.[8]

Daume was uncomfortable, forced to act as an apologist for a government policy that he did not agree with. Having lived through the war, Daume threw himself into sports administration in 1947, believing that if it could be kept apolitical, the playfulness of sport could help ease the trauma left by the war. For this reason, he found the impasse between the two Germanys distressing. Rather than embracing the tolerance, respect, and camaraderie inherent in Olympism, politicians were playing out Cold War battles on sporting arenas. Worst of all, Daume was being drawn into their machinations.

The construction of the Wall threatened the demise of the all-German team. To salvage the facade of Pax Olimpica, Daume developed an audacious plan for East and West Berlin to jointly host the 1968 Olympics.

Bids could only be made by cities, so, on 21 January 1963, Daume phoned Willy Brandt, the mayor of West Berlin, and asked him whether he would support a joint bid. Daume's proposal struck a chord with Brandt, who, three months earlier, had delivered two lectures at Harvard University on 'Co-existence'. He outlined a new approach to dealing with Cold War tensions that would become known as 'Ostpolitik': a policy for normalising relations with East Germany. While not specifically mentioning sport, he said that West Germany should 'welcome projects of the kind that are conducted jointly by East and West'.[9]

The proposal Daume pitched to Brandt tried to anticipate and address the inevitable practical problems. The opening ceremony would be held in the stadium built for the 1936 Olympics; events would be distributed equitably between East and West Berlin; and a non-political organising committee would be in charge. Since 1952, the host city was expected to build an Olympic Village to accommodate athletes and officials. Daume knew that East Germany lacked the financial resources to build new accommodation so he recommended that the men would be housed in newly constructed dormitories in West Berlin, with the much smaller contingent of women staying in refurbished buildings in East Berlin. At the time there was a large disparity between West Germany's Deutschmark and East Germany's Ostmark, so Daume proposed that a special Olympic currency be created, as had been done in 1952 for the Helsinki Olympics. To placate the federal government in Bonn, who objected to anything that would identify East Germany as a sovereign nation, the only flag allowed to fly over the stadium during Olympic events would be the black, red, and gold German tricolour with the Olympic rings at their centre, rendered in white. And while the honour of opening the Games was usually given to the head of state, Daume suggested that Brundage open the Games to avoid a political fight.

The next day, after getting Brandt on board, Daume phoned Brundage and told him to expect a late bid from Berlin to host the 1968 Olympics.

Brundage was supportive, despite knowing that East Berlin had not yet been approached and that neither part of Berlin had the sporting venues or accommodation needed to stage the Olympics and would be hard pressed to build them in time. Why then did Brundage put aside these seemingly insurmountable problems and encourage the bid? If, by some miracle, Daume could pull such a bid off, Brundage could claim it as the crowning achievement of Pax Olimpica. 'This would really be sensational and might do more than Kennedy and Khrushchev, together, for the peace of the world,' Brundage claimed.[10] He was no longer the hard-nosed president of the IOC but a knight-errant pursuing an impossible dream, like his hero Don Quixote.

Brandt was conscious that time was running out to put in a formal bid to the IOC. So, rather than waiting to secure approval from West Berlin's Senate, which was in the middle of an election campaign,[11] on 30 January 1963 he referred the proposal to Bonn, where it was considered by the federal government.

Bonn was in a bind. A joint bid would confer de facto recognition of the German Democratic Republic, reversing a key plank of West Germany's foreign policy. However, rejecting the proposal would open West Germany up to criticism that it had turned its back on an opportunity to reduce Cold War tension in divided Berlin. Rather than make a decision, the federal government engaged in carefully calibrated procrastination, waiting until Brandt ran out of time to meet the IOC's deadline for bids.

Frustrated by this delaying tactic, on 27 March Brandt sent a letter to IOC Chancellor Otto Mayer in Lausanne formally asking for Berlin to be considered as the host city: 'I assume that the East Berlin authorities – after appropriate negotiations of the two German National Olympic Committees – will express its willingness [to participate].' Keeping in mind that Bonn had actively worked to stop East German athletes from competing in international events, Brandt provided the improbable assurance to Mayer that 'all participants and visitors to the Olympic Games will not be hindered entering Berlin (West)'.[12] Somewhat presumptuously, there had been no approach to East Berlin before he sent this letter.

With time running out and no response having been received from Bonn, Daume decided to force the issue. On 9 April Daume approached Schöbel, his East German counterpart, who in turn referred the proposal to the Politburo.

The Politburo met on 14 May and its members were in a quandary over how to respond to the joint Berlin bid. Was this a deliberate provocation? If the Politburo rejected the bid, would West Germany use it for propaganda? As the Olympics would require freedom of movement across the Wall, how could the communist government prevent East Germans from fleeing to the West? The Politburo knew it could not accept the proposal, so instead it devised unacceptable conditions that would force West Germany to abandon the bid. This would allow peace-loving East Germans to claim that they wanted to reduce tensions in Berlin by embracing the joint bid but were frustrated by the West. Among their demands was that, as East Germany claimed 'Westberlin' (as they knew it) as theirs, the bid should be sponsored solely by East Germany. The East Germans also demanded that, as host, First Secretary Walter Ulbricht would open the Games, that its flag would fly over the stadium, and that its anthem would be played during the opening ceremony.

While the bid was being considered by the governments of East and West Germany, on 21 May news of the plan leaked to the press. A week later, a cartoon by 'Oskar' in the *Berliner Morgenpost* depicted Brandt ready to kick a football over the Berlin Wall.[13] It was the sort of reception that would have gladdened Brundage. Here was the essence of Pax Olimpica, with the Games overcoming the political and physical barriers that the Berlin Wall represented. As Peter Bender commented in *Die Zeit*, 'Even if this plan is not realized, it will have been valuable – as a sign for the direction in which Berlin and Germany should go.'[14]

Significantly, on 22 May Brundage was quoted in the *New York Times* giving the bid his support: 'This would be a great triumph for amateur sports and the Olympic movement, and it would put political wrangling to shame.' He qualified his statement by explaining that the bid 'would be impossible to consider unless authorities in East Berlin back it up'.[15]

Now that the bid was out in the open, the IOC summoned representatives from the two German Olympic committees to Lausanne to see whether they could agree on a joint bid. Meetings were held on 29 May and 4 June. After the second meeting, Schöbel told Brundage that little progress had been made. So, when the IOC's Executive Board met on 6 June it rejected the bid 'because it was not accompanied by an equal invitation from East Berlin'.[16]

Unwilling to pass up a propaganda opportunity, the leading East German sports newspaper, *Deutsches Sportecho*, ran as its headline: 'Bonn thwarts 1968 Games in Berlin'.[17]

### AND THEN THERE WERE FOUR

When Berlin's bid fell away, the IOC was again left with a shortlist of four cities: Detroit, Lyon, Mexico City, and Buenos Aires. On 18 October 1963, at the Kurhaus, a hotel and casino in Baden-Baden, these four cities would have an opportunity to put their case before the IOC voted on which city would host the 1968 Olympic Games.

Eight months earlier, the head of the US Olympic Committee, Douglas Roby, told the *Los Angeles Times* that it 'looks more and more as if the United States is going to get the Games'.[18] *Sports Illustrated* agreed: 'This may be Detroit's best chance yet; for the first time the city has all its big wheels of government and industry backing the effort.'[19] Such was Detroit's confidence that they had booked a ballroom at the Kurhaus for a victory celebration.

Lyon was also confident: it had booked the other ballroom. 'We're going to win hands down. There is no question about that,' said Tony Bertrand, one of the architects of the French bid. 'We've got all that Detroit lists – and much more besides. Detroit hasn't got a hope.'[20]

However, the favourites' bids were flawed: Detroit did not have a major stadium, but had promised to build one; and the French government had not fully committed to help fund the Lyon Games.

While Detroit and Lyon touted their status as favourites and tried to paper over the holes in their bids, Mexico City revelled in being the underdog. Its main problem was that the Games had never been held in a developing country or at such high altitude.

Buenos Aires should have been ahead of Mexico City. It had hosted the Pan-American Games in 1951 and had only missed out on hosting the 1956 Olympic Games by a solitary vote. However, the country had been racked by political instability since those Games: there had been a successful military coup on 29 March 1962 and an unsuccessful revolt by elements within the navy, which lasted from

21 September 1962 to 5 April 1963. By the time the Argentinian Olympic organising committee arrived in Baden-Baden, they were resigned to losing and put in only a token effort.

On the eve of departing for Baden-Baden, Detroit's Olympic organising committee staged a torch relay to draw attention to its bid. The 4,060-kilometre (2,521-mile) torch relay symbolically started in Los Angeles, the nation's previous Olympic host city, crossing Route 66 and I-94 before ending up in front of the Spirit of Detroit statue on 11 October 1963.

Three days before the torch arrived at its destination, civil rights leader Abraham Ulmer Jr wrote an open letter protesting the lack of support from Detroit City Council to end housing discrimination: 'If the white community can dictate and say to the Negro, no housing freedom, then the Negro can tell the world no Olympics for Detroit yet.'[21]

Activists had protested before on this issue with little effect. When they heard about the torch relay they saw a new way to draw attention to housing discrimination. Securing the Olympics was important for US prestige, and if their protest could cruel the bid, it would embarrass white America over its treatment of African Americans. This was an early example of discontents using their disruption of an Olympic event to amplify their protest, knowing the national media would cover it and that they might even attract attention from foreign newspapers.

As spectators waited for the arrival of the torch they were entertained by a police band. Not that it was easy to hear the band, which had to compete with the chants of around fifty demonstrators.

When the torch arrived at its destination, the City-County Building (now the Coleman A. Young Municipal Center), Mayor Jerome Cavanagh was there to receive it from Hayes Jones, an African American Olympic hurdler.

Protesters held placards, one of which read: 'Is Detroit's segregated housing ready for the Olympics?' Another showed a Klansman, carrying a flaming cross and a shotgun, chasing a black athlete carrying an Olympic torch.[22] Some sang *We Shall Overcome*. As Hayes Jones passed the protesters, one of them, 'Gen' Baker Jr, shouted: 'We've been running from the white man too long!'[23] Over the noise of the protest the police band struck up *The Star-Spangled Banner*.

Afterwards, Mayor Cavanagh attacked the protesters: 'The booing, catcalling and other disgusting antics during the playing of our

National Anthem calls for a public apology from the leaders of this demonstration.'[24] No apology was forthcoming, and six protesters were later arrested and unsuccessfully prosecuted for creating a disturbance in a public place.

The protest had no success in attracting the global media and only received passing attention from Detroit newspapers and television. Nevertheless, targeting an Olympic event was sound. Protesters might have attracted more interest from the media had the Detroit torch relay been an official Olympic event and had it featured the sacred flame from Olympia. Instead, it was a crass publicity stunt by the organising committee to generate enthusiasm among Detroit's residents, who, until then, had been apathetic towards hosting the Games.

In the days running up to the vote, teams of lobbyists from the contending host cities buttonholed IOC delegates and distributed gifts. None were more effective than the Mexicans, who handed out silverware and promised to fly IOC members and their wives to Mexico City should they win. Cultivating the wives was something the other cities did not do. It was small details like this that would be important. In its report from Baden-Baden, the Mexican daily newspaper *El Nacional* wrote that 'wives do not kiss their husbands goodnight without whispering the name "Mexico" in their ears'.[25]

The IOC meeting was held in the Kurhaus. Built in the early nineteenth century, the building displays all the elegance of *La Belle Époque*, white Corinthian columns running along its front and, during the meeting, flags of Olympic member countries fluttering in the breeze. On 18 October, starting at 10 a.m., each city was allocated 45 minutes to make its case. By then, Detroit was 2-1 favourite in the betting.[26]

Buenos Aires was first. There were no visuals, just long dreary speeches. Quite a few delegates escaped the room before the speeches even finished: no one believed that Buenos Aires was serious so they saw little reason to endure the tedium.

Detroit was up next, and their delegation asked for five minutes to sort out some technical issues. This was just a pretext, though, in order to give them enough time to round up the IOC members who had left during Buenos Aires's session. Detroit's presentation started with a film that included a short message from President John F. Kennedy, who papered over racial problems in the US, telling IOC members: 'People of almost every race and creed work harmoniously in an environment of respect for each other's dif-ferences.'[27] There was also a filmed endorsement from African American Olympic athlete Rafer Johnson, who posited that Detroit was striving for 'interracial brotherhood'.[28]

While they were considering the bids, IOC members received let-ters from African Americans who had protested during the torch ceremony in Detroit. They painted a different picture of Detroit: one that had little to do with racial harmony. One of those letters was written by Lloyd and Hazel Dolby: 'This country is not capable of accepting the many colored people from all parts of the world because it has not settled its differences towards the Negro, who is struggling to gain freedom.'[29]

Racial tensions were simmering in Detroit at the time, with whites fleeing mixed neighbourhoods. The city's racist police force ha-rassed African Americans, and white guys on the street, with their heads hanging out of their Chevrolets, yelled abuse as they passed through black neighbourhoods, liberally employing the 'N word'.

In the South, Jim Crow segregationist laws were still in place. Black kids and white kids went to different schools; there were restaurants where African Americans were not served; bathrooms were segregated. The Ku Klux Klan and other white terrorist groups were active, and on 15 September 1963 a bomb detonated at the 16th Street Baptist Church in Birmingham, Alabama, killing four young girls and injuring others.

In 1963 the US was a long way from achieving interracial brother-hood; it was unlikely to be much closer by 1968, when the Olympic Games would be held. The prevalence of racism would certainly have weighed heavily on the minds of IOC members.

After lunch it was Lyon's turn. Their presentation did not impress delegates, and nor did the poorly produced film that was shown to promote their city. IOC members were left wondering if Lyon would be just as amateurish in organising the Games.

The Mexican delegation was the last to present. They did not show a film. Instead their polished presentation painted a pic-ture of a country that was enjoying an economic miracle, with high growth rates and a rich culture that valued its pre-Columbian heritage. They were also able to point to their experience organis-ing the Pan-American Games in 1955 and the Modern Pentathlon World Championship of 1962. The most important segment was de-livered by Dr Eduardo Hay, who was able to dispel fears that Mexico

City's altitude could risk the health of athletes as well as affect performance. He was interrupted by General Vladimir Stoychev, a Bulgarian equestrian Olympian, who asserted: 'Horses never have trouble getting acclimatized down there. And if horses can stand it, so can the humans.'[30] The Mexicans concluded their presentation by pointing out that no Latin American country had ever hosted the Olympics. For an organisation that prided itself on being global, this was a persuasive argument.

The IOC then adjourned, and after a discussion that lasted around an hour members cast their votes in a secret ballot. After the votes had been tallied, Danish IOC member Ivar Vind announced, 'Mexico obtained thirty votes ...'. Before he could finish, the room burst into applause and cries of joy from the Mexicans. As there were a total of 58 voters, Mexico City had gained an overall majority on the first ballot, much to everyone's surprise.

The Mexicans wanted to celebrate their unlikely victory, but there was a problem: the American and French delegations had booked the only available ballrooms for their hoped-for victory celebrations. However, as both those delegations had left immediately after the vote, the hotelier invited the Mexicans to wine and dine in Bel Etage, a fine restaurant on the first floor of the Kurhaus, paid for by the defeated teams.

Back in Mexico, the country's main daily newspaper, *Excélsior*, welcomed the victory with the headline: 'Mexico's time has come'.[31]

# True Colours

Spurious optimism. That's the traditional South African drug. That and sport.

Dennis Brutus, *Cattle* (1962)

## STRANGERS IN THEIR OWN LAND

Of African, French, and Italian ancestry – which legally made him Coloured – Dennis Brutus dedicated much of his life to campaigning to rid South African sport of institutional racism. When white and non-white sportspeople were treated alike, explained Brutus, 'a small crack in the grim edifice of apartheid' opens and 'the entire indivisible structure of racial rule is threatened by collapse'.[1]

While at university Brutus enjoyed playing soccer, table tennis, and rugby, and he was a handy left-arm medium-fast bowler in cricket. However, he admits that he 'was never a good athlete. Let's not kid ourselves about that,' adding that he was 'reasonably good at organizing. That's how it began'.[2]

His involvement in sport drew his attention to how profoundly unjust apartheid was. Brutus saw 'some absolutely brilliant black athletes whose performances were better than those of the [white] South Africans who are being selected to go to the Olympic Games and everywhere else, but because Blacks were black, they couldn't get on the team'.[3]

And not only would most South Africans never be considered for Olympics selection because of the colour of their skin, they would not be granted the honour of wearing the national uniform – the Springbok Colours – either. More than a uniform, it defined and celebrated apartheid sport.

These colours were first worn by members of the national rugby team who toured Great Britain in 1906. They wore green jerseys with yellow trim. The team was captained by Paul Roos, an Afrikaner, who suggested the team be called the *Springbokken*, the Springboks. The springbok is a graceful species of antelope found mainly in southern and southwestern Africa. They have white faces and a cinnamon-coloured coat marked by a reddish-brown stripe that runs along their flanks; the rugby Springboks were, by contrast, all white.

When the Springbok Colours were also adopted by South Africa when the country attended its first official Olympic Games in 1908,[4] a tradition was born.

Springbok Colours consisted of a green and gold emblem and were awarded to individuals and members of teams who represented South Africa in international sporting competitions. It was a tradition that grew in its symbolism, with the Colours awarded with the same ritual solemnity as medals would be during a war. Revered by white sportspeople, it was the highest honour that their country could bestow on them.

Athletes who wore the Colours were not just sporting heroes. In the years that followed, as the world turned against South Africa's apartheid policies, they were warriors representing the strength and determination of white South Africans to assert their superiority.

In 1948, just as Brutus was graduating, the situation for non-whites considerably worsened when the National Party won the election. Dominated by Afrikaner hardliners, it aggressively promoted apartheid. Up to this election, racial segregation had been governed by custom. Called 'petty apartheid', it was a patchwork of customs and informal rules. With the change of government, Parliament enacted laws to separate the races. This system became known as 'grand apartheid'.[5]

One of the foundations of this new approach was the Group Areas Act. Passed in 1950, it set aside specific zones for each racial group. Then, in 1951, the Bantu Authorities Act created the administrative framework for the *bantustans*, or black 'homelands'; some would become 'self-governing' and others semi-autonomous. These states could have their own governing councils, flags, and national anthems, but they were controlled by their white overlords in Pretoria. The *bantustans* amounted to 13 per cent of the total land area of South Africa, even though non-whites made up around three-quarters of the country's population. The best agricultural land was reserved for whites, too, as were the areas rich in valuable minerals.

Outside the *bantustans* non-whites had to carry passbooks, which administered their movement within the country. They became a despised symbol of apartheid. Legally, non-whites had become strangers in their own land: the place where they were born and where many had roots that went way back.

Sport was not exempt from apartheid, and interracial sport was rare. Even blacks kids playing a game of football on the street with white kids could find themselves in trouble with the police. Spectators were segregated at sporting events and there were sporting clubs for each race: white Europeans, Asians, and mixed raced Coloureds and black Africans.

For international events, only whites could represent South Africa, and they could only play against whites. Non-whites could compete overseas, but only against non-whites, and they would represent their *bantustan*, not South Africa. Nor were they given the honour of wearing Springbok Colours, because legally they were citizens not of South Africa but of the *bantustan* on their passbook.

These rules were to preserve a cardinal tenet of apartheid: *baasskap*. This is an Afrikaans word that directly translates as 'boss-ship' and that, when rendered into plain English, means 'white supremacy'. If whites played and were beaten by non-whites, what might that mean for *baasskap*? Even worse, in a sport like boxing, the bloody defeat of a white boxer would be humiliating.

There was much that Dennis Brutus wanted to change. During the 1950s he made his name as a formidable activist, working primarily to promote multiracial sport. But what sort of activist was Brutus? As a public figure he was often dressed in a suit and tie and wore dark rimmed glasses, giving him a bookish look, and he had thick black hair that rippled back off his forehead, barely tamed. He looked anything but a wild-eyed revolutionary. But in front of an audience he came to life: fiery and charismatic. His language was evocative – not surprising as Brutus was also developing as a talented lyric poet and would one day be regarded as one of the best in South Africa. In fact, Brutus saw himself in poetic terms, as a knight-errant or troubadour: 'the man who can be both fighter and poet,' he explained.[6] He was a man who used his pen as a lance and his tongue as a sabre. More than a knight-errant, he was a superb organiser, strategist, and leader.

Brutus saw sport as the soft underbelly of apartheid: 'If you hit them hard on that [international sport] you are going to get the message across that they [white South Africans] were not welcome in the world as long as they practised racism in sport.'[7]

## A FAUSTIAN BARGAIN

Brutus's first campaigns were directed at reforming sporting organisations within South Africa, and removing barriers to the participation of non-white athletes in international events like the Olympic Games.

To put an end to these campaigns, on 26 June 1956 Dr Eben Dönges, South Africa's Minister of the Interior, made official what had before been an informal rule: 'Whites and non-whites should organise their sporting activities separately, there should be no interracial competition within South Africa, the mixing of races and teams should be avoided.'[8] He went on to warn that 'non-European sport organisations seeking international recognition must do so through the aegis of white Associations already enjoying such benefits'.[9]

This arrangement was a Faustian bargain. To compete overseas, non-white sportspeople had to accept being governed by white sporting officials. And even then, they knew they would never be allowed to compete for South Africa.

As the 1960 Olympic Games approached, eyes turned to the all-white South African National Olympic Committee (SANOC)[10] to see whether they would toe the government line. One of its officials was Reg Honey, who was also an IOC member. He addressed the issue at an IOC meeting held in Munich in May 1959. Dissembling the truth, he claimed that 'should a [black] champion be discovered in his country, it is most certain that he would belong to the Olympic team of South Africa'.[11] The IOC accepted Honey's assurance, making no effort to test its veracity.

SANOC was soon tested on how it would reconcile the assurances given by Honey with government policy when Coloured weightlifter Precious McKenzie lifted more than anyone else in South Africa, black or white. He was an obvious selection for the 1960 Olympic Games. Known as the 'Pocket Hercules' (he was just 147 centimetres tall, or 4' 10"), officials from SANOC told him that to be considered for selection he had to join the non-European section of the South African Weightlifting Union. The segregated Union was controlled and managed by white officials, making the non-European section nothing more than a vassal. McKenzie refused to be dependent on the good graces of white officials and he was therefore not considered for selection. Considering the government's explicit ban on non-whites representing South Africa, even had he joined the Union he would have undoubtedly been excluded on some technicality.

On 25 August 1960 the opening ceremony for the Rome Olympics took place. As athletes entered the Estadio Olímpico Universitario for the Parade of Nations, they hit a wall of oppressive heat. Team members dressed in full uniform sweated profusely under their jackets. Spectators were suitably dressed for the weather, with one taking things even further: a streaker wearing just Bermuda shorts dashed across the stadium before the athletes entered.

The South African team was one of the last to enter the stadium. Led by wrestler Manie van Zyl, who carried the flag, the team consisted of fifty-three men and two women, all white, and all proudly wearing the Springbok Colours.

## THE LONG GAME

After the Rome Olympics, worried that Brutus might jeopardise South Africa's participation in future Games, the South African government issued him with the first of a number of banning orders in October 1961. He could not attend gatherings of more than two people. Anything he said or wrote could not be printed, published, or distributed. He was also banned from teaching. But despite these banning orders making life difficult for Brutus, he surreptitiously continued campaigning, directing his energies to the Tokyo Olympic Games, to be held during October 1964.

In early June 1962 Brutus received encouraging news from the IOC. At its meeting in Moscow, Avery Brundage, the IOC president, chastised SANOC for sending an all-white team to Rome and warned that if nothing was done to address racial discrimination, 'the International Olympic Committee will be obliged to suspend this Committee [SANOC]'.[12] The IOC decided to revisit the matter at its meeting in Baden-Baden in October 1963 (the same meeting at which it decided to grant the 1968 Games to Mexico City).

Looking ahead, on 13 January 1963 Brutus created the South African Non-Racial Olympic Committee (SAN-ROC),[13] which he hoped would replace the all-white SANOC should the IOC no longer recognise it as South Africa's official representative for the Olympics.

The IOC sent the Swiss journalist Rudolf Balsiger on a fact-finding mission to help it decide whether South Africa's racial policies breached the anti-racism clause of the Olympic Charter.[14] On 29 May, Balsiger met SANOC president Frank Braun. Brutus also waited at the hotel, hoping to meet Balsiger, but before he could he was arrested for breaching one of his banning orders. Who had tipped off the police? Brutus believed it was Braun, and he was probably right.

When he was released on bail, Brutus fled to neighbouring Swaziland and from there to Mozambique's capital, Lourenço Marques (now Maputo). It was the end of August, which gave him plenty of time to fly to Baden-Baden for the IOC meeting. But while he was in Lourenço Marques, Brutus was arrested by the Portuguese secret police, who handed him over to South African police. He was taken into custody by Warrant Officer Helberg and Sergeant Kleingel, who drove Brutus back into South Africa.

Arriving in Johannesburg on 17 September, the car pulled up outside John Vorster Square (now called Johannesburg Central Police Station). Brutus's handcuffs were removed and he was told to collect his suitcase from the boot. One of the policemen said: 'I hope you will try and escape so we can kill you.'[15] Brutus didn't believe they would shoot him; after all, it was 5 p.m. and the street was crowded with pedestrians heading home from work. Taking a calculated risk, Brutus made a run for it, if for no other reason than to draw attention to his whereabouts. Brutus feared that if his family and supporters didn't know he had been arrested he could easily be 'disappeared'. As he ran, Brutus heard a loud report and felt like someone had punched him in the back. He then noticed a spreading red stain on his shirt. As he lay in a pool of blood, an ambulance arrived and then left without Brutus. When he asked why, Helberg explained: 'But Brutus, you know that these men would lose their jobs if they took you in their ambulance. That is an ambulance for whites only, and you will have to wait for a non-white ambulance.'[16] When a Coloured ambulance finally arrived, Brutus was taken to Coronation Hospital, where a surgeon discovered that the bullet had passed through his body, perforating his intestines. The trauma had also collapsed one of his lungs.

Brutus missed the meeting in Baden-Baden while on remand. Nevertheless, his predicament was drawn to the attention of the IOC by Chancellor Otto Mayer, who expressed extreme concern at not knowing whether his life was in danger or not.

Reflecting on these events, Brutus believed that 'the mere impact of the bullet which had been fired into me, and the publicity surrounding the event and the outcry at the United Nations, in Britain and elsewhere ... created a climate in which it was much easier for the IOC to take the kind of decision which it was most reluctant to take because so many of the Olympic committee countries were sympathetic to apartheid'.[17]

On 9 January 1964 Brutus was sentenced to eighteen months and was sent to Leeuwkop Prison. For exercise, Brutus was made to run in circles, with guards beating him whenever they decided he wasn't going fast enough. After one such session he went to see Dr Greenberg for treatment. Rather than compassion, the prison doctor taunted him: 'Brutus, you are the man who wants to get the blacks into the South African Olympic team, so you should be grateful for the opportunity to have this exercise.'[18]

After two months at Leeuwkop Brutus was transferred to the prison where he would spend the rest of his sentence. 'You think you have gone to Robben Island, but you are wrong,' a guard taunted him when he disembarked. 'You'll find out that you have come to Hell Island.'[19] During the day Brutus broke rocks in the island's lime quarry with Nelson Mandela, Walter Sisulu, and other liberation leaders. Brutus was severely punished for any minor infraction, and from his nape down to his ankles was a carpet of purple and green bruises. Despite the frequent punishments, Brutus continued his campaign from Robben Island, smuggling letters out to activists.

At Baden-Baden, SANOC had promised to send a multiracial team to Tokyo. Unwilling to accept such an outrageous proposition, on 27 June 1964 South Africa's Minister of the Interior, Senator Jan de Klerk, set out the government's position: 'Where whites participate individually in international tournaments they must do so as representatives of the whites of South Africa,' he said. 'Nonwhites must represent the nonwhites of South Africa.'[20] By this he meant that non-whites would represent their homelands: their *bantustans*. Based on this policy pronouncement, non-whites would not be allowed to be part of South Africa's Olympic team.

The IOC had little choice but to withdraw South Africa's invitation to the Tokyo Olympic Games.

When the news arrived on Robben Island from a prisoner who had recently been jailed, 'it gave us great satisfaction,' recalled Brutus. 'The cheering in the quadrangle at Robben Island, where we were breaking stones, must have deafened the guards.'[21]

### THE GATHERING STORM

On 8 July 1965 Brutus was released from prison. Realising that he would achieve little if he stayed in South Africa, Brutus left for London, which would become his new base.

In a new phase of his campaign, Brutus travelled the world, raising awareness of conditions for sportspeople in South Africa. He was sympathetically received, in part because reports of his arrest and of then being shot, and then his mistreatment on Robben Island, had been widely covered by the mass media. Now Brutus had the aura of a martyr, without the inconvenience of sacrificing his life.

There was little comfort for anti-apartheid activists during the 1960s from the United Nations. Efforts to impose economic sanctions were undermined by South Africa's main trading partners, who continually voted against the introduction of mandatory sanctions in the Security Council.

Activists needed to look elsewhere, according to Brutus, to put pressure on South Africa. He argued that sport 'was an area in which protest against apartheid, which so often seemed futile and ineffective, had actually made some real gains'.[22] Making South Africa a pariah in the world of international sport, Brutus believed, would sap the morale of sports-crazy white South Africans and challenge the resolve of the Nationalist government to maintain apartheid.

He hoped that countries, particularly in Africa, would boycott the Mexico Olympics to show their opposition to the racist South African regime. With 112 countries due to participate in the Olympics, local media around the world closely followed the progress of the boycott because it could affect the fortunes of their athletes. For '68ers opposed to apartheid, the boycott campaign provided a rallying point, a common cause, in which they felt part of a transnational community of affinity.

Unsurprisingly, Brutus's first targets were black African countries. On 14 December 1966 Brutus attended the inaugural meeting of the

Supreme Council for Sport in Africa,[23] held in Bamako (Mali). He
was able to convince its thirty-two member countries to campaign
against apartheid. 'The meeting in Bamako was pivotal,' Brutus believed. 'It meant that there was a united body for sports in Africa
that could take unified action.'[24]

On 11 April 1967, in an attempt to disarm his country's critics,
Prime Minster 'BJ' Vorster announced a number of concessions.
The government would permit a multiracial team to compete in
the Mexico Olympics. Each of the four population groups – white,
Bantu, Indian, and Coloured – would select its own representatives, and the final decision would be made by the all-white SANOC.
The Olympic Games, however, would be treated as a 'unique
event' and the arrangements he outlined would not extend to
other events.

This new policy was risky for Vorster. He wanted to avoid the humiliation of once again having South Africa excluded from the
Olympics. On the other hand, the right-wing of the National Party,
called the *verkrampte*, was critical of government compromises
and made it clear that 'no decent white athlete will wear the same
Springbok [Colours] badge as an African or non-white'.[25] This was
important because the Springbok Colours were an important symbol of white supremacy in sport.

To placate hard-line supporters of apartheid, on 24 March 1968
SANOC announced that team members would not receive the Springbok Colours, breaking with the past. Instead, all members of the
multiracial team would wear a specially designed blazer that would
not include the national emblem, the Springbok, but would instead
display the Olympic rings.[26]

The South African government's offer to send a multiracial team
did little to allay scepticism among some IOC members. It smacked
of tokenism, and there was little evidence to suggest that the government intended to make meaningful changes to its racist policies
towards nonwhite sports. To resolve the matter, the IOC sent a
fact-finding Commission to South Africa. It was headed by Lord
Killanin of Ireland and included Reg Alexander, the president of
Kenya's Olympic Association, and Sir Adetekumbo Ademola, the
Chief Justice of Nigeria and the only black on the Commission.

Brundage, regardless of the Commission's findings, had already
made up his mind, as Brutus discovered. When the two men met,
Brundage said that even if he was the 'only spectator in the bleachers

and South Africa is the only country in the stadium, the games will still go on'.[27]

When the Commission arrived in South Africa, Ademola needed to be classified as an 'Honorary White' so that he could travel freely around the country. He was also sufficiently 'white' to be allowed to stay in the same hotels as the other two commissioners, but he wasn't sufficiently white to be allowed use the gents' cloakroom in the lobby.

On receiving the resulting report, the IOC held a postal vote. A majority voted to allow South Africa to participate in the Mexico Olympics: thirty-six to twenty-five, with one abstention. After the vote, Brundage issued a press statement: 'There has been a lot of talk about underprivileged Non-Whites in South Africa; now, for the first time something has been done for them and they have been given an opportunity to appear in the Olympic Games on the same basis as everyone else. Who would have thought it possible a few years ago? It is a great step forward that could only be accomplished by the International Olympic Committee. South African Non-Whites have long sought this opportunity and it is unfortunate that some who pretend to be their friends would deprive them of it.'[28]

For Brundage, it was an opportunity to demonstrate the power of the IOC as an agent of the global moral order: whereas international political and economic pressure had failed to convince the South African government to reform apartheid, the IOC had succeeded.

Brutus disagreed: 'Frankly, we think it's a fraud. It presents to the outside world a pretence of change, but Vorster, the Prime Minister, has made it clear that this is the end of change. There will be no further change. So it is wrong to admit people who intend to continue to practice racial discrimination.'[29]

On the same day as Brundage announced that South Africa would compete in Mexico, Brutus was in Brazzaville, the Congolese capital, where he convinced the Supreme Council for Sport in Africa to boycott the Olympics. After the meeting, André Hombessa, chairman of the Council, said: 'The black men of South Africa would be like trained monkeys who would be shown at the fair and who would go back to the forest once the party was over.'[30]

With African countries united in threatening boycotts, Brutus looked to other parts of the world to boycott the Olympics. His travels took him to the Caribbean, Latin America, Europe, Iron Curtain countries, India, and the United States. He believed that as the Mexico Olympics approached, about fifty countries would not participate.

For all his bluster, Brundage was a realist. As the boycott movement grew, he was left only with bad choices: the IOC could cancel the Mexico Olympics or it could accept that around a third of countries would withdraw. In either case, the reputation of the Olympic Games, as the greatest sporting show on Earth, would be harmed; perhaps even irreparably crippled. Furthermore, the IOC could lose millions of dollars of TV income, which could bankrupt the organisation. Giving in was not palatable either, as it undermined the IOC's authority and Brundage's Olympian-sized ego.

Brundage flew to South Africa on 15 April, purportedly to visit Kruger National Park, but in reality to try to find a face-saving way out of the impasse. During his visit he secretly met Frank Braun, SANOC's president. Brundage urged South Africa to pull out of the Games, giving as his reason that there might be violence directed at its athletes. Braun laughed: 'I would rather be shot in Mexico City than lynched in Johannesburg.'[31]

When Brundage returned empty handed, the IOC decided to hold a postal ballot. The vote was now decisively against allowing South Africa to compete: forty-seven in favour and seventeen against, with eight abstentions.

To protect the status of the Olympics as a universal movement, the IOC could not afford to ignore the threat that a large number of countries would boycott. It had little choice but to surrender.

In a wavering voice, Brundage told the press that the IOC was forced to withdraw South Africa's invitation because of the threat of 'violence and turbulence', adding that the IOC was solely concerned with 'the safety of participants and the dignity of the Games'.[32] This was a fiction. There had been no threats of violence. What Brundage would not admit was that the boycotts had forced the IOC to act.

In South Africa, the government was livid: 'If what has happened is to be the pattern of how world events are going to be arranged in the future we are back in the jungle,' said Prime Minister 'BJ' Vorster. 'Then it will be no longer necessary to arrange Olympic Games but rather to have tree-climbing events.'[33]

So was Brutus's campaign effective?

Once the Mexico Olympics commenced, few if any spectators noticed that South Africa was absent from the Parade of Nations at the opening ceremony. Nevertheless, participation in the Parade of Nations confers de facto recognition of the legitimacy of a country – it is arguably even more important than membership of the United Nations as it is so visible. The absence of South Africa at the Olympic Games allowed its critics to argue that it was a rogue regime. For the South African government, the country's absence meant it could no longer bask in the halo effect of being associated with the Olympic Games. Commentators also did not note the absence of South African athletes from events in which they would have had a chance of a medal. For the global media in Mexico, it was a non-story.

The greatest impact was psychological. White South Africans now saw that its apartheid policies could see it excluded from international competitions. Sport was important for cohesion within the country. After the trauma of two Boer wars (the last ended in May 1902), playing international matches against other countries helped forge a national identity and build solidarity among the white nationalities – Anglo and Afrikaner – which otherwise differed in many ways. In the 1960s and the years that followed, South Africa's increasing isolation exacerbated divisions between the white nationalities and sapped their morale.

## JUKSKEI IN ITS OWN BACKYARD

Brutus had foreseen the psychological impact that isolation might have on the psyche of sport-mad white South Africans ten years earlier, when he predicted that unless South Africa ended apartheid, sport would be 'doomed to dispirited games of jukskei in its own backyards'.[34] Popular among white Afrikaans, jukskei involves four players throwing pins, called *skei*, over a fixed distance. Players score by knocking over a peg that is planted in a sandpit. The closest analogy is a game of horseshoes.

To counter the psychological impact of being excluded from the Olympics, the government organised the South Africa Games.[35] Not only would it provide consolation for the members of its team who had not been allowed to compete in Mexico City, but it would also be an international event. The participation of other countries was to give the impression that South Africa was not isolated in the sporting world.

The Games were divided into two: whites would compete in Bloemfontein,[36] non-whites in Johannesburg.[37] Only whites who

Figure 2.1    Postage stamp issued to celebrate the South
Africa Games.

competed against international opponents were awarded the
Springbok Colours: an honour not extended to non-whites. In
these ways, the South Africa Games were the apartheid version of
the Olympics.

To assure the white population that South Africa was held in high
regard by the sporting world, it was important to have a large contingent of international competitors at the Bloemfontein Games. To
this end, nearly 100 invitations went out to foreign athletes; white

athletes. There were, however, some embarrassing slip-ups. Inadvertently, the organisers invited German weightlifter Günter Wu, who was Chinese, and New Zealand runner Kevin Ross, who was Maori. Both invitations were promptly withdrawn when this unforgivable mistake was discovered.

In the months running up to the South Africa Games, Brutus lobbied athletes, asking them not to participate. As a result of his campaign, athletes from fifteen countries withdrew. By the time the Games started, fewer than twenty foreign sportspeople participated, some in defiance of their national sporting association. Rather than proving apartheid had not isolated South Africa from the sporting world, these Games proved that it had.

The organisers consciously tried to replicate the ceremonies and rituals of the Olympics. On 15 March 1969 the whites-only Games started with an athletes' parade through Bloemfontein's streets to the Vrystaatstadion stadium. There was also a torch, but not one lit from the sacred flame of Olympia of course. In the stadium, a large flag displayed faux Olympic rings, and 2,000 pigeons were released. Any pretence that the South Africa Games were, like the Olympics, a celebration of peace was dispelled when the opening ceremony ended with a flypast by four Mirage fighters.

In a half-full stadium, 30,000 spectators watched Jim Fouché, the South African President, open the South Africa Games. His message was that the Games were much purer than the Olympics, which had become corrupted by politics.

The first three place getters were presented with gold, silver, and bronze medals, on which a springbok pranced over slightly modified Olympic rings. Stamps were also issued to mark the event. And despite a concerted effort to mimic Olympic ceremonies, all the organisers could offer was a poor imitation of its rituals. They certainly lacked the symbolic power of the real thing.

The South Africa Games were quickly enveloped in controversy when the Bloemfontein municipality banned non-white spectators from its stadium. The government believed that this would be pounced on by anti-apartheid activists, and it forced the municipality to back down. Up to 750 non-whites were allowed into the Vrystaatstadion, segregated behind a fenced-off section. They also allocated 150 seats to non-whites who wanted to see tennis and cricket matches. No seats were available, however, for non-whites who wanted to watch the boxing, karate, or swimming competitions.

In karate, South Africans competed against a British team. As an international event, arrangements were made to award the three-man South African team with the Springbok Colours, which should have included Glen Popham, the team's captain. However, he was not invited to the ceremony. The problem was that after the Games, officials discovered that Popham was Coloured, and therefore not worthy of receiving this honour. Only the other two white members of the karate team, Lionel Marinius and Rob Ferriere, were presented with a Springbok jacket and tie at a formal ceremony in the Eden Rock Hotel in Durban, attended by family and friends.

The South Africa Games themselves included Olympic events, like track and field and swimming. And with unintended irony, just as Brutus had predicted, the programme included jukskei.

According to the Johannesburg *Sunday Express*, the South Africa Games 'failed as a spectator spectacle, as a national sports summit and as a counter to our expulsion from the Mexico Olympics'.[38] Reporting for *The Times* (London), Derek Du Plessis concluded that the Bloemfontein Games 'have provided a symbol of White supremacy and, whether we like it or not, flouted the Olympic principle of equality in sport'.[39] *The Times of India* also warned that 'South African white sportsmen should be convinced that there is no hope of their being able to take part in international competitions unless their country gives up *apartheid* in sport'.[40]

# 3

# Manufacturing Discontent

*A ce perfide Anglois, gent cruelle et barbare.*
[To this perfidious Englishman, cruel and barbarous.]

Jacques-Bénigne Bossuet

## TOUCH THE SKY

On 13 July 1968 an Olympic Ball was held in the plush Harry Margolis Hall in Salisbury (now Harare, Zimbabwe). At 10.30 p.m., Prime Minister Ian Smith rose to his feet to announce the names of the seventeen-member team who would represent Rhodesia (also known as Southern Rhodesia) in Mexico. After congratulating the athletes, Smith said that Rhodesia would participate 'in spite of all the yelling jackals'.[1]

Foremost among the yelling jackals was Great Britain, which was angry at Rhodesia's Unilateral Declaration of Independence (UDI). Announced on 11 November 1965, UDI cut Rhodesia's colonial ties to Great Britain, entrenching white-minority rule.

At an Olympic fundraiser in Bulawayo, held on 12 January 1968, Smith said that sending a team to Mexico would be 'a wonderful breakthrough for Rhodesia, not only in the sporting world but in general as far as Rhodesian acceptance throughout the world is concerned'.[2] Winning medals was a secondary objective. For Smith, it was more important to attend the Olympic Games as a sovereign nation, which would confer de facto recognition on newly independent Rhodesia. For the same reason, it was important to the countries that opposed UDI – those yelling jackals – to prevent Rhodesia from participating.

Luckily for Rhodesia, most of the attention had been on apartheid South Africa. This changed after 21 April 1968, when South

Africa was 'uninvited' from the Mexico Olympics.[3] Rhodesia's participation subsequently received considerably more attention.

The issues surrounding Rhodesia were different from those for South Africa. Rhodesia eschewed apartheid, and it had sent multiracial teams to the 1960[4] and 1964[5] Olympics. While Rhodesia had yet to win a medal, it hoped that that would change in Mexico, with its best chances vested in its two black athletes: Bernard Dzoma and Mathias Kanda.

It would be Bernard Dzoma's first Olympics; he had been selected to compete in the 5,000 and 10,000 metres races. On hearing his name read out he was excited: 'I felt like I would get to touch the sky,' he recalled.[6] His teammate and good friend Mathias Kanda was just as excited, although this would be his second Games. In 1964 he had finished in the bottom half of the field in the marathon. Now, four years later, and at his peak, Kanda hoped to do better.

From his birthplace in the black township of Enkeldoorn (now Chivhu), Kanda moved to Bulawayo, where he worked as a machinist in a clothing factory. In his spare time – at dawn before work, and after work until it became dark – Kanda would run around the streets of Bulawayo or up and down the nearby hills and along rock-strewn tracks, averaging thirty kilometres a day. He was a familiar sight in Bulawayo, running barefoot and wearing Rhodesian green and yellow shorts. When running along a road he would break into a sprint when a cyclist or truck approached, just for the sheer joy of running. Local lads would try and outrace him, while stray dogs provided him with good reason to accelerate.

An uncut diamond of an athlete, Kanda was largely self-taught. In 1968 Kanda was twenty-six years old and he realised that Mexico might be his last shot at Olympic glory.

Bernard Dzoma was eight months older than Kanda, and he had come to competitive racing in 1966. In his first race, which was over three miles, he looked anything but a future Olympian. He wore a pair of khaki work shorts and he ran barefoot, having never owned a pair of spikes. Nevertheless, he won the provincial title. The following year, at the same meet, he won the Ranger Trophy for the outstanding athlete at the Mashonaland Senior Athletic Championship. He continued his winning streak over the next fifteen months, beating all-comers over one, three, and six miles.

As the Olympics approached, Kanda secured a job at the *Rhodesian Herald* in Salisbury, so he and Dzoma could train together, and

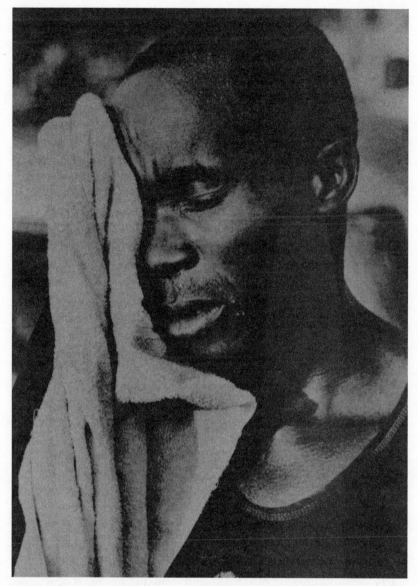

Figure 3.1   Rhodesia's Olympic hopeful Mathias Kanda after a training run.

every evening they could be found pounding the track at the Borrowdale Racecourse.

Believing that with professional training Kanda and Dzoma could win medals at the Olympics, the Rhodesian Sports Foundation provided funds to pay for an experienced coach. Looking to the future, the coach would also nurture emerging talent among the juniors. In a country that was struggling under the burden of sanctions, this was a major commitment.

As no local coaches with sufficient experience were available, the Foundation chose an Australian, John Cheffers, who had recently coached athletes in Papua New Guinea. A former athlete, Cheffers's career ended when he wrecked his leg while long jumping. He limped following the accident, throwing out his right leg as he walked. Just twenty years old when his athletics career ended, Cheffers sublimated all his energy into mastering the skills needed to be a first-rate coach.

Cheffers knew very little about Rhodesia: only what he had read in the Australian newspapers. 'I eagerly awaited confrontation with the people and geography of this controversial land.'[7]

After touring through the country, Cheffers noticed that sport was not mired in South African-type apartheid. Instead, divisions between black and white were based on wealth, social status, and unwritten social customs. Cheffers also saw that white kids preferred rugby, cricket, hockey, tennis, and swimming, while black children favoured soccer and running, probably because they were sports that cost less to pursue.

Cheffers was particularly pleased to discover that athletics was surprisingly well resourced among Africans, as each mining company invested in sporting facilities and provided time off for training.

After Cheffers met Kanda and Dzoma he worked them hard, putting more kilometres into their legs and correcting their technique. 'Bernard's beautifully relaxed running style, which he maintained throughout, even when fatigued, gave me just cause for optimism.'[8] Kanda was more experienced, but there were areas that Cheffers was keen to improve, not least Kanda's rather unsophisticated understanding of tactics, which was to stay as close as possible to the leaders for the whole race.

Cheffers was also keen to nurture the next generation of Rhodesian champions, and he gave clinics at black and white schools, at mining camps, and in black townships.

Cheffers's first opportunity to see up-and-coming talent was at the Mashonaland Junior Championship, held in March 1968. When he arrived he met the formidable Burnice Davies, a bundle of energy, who organised the meet. As for previous Championships, she wanted to hold the competition in the grounds of the Churchill Boys School. It had a grass track, which was kind to unshod feet; many black competitors could not afford spikes or just disliked wearing them. But Davies ran into a problem. In June 1967 Philip Smith, the Minister of Education, had restricted multiracial sport on school lands.[9] The alternatives were church or police properties, which were far from ideal as they had cinder tracks, which were hard on bare feet. This administrative directive showed that some members of the government were keen to move towards the harsh form of apartheid practised in South Africa. Many in the white community, particularly parents' groups, did not support such bigotry. Burnice Davies, in particular, was outraged, and she vigorously fought the minister's racist edict. A compact woman with short brown hair, Davies pestered Education Department bureaucrats until she eventually got her way.

The Championship was a splendid success, with 909 competitors, black and white, competing against one another. This would never have been allowed in South Africa.

Spectators sat in a wooden stand or on blankets spread on the lawn surrounding the Churchill oval, finding shade under jacaranda trees or umbrellas. The majority were white, and the few blacks who attended sat separately, by choice. There was no formal segregation among athletes; black and white changed in a pavilion adjacent to the school building and mixed freely, although friendships were rare.

Blacks followed informal rules in Rhodesia, although the system was nowhere near as oppressive or rigid as that of South Africa. Nevertheless, outside sport Africans knew which toilets, hotels, restaurants, and cinemas they could not go into: 'I was careful not to go into the wrong place,' Dzoma shrugged. 'You just get used to it.'[10]

The young talent that Cheffers saw at the Mashonaland Junior Championship was encouraging. His immediate priority, however, was to prepare those athletes who were ready to compete in the 1968 Olympics.

To assess and develop his pool of talent, he invited promising athletes to an acclimatisation camp located on Mount Nyangani. The camp was at a similar altitude to what the athletes would encounter in Mexico City.

On the evening of 5 April 1968, Cheffers and a number of Olympic hopefuls left Salisbury for the training camp by bus. The last part of their journey was along an unmade road. When the bus's wheels came perilously close to a deep precipice, some of the athletes screamed at the driver, who stoically replied: 'We must be getting close to Jesus!'[11] The athletes continued to complain and made it clear to the driver that they were not ready to meet Jesus just yet. They arrived at the camp at midnight and collapsed into bed.

At 6.15 a.m. the next day a bell rang out and everyone had fifteen minutes to get ready for their morning seven-kilometre run, with the long-distance runners doing twice that distance. After their run, everyone sat down in the dining room for a hearty breakfast of eggs and bacon, after which came weight and skills training. The morning ended with a vigorous callisthenics session.

Cheffers devoted his afternoons to Kanda and Dzoma. As the athletes pounded the tarmac, Cheffers would catch up with them in his ancient Toyota Corona. With someone else driving, he would hang out of the passenger window and measure their heart rates with a stethoscope while they were still on the move.

After dinner everyone gathered in a large carpeted recreation room to relax, with an open fire taking the chill off the mountain air. Most of the athletes – black and white – had seldom if ever mixed socially, so initially there was some awkwardness as they passed their time playing table tennis, doing jigsaw puzzles, and reading. Myra Fowler, a white pentathlete, had always found black athletes to be particularly reserved around white women. Then someone put a record on a portable player and the chairs and tables were moved out of the way. 'I saw a side of them that was quite unexpected,' Fowler explained. 'They [black athletes] were boisterous and great fun. When the music started and the adrenalin kicked in they just wanted to boogie.'[12]

While Cheffers and his athletes trained in a remote corner of eastern Rhodesia, they had reason to be optimistic that they would be welcomed in Mexico. After all, hadn't Rubén Hernández from the Mexican Olympic Organising Committee attended a formal ceremony in the Bulawayo City Hall on 20 November 1967 to personally present Rhodesia with its invitation. Ordinarily, invitations were posted out, so the Mexicans had gone to some trouble to ensure that Rhodesians felt valued by their future host. This good-news item appeared in the Rhodesian press, but bad news was often censored, so athletes knew little about the 'yelling jackals' who were plotting to cruel their Olympic dreams.

## DENYING COMFORT

Heading the pack of jackals was the British government. Following UDI, the British government encouraged countries to apply sanctions on Rhodesia, including cutting off sporting contacts, which it argued provided comfort to the rogue regime.

An early test was the British Empire and Commonwealth Games, held in August 1966, when a number of African countries threatened to boycott the Games in protest if Rhodesia attended. The Rhodesian government withdrew its team, unwilling to take the blame for ruining the Games.

In late 1966 the British government dissuaded the Field Hockey Association from inviting a Rhodesian team to England. It also convinced the Spanish government to deny visas to members of the Rhodesian field hockey team, who were due to compete in an international tournament in Madrid in April 1967.

The British government also faced setbacks, as some countries argued that politics should not intrude into sport. For example, in November 1966 Australia sent its cricket team to Rhodesia; a French rugby team played against Rhodesia in July 1967; Mauritius played two soccer friendlies there in November 1967; and West German tennis players, including Wimbledon finalist Wilhelm Bungert, visited Rhodesia in January 1968.

The British campaign to isolate Rhodesia also faced resistance in its own backyard. This created a headache for the Foreign Office because 'it would make it almost impossible to convince foreign governments that we were serious in our prosecution of sanctions against the illegal regime if HMG [Her Majesty's Government] failed to take a very strong line against British international teams who wish to play football or cricket against the territory which is in rebellion'.[13]

The first to test the British government's resolve was a tour by Oldham Athletic Football Club, which had been invited to play a series of games in Rhodesia in the summer of 1967. George Thomas, the Minister of State for Commonwealth Affairs, told Parliament: 'We deplore organised tours of this kind while the state of illegality exists in Rhodesia, and we made our views clear.' The problem was that the government had 'no powers … to prevent private citizens from going to Rhodesia,' explained Thomas.[14] The tour went ahead and provided a propaganda win for the Rhodesian government when its Ministry of Information published a photograph of Ken Bates, Oldham's chairman, with Prime Minister Ian Smith.[15]

Next, the British government tried to stop a tour by the Yorkshire County Cricket Club. Rather than suffer another public rebuff, as had happened with Oldham, Thomas wrote to some Yorkshire members of parliament 'in confidence' to express his 'deep anxiety' about the tour. He was concerned that if the tour went ahead, it 'would be bringing comfort and encouragement to those who have rebelled against The Queen's Authority'.[16] When news leaked out about the government's intervention, prominent cricketers weighed into the controversy. 'I don't know what the hell the fuss is about,' cricketing legend Freddie Trueman told the *Daily Express*. 'All I know is that I want to go and play cricket and nowt else.'[17] The government was further shaken when the *Daily Telegraph* attacked its intervention in an editorial: 'Fascist Italy and Germany used to align their athletics closely to their foreign policies, and Britain is in danger of making the same pernicious mistake.'[18] In Yorkshire, where cricket is a religion, the reaction was also critical, although it was tempered with levity. The *Yorkshire Post* explained that rather than providing 'comfort to the enemy … the Yorkshire team never goes anywhere to offer aid and comfort to anyone; its object is always to hammer them into the ground'.[19] Buckling under the pressure, the Yorkshire County Cricket Club ungracefully announced that it had abandoned the tour, blaming 'political pressure' for its decision.[20]

The government's credibility was tested again when the British and Irish Lions rugby side refused to call off its tour of Rhodesia. The government hit back: 'We regard this as a political act – going to a country led by an illegal regime,' said Denis Howell, Minister for Sport.[21] 'I have pointed out to the Lions committee several times that a visit to Rhodesia would be used politically by the Smith regime. They will make a great song and dance of it.'[22] Rugby is sacred to Rhodesians and the tour raised the morale of the beleaguered nation, as Prime Minister Ian Smith recalled in his memoir: 'It was a warm feeling to know that there were some sportsmen in the world who had the courage to stand up to the politicians and tell them to keep their noses out of sport.'[23]

The next major challenge to its campaign to isolate Rhodesia was beyond the British government's ability to exert pressure. The International Tennis Federation allowed Rhodesia to compete in the 1968 Davis Cup. This was Rhodesia's first international sporting event since UDI, and participation was important to Ian Smith as it bestowed de facto recognition on his regime.

Rhodesia's first match was against Sweden, and university students from Stockholm, Uppsala, and Gothenburg announced they would protest, as did militant activists. Their complaint was with racism, not UDI.

When the Swedish Lawn Tennis Association heard about the demonstration it moved the matches to Båstad, a seaside resort in the south of Sweden. Båstad had the advantage of a highly conservative population, who were looking forward to hosting an international tournament. Local burghers even talked about creating vigilante groups to teach the protesters a lesson, but they were dissuaded from doing so by the police.

On 3 May 1968, match day, around 1,000 demonstrators arrived in Båstad by train, bus, and in cars. They marched to the stadium carrying placards: 'Stop the match', 'White Sport, White Racism', 'Rhodesians Go Home!!', and 'Kill Smith'. And they chanted: 'Zimbabwe! Zimbabwe!', 'Crush Fascism!', and 'Stop the match!'

As they approached the stadium, the demonstrators were confronted by 1,200 police. The protestors took up positions at the two gates leading into the stadium and chanted their slogans. A small group of radicals then crashed through the northern gate, breaking the chain that had secured the entrance. They were pushed back by a high-pressure fire hose; that is, until one of the students cut the hose with a knife. After a short break, a new hose was found and protesters were driven back. Batons and tear gas were also used on the protesters.

Some students had bought tickets and were sitting in the stands. Once the match started, they threw eggs and plastic bags full of rapeseed oil, which burst when they landed on the court, making the surface unplayable.

Eventually, the stadium was cleared of protesters, many bloodied and soaked to the bone, with tears streaming down their faces. Nevertheless, they left Båstad triumphant when they heard that the match had been called off.

Later that afternoon all the competitors left Sweden in a private aircraft for the French Riviera. The match was played in secrecy two days later in a private club in Bandol. Sweden won 4–1 and Rhodesia was knocked out of the Davis Cup, much to the relief of its organisers.

On 9 May 1968 the British Foreign Office sent a coded telegram to Peter Hope, the UK's ambassador in Mexico City. It asked him to draw the attention of Mexican officials to the Båstad riot and suggested that if a Rhodesian team was allowed to compete in the Olympic Games it could face similar disturbances.[24]

### PERFIDIOUS ALBION

Back in Britain, the government's campaign to have Rhodesia thrown out of the Olympics was in the hands of two ministers of the Crown: George Thomas and Dennis Howell. They were supported by a host of ethereal civil servants in the Foreign Office, who had never mistaken virtue for diplomacy, and who firmly believed that duplicity and hypocrisy were companionable attendants to state-craft. 'Perfidious Albion' had long been used to describe Britain's reputation for bad faith and outright treachery when it came to dip-lomacy, and it was fully employed to exclude Rhodesia from the Mexico Olympics.

From the start, whenever possible, British officials stayed in the shadows: the natural habitat of the Foreign Office. If 'Rhodesia should be seen to win after all our influence has been thrown into a lobbying exercise with governments, it would seem to represent a much greater victory politically for Rhodesia than if we were to take a relaxed line from the start,' advised James Bottomley, assistant under-secretary for the Commonwealth Office.[25]

The campaign would be won quickly, the Foreign Office believed, if the IOC could be persuaded to withdraw Rhodesia's invitation. To this end, Minister Howell met with the Marquess of Exeter and Lord Luke, British members of the IOC. The two peers quickly disabused the minister on where their loyalties lay. They were not British rep-resentatives on the IOC. When it came to sport, their first allegiance was to the ideals of the Olympic movement. Exeter then warned Howell that the IOC might 'cancel the Games sooner than accept this kind of political interference'. When the minister pointed out that a number of African countries could boycott the Games, Exeter told him that such a boycott was of no consequence as it would only be 'countries that had little to contribute athletically'.[26] What How-ell discovered during this meeting was that the IOC was a sovereign power, and its members were its ambassadors, representing its inter-ests, even when they were against the policies of their own country.

In March 1968 the Foreign Office faced a new problem. They discovered that there was a second international sporting event that Rhodesia had been invited to: the Paralympic Games (then known as the International Stoke Mandeville Games). While these Games had nowhere near as high a profile as the Olympics, they would nevertheless allow Rhodesia to flaunt its sovereignty.

The Paralympics were normally held in the same city as the summer Olympics and were scheduled to follow them. Mexico City could not handle both games, so the Paralympics were moved to Tel Aviv (Israel).

The Foreign Office worried that Great Britain could 'expect a good share of Press criticism if at our insistence the Israelis were to make an issue over the type of passport held by Rhodesian cripples'.[27] Determined to 'turn a blind eye to the paraplegic sports',[28] the Foreign Office devised a face-saving solution. It asked Israel to not recognise Rhodesian passports but to allow athletes to complete landing forms to which Israeli immigration officials would attach stamped visas. Israel agreed to this arrangement.

The Rhodesian team participated in the opening ceremony and its members had considerable success on the field, winning six gold medals, seven silvers, and seven bronzes. The Foreign Office was relieved when Rhodesia's participation in the Paralympics was largely ignored by the international media.

When South Africa was thrown out of the Olympic Games in April 1968, the Foreign Office renewed efforts to manufacture discontent towards Rhodesia among African countries. This was done behind the scenes. By 'not exposing ourselves too much',[29] the Foreign Office hoped to avoid opprobrium should the campaign fail. Through its embassies, the Foreign Office encouraged African countries to boycott the Olympics. They found few allies, receiving only tepid support from Ethiopia, Nigeria, and Kenya.

While the Mexican Olympic Organising Committee was aware that only a few countries threatened boycotts, it worried that the number might grow. It also saw that the IOC was staunchly behind Rhodesia and was unlikely to blink as it had on South Africa's participation.

The Mexicans were handed a legal way to resist IOC pressure when, on 28 May 1968, the UN Security Council approved a resolution that contained economic and diplomatic sanctions against the rogue regime. It also called on its members to prevent the entry into their territory of people on Rhodesian passports or those who were 'likely to further or encourage the unlawful actions of the illegal regime'.[30] This allowed Mexican border control to exclude Rhodesian athletes.

Having stuck its neck out, the Mexican government told Ambassador Hope that it wanted a public statement from the British government supporting its blanket ban.[31] This presented the Foreign Office with a problem, as they explained to Hope: 'We find ourselves embarrassed by the full-blooded way in which they [Mexican government] have interpreted ... the Security Council resolution.' The Mexicans believed that they could stop not only athletes with Rhodesian passports, but also Rhodesians travelling on foreign passports. Having sponsored the UN resolution, the British Foreign Office knew that this interpretation was wrong. The telegram went on to say: 'We should not want to make a public statement pointing out these differences of interpretation. On the other hand we should be reluctant to make a statement endorsing the Mexican government's position since this could lead us into considerable difficulties in other fields.'[32]

When the IOC heard that the Mexican government intended to prevent Rhodesian athletes or officials from entering the country, it threatened to cancel the Games. Caught between his government and the IOC, the president of the organising committee, Pedro Ramírez Vázquez, issued a masterfully vague statement that said that 'it is clear that the sports delegation from Southern Rhodesia which had been invited to take part in the sports competitions of next October will find itself unable to participate in them'.[33] The statement avoided banning Rhodesia, but instead observed that the country would be unable to attend because of the bans on travel contained in the UN resolution. This equivocal wording was needed to placate IOC president Avery Brundage and to not upset the Mexican government.

The question of using passport controls to stop Rhodesian athletes entering Mexico became problematic when, on 13 July 1968, the Rhodesian team was announced. It included two black athletes: Bernard Dzoma and Mathias Kanda. According to Richard Faber from the Foreign Office, 'the only members whom we knew we could stop were the two Africans in the team', because they were the only ones that the Foreign Office was certain had only Rhodesian passports.[34] Most, if not all, of the white athletes had passports from other countries. Cheffers held an Australian passport, while others held either South African or British passports.

As it turned out, Salisbury Radio understood how the IOC worked better than the Foreign Office did. As one of its commentators explained: 'All athletes will be issued with Olympic credentials for the journey to Mexico and home again, and these will be their passports. So the Mexican immigration authorities will be spared the ticklish decision of whether to stamp Rhodesian passports or not.'[35]

## A WILDERNESS OF SPITE

The National Olympic Committee of Rhodesia also understood that they could rely on Olympic identity cards rather than passports that may or may not be recognised by the Mexican government. The Mexican Olympic Organising Committee (MOOC) was obligated to provide all athletes with entry documents. But by the end of August the identity cards had not arrived. The Rhodesians sent numerous cables asking the Organising Committee when they would receive the cards but received unhelpful replies: they were being processed; their application had been mislaid; the cards were in the mail. Sometimes they received no reply at all. It was only a month before the Games and athletes in every country except Rhodesia had received their documents. The Rhodesians underestimated the capacity of the MOOC for masterful obfuscation and inaction.

The British were privy to the tactics being employed by the MOOC. It had 'unilaterally decided not, repeat not, to send any Olympic identity cards to Salisbury for the Rhodesian team,' Ambassador Hope explained in a telegram to the Foreign Office. Success could not be assured, warned Hope, because 'should any member of the Rhodesian team succeed in landing in Mexico the O.O.C. [Olympic Organising Committee] would have no alternative under the Olympic rules but to give them identity cards and allow them to compete'.[36]

By 30 August the president of the National Olympic Committee of Rhodesia, Douglas Downing, realised that his telegrams to Mexico would not be answered and that identity cards would not be sent. Bitter at the 'enforced exclusion' of Rhodesia from the Olympics, Dowling raged at the 'wilderness of spite' that had conspired to defeat Rhodesia's bid to compete. Next, he addressed those who would suffer most from this decision: 'To our own sportsmen of all races, selected but denied the privilege of competing, we apologise.'[37]

This communiqué was telexed to Coach Cheffers, who was in the offices of the *Rhodesian Herald* with Mathias Kanda. When Cheffers read it he buried his face in his hands: 'I reread the telex, searching for some ray of light, something to which I could attach optimism.'[38] Kanda's eyes were fixed on Cheffers, knowing that his Olympic hopes were vested in that telex. The room was thick with emotion. Kanda had sacrificed so much; he had moved away from his family and friends to live in Salisbury so he could train under Cheffers. He spent every hour when he wasn't working or sleeping, training. He knew little else but running. After Cheffers told Kanda that he was not going to Mexico, the athlete, bewildered, gazed blankly out of the window. 'You have earned the highest honour this country can give, but it is of no use,' said Cheffers. 'But you, Mathias, have done nothing wrong.'[39] As Kanda left the room he told Cheffers, blinking back tears: 'I will not train tomorrow.'[40]

After he'd spoken to Kanda, Cheffers drove to the Borrowdale Racecourse. Dzoma interrupted his training and went over to Cheffers's car and sat down. After telling him the bad news, Dzoma turned his head towards the car window and started to cry. When he'd recovered his composure, he angrily reflected on all the sacrifices he'd made: the hard training that he did not enjoy; the aches and pains; the cost of his spikes; living away from his home in Umtali; and postponing his wedding to Renica, the love of his life. And then there was the pure injustice of it all: 'I cannot understand why, as a black man, I am made to suffer by people a long way off, who, for reasons I don't understand, don't like Ian Smith, and wanted to throw me out of the Olympics in the interests of black people in my country.'[41]

Dzoma did not return to training the next day or the one after that. He felt depressed and humiliated. 'That was the end of the road,' he decided.[42]

After delivering the news to his athletes, Cheffers was in a dark mood: 'What right had vindictive and smelly politicians to deprive this lad of his life's ambition – an ambition so full of merit? Yet, here in Africa, they were to be used as another pawn in the highly amoral game of politics, and the little people – should we say the really big people? – in this world were being made to suffer.'[43]

Cheffers was too emotionally involved with his athletes to be objective. But was he right to argue that there was no justification for excluding Rhodesia from the Olympic Games?

There was much wrong with Rhodesia in the way it treated its black population.[44] However, its sport was multiracial and selection was based on merit. The inclusion of Bernard Dzoma and Mathias Kanda in the team was proof of this. Nevertheless, there was black disadvantage in sport; the situation wasn't much different from that in Jim Crow America in the 1960s but was nowhere near as severe as that in South Africa, where apartheid was integral to the way sport was organised.

However, racism in Rhodesia was a secondary consideration for the British government. Its campaign was to deny the rogue country the opportunity to display its symbols of sovereignty in the global space of the Olympics because it would help legitimise UDI.

On his way home to Australia Cheffers stopped off in Mexico City to watch the Olympics. At the opening ceremony, as he later recalled, he 'sat motionless, bitter once again in the midst of all this festivity'.[45] Later, as he walked around the Olympic Village, sat in the stands of the Estadio Olímpico Universitario stadium, dined with athletes, and walked around Mexico City's shopping centres, he 'saw the faces of Mathias and Bernard'.[46] And he obsessively noted down the times for the events that his athletes would have competed in. They were slow by world standards, leading Cheffers to believe that 'Mathias Kanda might have medalled in the marathon, and [Bernard] Dzoma would certainly have acquitted himself well in the final of the 5,000 metres'.[47] But they never had a chance of testing themselves against the world's best in Mexico City; they never had the opportunity to touch the sky.

# 4

## Revolt of the Black Athlete

Will you, won't you, will you, won't you, will you join the dance?
Will you, won't you, will you, won't you, won't you join the dance?

Lewis Carroll, *The Mock Turtle's Song*

### MOBILISING THE MOVEMENT

In early September 1967, while competing at the World University Games in Tokyo, sprinter Tommie Smith created a firestorm when he answered a question from a Japanese sports reporter, who asked whether African American athletes would compete in Mexico City. Smith answered: 'Some athletes have been discussing the possibility of boycotting the games to protest against injustice in America.'[1]

Through wire services, Smith's interview was widely reported in the US. He only realised just how seriously his off-the-cuff remark had been taken when he arrived back home. At San Francisco airport he was met by a thicket of TV cameras and microphones, with reporters screaming questions at him. Smith told them: 'The Negroes feel if they can represent the US before the world, why can't they be treated as full citizens at home?'[2]

As a committed athlete, Smith was not in a position to organise a boycott, so he turned to Harry Edwards, his sociology lecturer at San José State College, to take up the baton. Outside class they talked about black empowerment and racial justice, and Smith looked on Edwards as a mentor, as well as being a friend.

Smith respected Edwards because he understood the problems that African Americans on athletic scholarships had, having gone down that path himself to escape poverty. For most it was a temporary escape, as few graduated or forged successful careers as professional sportspeople. Smith admired Edwards because he had created his own opportunities outside athletics, despite a difficult childhood.

Harry Edwards grew up in East St. Louis, Illinois: a ghetto where the smell of barbecuing pig snouts mixed with the tang of outhouses and the stench of poverty.

Before Harry was born, his father, Harold Senior, had spent eight years in Joliet State Penitentiary for burglary. Harold was from a broken home, and he had ended up running with the wrong crowd. After being released, he tried prizefighting, hoping that one big win would launch him 'on that golden road'.[3] Sport was the best way out of the ghetto, and heavyweight boxer Joe Louis was Harold's hero. He never had that big win, though, and struggled to earn enough for his growing family.

In the ghetto, education was not seen as a way out of poverty. Black schools were overcrowded; most teachers were overworked, while some were overwhelmed and had just given up. Even though Harry went to a segregated school, corporal punishment was used to reinforce racial norms. Once, when Harry was punished for a minor infraction, his well-intentioned teacher explained: 'I'm going to paddle you good here to keep white folks from killing you outside.'[4]

His teacher was not exaggerating. On 21 August 1955, fourteen-year-old Emmett Till visited relatives in Money, Mississippi. Three days later, he and some friends went into town and, in Bryant's Grocery & Meat Market, Till made the mistake of flirting with Carolyn Bryant, a white woman. Four days later two white men abducted Till and then tortured and killed him. Tried for murder, the all-white jury acquitted the accused after 67 minutes of deliberation.

When Harry saw a photograph of the mutilated body of Till in *Jet* magazine, he went to his father: 'Hey, the same thing could happen to me.' His father admitted he might not be able to protect his son or even himself from such violence.[5] It hit Harry that no African American was safe from lynchings, unless they were willing to be docile and behave like the white man wanted; to play the 'good Negro'.

At school, it was drummed into young Harry that black kids like him 'shouldn't even aspire to learn, that learning *naturally* just wasn't our calling'.[6] Sport, however, was. Just as his father once pursued boxing as a way out of the ghetto, Harry too looked to sport. An apathetic student, Harry was, thankfully, a talented athlete, playing football in the autumn, basketball in winter, and track and field in spring.

For a year after he left high school, Edwards attended Fresno City College on an athletic scholarship. For the first time in his life he discovered books and took joy from learning. It gradually became a passion, even more important to him than sport. This was not expected from an African American student on an athletic scholarship, but Edwards was happy to dance to his own tune.

In 1960 Edwards was recruited by San José State College on another athletic scholarship. He confounded expectations by asking to enrol in a meaty course: a Master of Social Work. This was unprecedented. Jocks were invariably enrolled in easy courses like physical education, which Edwards mockingly referred to as 'Badminton 1'.[7] Despite being discouraged from taking on an academically challenging subject, Edwards persisted, and he was eventually, grudgingly, allowed to pursue his chosen course; he was on probation, though, and had to submit weekly progress reports. If his grades dropped he would be immediately transferred to the physical education course, where the professors knew the rules: keep passing athletes on scholarships so that they could continue playing for the glory of the college. Harry astonished his professors by achieving a B-average. African American jocks were not supposed to get a B-average, and certainly not in the demanding subjects that Edwards was studying.

Harry Edwards graduated with distinction in 1964, and rather than accept lucrative offers to try out for the San Diego Chargers and the Minnesota Vikings, he turned his back on pro football and took the road much less travelled by African American athletes in the 1960s. Edwards gave up sport and, against stiff competition, he won a Woodrow Wilson Scholarship. This allowed him to go to Cornell University, where he undertook a Master's degree in sociology, which he successfully completed in the spring of 1966. The following fall he was offered a part-time lecturing position at San José State.

When Tommie Smith returned from Tokyo, Edwards was in the midst of organising a protest on campus. Discussion about an Olympic boycott would have to wait.

It was just before the opening game of the intercollegiate football season, and on behalf of United Black Students for Action, Edwards put a series of demands to the administration that addressed 'racism in the fraternities and sororities, racism in housing, racism and out and out mistreatment in athletics, and a general lack of understanding of the problems of Afro-Americans by the college administration'.[8] If these demands were not met, students would disrupt the first football game of the season. Edwards warned: 'Try and play this game, and you'll see the stadium burn to the ground. I can't promise to control the people who've hit this town in support of my program.'[9] A day before the game, the university president, Robert Clark, cancelled it. He then ordered an inquiry into the complaints Edwards had raised, which would eventually lead to reform.

After this victory, Edwards said: 'At San Jose State, the mold had been forged: By exploiting sports we had compelled long-overdue change.'[10]

The success of this protest confirmed Edwards's belief in the power of sport to attract the attention of white America: 'If there is a religion in this country it is athletics. On Saturdays from 1 to 6, you know where you can find a substantial portion of the country: in the stadium or in front of the television set. We want to get to these people, to affect them, to wake them up to what's happening in this country, because otherwise they won't care.'[11]

This was only the start. 'If it can be done at San Jose State College, I don't see why it couldn't be done in Detroit, Newark and Watts,' he said.[12] Edwards could have added Mexico City to his list, as the Olympic boycott provided African American activists with an opportunity to address a global audience.

The Olympic boycott would define Edwards's strategy, which he would later call the 'revolt of the black athlete'.[13] It would be this campaign that would mark him as a prominent '68er, and a formidable one.

## THE BOYCOTT CAMPAIGN BEGINS

Once the protest at San José State had come to a satisfactory conclusion, Smith and Edwards had time to consider their next move.

To see whether there was support among athletes for an Olympic boycott, Edwards organised a workshop that was held on 23 November 1967 in a Sunday school room of the Second Baptist Church in Los Angeles. Around 200 people attended. Many turned up in colourful African dashiki shirts, sporting Afro hairdos, and wearing T-shirts displaying images of Malcolm X. Only a quarter of the audience were elite athletes, however, and even fewer had a chance of being selected for the US Olympic team. They included Smith and his fellow runner Lee Evans, the high jumper Otis Burrell, the hurdler Ron Copeland, and the basketball star Lew Alcindor, who later changed his name to Kareem Abdul-Jabbar.

At 2 p.m. Edwards kicked off the meeting: 'Wasn't it about time that black people refuse to be utilized as performing animals for a little extra dog food?', he asked.[14] He went on to say that the boycott would succeed because the 'fastest cats in the world on the track and the best basket stuffers and weightlifters and boxers are striking a blow for human rights. If their country won't do a damn thing for 22,000,000 oppressed people why should they flog their butts and sweat and strain under the Yankee flag?'[15]

By comparison, when it was Smith's turn to speak, he was the voice of moderation, as was his nature: 'I can't tell another black athlete that it is his duty to forget a goal that he has sought for himself. In fact, I hope the boycott won't be needed to bring about the necessary changes in our country. But if a boycott is deemed appropriate, then I believe most athletes will act in unison.'[16]

Edwards was a force of nature: like a human tsunami, carrying along all before him. After two and a half hours Edwards asked: 'Well what do you want to do?' The response was loud cries of 'Boycott! Boycott!'

With the threat of a boycott in the air, journalists tracked down athletes who were likely to qualify for the Olympics and asked for their opinion. Triple jumper Art Walker said: 'I believe every person has to do what his conscience tells him to do. Mine tells me to go to the Olympics.' Long jumper Ralph Boston said: 'What boycott? I've put too much time and effort into track and field to give up.'[17] Lee Evans said that he wouldn't participate in the Olympics if it meant 'slamming the potential door in the face of black people'.[18] According to a quick poll conducted by the African American magazine *Ebony*, 71 per cent rejected a boycott and another 28 per cent were undecided.[19] Only one per cent agreed with the boycott.

Many white newspaper columnists were critical. Jim Murray wrote in the *Los Angeles Times* that he was 'getting mighty bored with downy-cheeked youngsters trying to general manage the world just because they have an interesting little athletic talent'.[20] More worrisome were the critics who dwelt on a racist trope that was current at the time. For example, Charles Maher, also from the *Los Angeles Times*, warned that a boycott would 'anger them [the white

majority] more and thus resist future Negro demands'.[21] Behind
his remark was the conviction that greater equality was a gift that
whites would bestow on African Americans once they could demonstrate that they were well behaved and asked politely for their civil
rights. This position was unapologetically rejected by a new generation of African Americans, who argued that they would take their
civil rights whether the white majority liked it or not. Often under
the rubric of 'black power',[22] this approach to race relations evoked
visceral anger among many whites.

After reading about the proposed boycott, IOC president Avery
Brundage issued a veiled warning: 'If these boys are serious, they're
making a very bad mistake. If they're not serious and are using the
Olympic Games for publicity purposes, we don't like it.'[23] Referring
to the African Americans as 'boys' was the sort of racist language
used in the Jim Crow South, and it angered rather than intimidated
African American athletes.

To build momentum for a boycott, Edwards organised a second
meeting on 14 December 1967. Held in New York City's Americana
Hotel, those at the meeting decided to create the Olympic Project for Human Rights (OPHR), which would pursue six demands. It
called on the IOC to ban apartheid South Africa. Another demand
was for the resignation of Brundage, who African American athletes
considered to be racist. It also called for the appointment of an African American coach to the Olympic team and demanded that an
African American be added to the all-white US Olympic Committee. The remaining two demands were domestic and had nothing
to do with the Olympic Games: that Muhammad Ali's heavyweight
championship title be reinstated[24] and that the New York Athletic
Club allow African Americans and Jews to join.

At the press conference after the meeting, Dr Martin Luther King
Jr lent his support to the boycott. He argued that the athletes' sac-
rifices were necessary to restore 'our manhood and our dignity'.[25]
Afterwards, in an interview with *New York Times* columnist Robert
Lipsyte, Edwards took up this theme: 'We must reassert the basic
masculinity of the black people.'[26]

This gendered language played to a widely held belief among
male civil rights leaders (and they were all male). It can be traced
back to the slave past, when white oppression had emasculated African American men, robbing them of power over their own bodies,
their livelihoods, and their families. Not only did they have to grovel

to their white masters, they were even lower than white women and children, who called them 'boy'. Consequently, the recovery of their lost manhood became indelibly linked to civil rights, as largely seen through male eyes.

This attitude caused a problem for women. According to the activist Elaine Brown, male leaders were threatened by women activists who wanted to play a prominent role in the civil rights movement because they were seen as 'eroding black manhood'.[27] The allotted role of black women in the movement was to provide emotional and material support, and, importantly, to help men assert their masculinity. Above all, they were expected to unquestioningly follow the lead of the male activists.

To drum up support for the OPHR, Edwards toured the country speaking to African American athletes. Male athletes only. This is not surprising, as Edwards believed 'that when the men take a stand, the women will follow'.[28]

But some black female athletes were not content to just follow: 'It appalled me that the men simply took us for granted. They assumed we had no minds of our own and that we'd do whatever we were told' said the sprinter Wyomia Tyus.[29] Long jumper Willye White agreed: 'You know, they [male track athletes] never consulted us on this black boycott issue.'[30] It was only on the eve of the Games, almost as an afterthought, that some of the women were approached. Sprinter Jarvis Scott was not impressed: 'If they didn't care to have our opinion from the beginning, they certainly didn't need it now.'[31]

Edwards's tour to drum up support coincided with changes in his wardrobe, which went from jacket and tie to radical chic: a multicoloured dashiki shirt, a beret, heavy boots, love beads, jeans, shades, and a black leather jacket. He chomped short cigars and breathed fire at public meetings. Black students loved it. Harry Edwards was just *so* cool. Here was an African American enthusiastically hitting out at their white oppressors, who he called 'honkies', 'crackers', and 'whitey'. Edwards's new image was deliberately crafted to appeal to television audiences, who lapped up his antics and his rhetoric, which were calculated to outrage. For Edwards, it was all theatre, and he sometimes had trouble keeping a straight face: 'When I couldn't bedazzle them with brilliance, I bamboozled them with bull.'[32]

Edwards soon discovered that his 'mystique worked too well',[33] as he attracted violent racists who were willing to show Edwards just how unhappy they were. In 1967, just before Christmas, Edwards's pet Scottish terrier Milo went missing. Searching the neighbourhood he found his dog, cut up into pieces and scattered in an orchard across the road. Someone scratched 'KKK', for Ku Klux Klan, on his apartment door and car. Afterwards, Edwards had nightmares, and possibly flashbacks to the photograph of the mutilated body of Emmett Till that had so disturbed him when he was a teenager.

## WILL WE, WON'T WE?

One of the demands of the OPHR was to integrate the lily-white New York Athletic Club. While African Americans could not join the club or dine in its clubhouse, they were welcomed on the track to compete in the club's annual meet. Held in Madison Square Gardens, it consistently drew large crowds, and, as an amateur event, the club didn't have to pay the athletes. This sweet combination made the meet a highly profitable enterprise for the club.

This meet allowed Edwards to draw attention to the club's racism, by organising a boycott. He hoped that a successful protest would build momentum for its ultimate objective of boycotting the Olympic Games. Many African Americans did not require much persuasion to boycott the event as they detested the racist New York Athletic Club, and some white athletes joined in too.

On 16 February 1968 between 1,500 and 2,000 picketers gathered outside the main entrances. The American Jewish Congress lent its support to the protest, but its members did not join the picket line because the meet was held on the Sabbath. Yelling 'Racism must go', picketers intimidated athletes about to enter the stadium. As the demonstration looked like it might get violent, with militants screaming 'let's tear the goddamn building down', Edwards subtly moved protesters away from possible confrontations. Seeing what he was up to, the police handed Edwards their bullhorn so he could get his message out.[34]

The protest was a partial success. There were many empty seats in the stadium, and of the 15,972 tickets sold, around 3,000 people did not show up.

For Edwards, however, there was reason to be worried. Despite intense pressure, nine black athletes participated. If this was repeated at the Olympics, the protest would fall flat. So Edwards ramped up his rhetoric, writing in the *Saturday Evening Post* that 'any Negro athlete who doesn't [join the Olympic boycott] is, in my opinion, a cop-out and a traitor to his race'.[35]

Smith was becoming uncomfortable with Edwards's overheated rhetoric. While continuing to advocate a boycott, in March 1968 Smith pointed out, in an article he wrote in *Sport* magazine, that athletes would be making a great sacrifice. He went on to argue that the boycott's credibility 'depends on Negroes acting as a group'. If it was not possible to obtain unanimity among black athletes, then he too would 'go on to fulfil my ambition of becoming an Olympian'.[36]

On 4 April 1968 Dr Martin Luther King Jr was gunned down in Memphis. This had a profound impact on black athletes, and it hit Edwards particularly hard: 'My first emotion was grief and anger. By the time I arrived back in San Jose, the anger had turned to a blistering rage.' He saw King's assassination as exposing just how quixotic his nonviolent strategy was. While Edwards's language had intimated violence, he had never seriously entertained its use. Now he wondered if it was inevitable.[37] As his anger ebbed, he announced that the Olympic boycott should become 'a solemn memorial to Doctor King and his family'.[38]

On 21 April the IOC decided that it would no longer allow South Africa to participate in the Mexico Olympics. This announcement took the wind out of the sails of the OPHR as one of its main demands had been met. Athletes who had been wavering now felt that they could go to Mexico City with a clear conscience.

But that was not how Edwards saw it, as he explained in an interview with the *New York Times Magazine*. He warned athletes that the black community would see them as 'the devil, with his medal around his neck'. While not directly inciting violence, he issued a warning: 'Some of them are going to have accidents. You can't live with the crackers and come back to Harlem. The athlete who goes will face ostracism and harassment.'[39]

## PLAN B

The track and field trials for Olympic selection were held over the last weekend in June in the Los Angeles Coliseum. As all the hopefuls would be together, Edwards was also there to drum up support for a boycott.

In an effort to attract spectators and to fill their coffers, the US Olympic Committee (USOC) put on a show: an anaemic imitation

Figure 4.1 Facsimile of the badge worn by many African American athletes.

of an Olympics opening ceremony. There were balloons aplenty, pigeons were released as a symbol of peace, and skydivers trailed multicoloured smoke as they dropped into the middle of the stadium. Bands played, choirs sang, and three trumpeters belted out a fanfare to welcome the athletes. Around 50,000 spectators came to enjoy the show, half filling the stadium: a disappointing turnout.

Black activists chanted slogans from the bleachers, with one holding up a placard that read 'WHY RUN IN MEXICO AND CRAWL AT HOME'.

If the number of OPHR badges worn by black athletes was a guide, then it looked like a healthy majority were onside. But this was not the case. While athletes agreed with the demands made by the OPHR, many did not support a boycott. This did not mean that African American athletes – whether they were for or against a boycott – wanted to make life easy for the USOC, which they detested. Before the Los Angeles trials, some athletes announced that they would refuse to mount the victory podium to accept their awards or join the traditional march of athletes around the Coliseum at the end of the trials. Taking these threats seriously, the USOC cancelled the victory ceremonies and the march.

Sitting in the cheap seats in the stadium, Edwards held court, listening to athletes to gauge their mood and trying to persuade and cajole them into joining the boycott. He realised he had his work cut out. Many of the athletes he spoke to had made great sacrifices in the name of sport and would not easily give up the ultimate prize of an Olympic medal. Others, he knew, had come from desperately poor backgrounds, and a gold medal might mean good jobs or big pay cheques as pro footballers or basketballers. With few other opportunities, success at the Olympics was their passport to a better future.

Before the Los Angeles trials, the USOC had told male athletes that the first three place getters in each event would qualify for the upcoming Olympics. Much to the surprise of athletes who thought that they had made the cut, after the trials the USOC announced that there would be a second set of qualifiers at Echo Summit (California) that would decide the Olympic team. The rules had been changed so that the top ten finalists in Los Angeles (and twelve for some events) would have to compete again for spots on the team. Smith smelled a rat: 'I think the two trials were held to weed the blacks out.'[40] He was probably right, as the new rules gave the USOC time to see which athletes would commit to the boycott. This was a clever tactic: the USOC could easily substitute other athletes if it needed to, allowing a full-strength team to compete in Mexico City.

Echo Summit was chosen because it had a similar elevation to Mexico City. Held in the first half of September, 193 track and field athletes gathered to see who would qualify for the Olympics. Located in the Eldorado National Forest, athletes found the setting wondrous; the track wound through thick woodland and runners would disappear behind thickets of Ponderosa pines before appearing down the backstretch, with spectators watching the competition perched on huge granite boulders. A synthetic Tartan track, like the one that athletes would race on in Mexico City, had been put down for the trial, and the men stayed in trailers or junior-college dormitories down the hill in South Lake Tahoe. After the day's competition was over, it wasn't unusual to see an Olympic athlete standing by the side of the road in the early evening, thumbing a ride to the Tahoe casinos.

The women's trials were held at Los Alamos, which was also at a similar altitude to Mexico City. Because it had been a nuclear testing site, there were no-go areas where the women could not wander: it was nowhere near as pleasant as Lake South Tahoe. 'What on Earth are we doing here,' wondered the hurdler Patty van Wolvelaere: 'It's in the middle of nowhere.'

The trials were held at the local high school, which also had a Tartan track installed. After training, the women could treat themselves at the Baskin-Robbins ice cream outlet in town, which dispensed free cones to Olympic prospects. The main option for recreation was the local cinema, which was featuring Clint Eastwood movies. After a week watching Clint Eastwood, though, even he became tiresome. And when they were not at the movies, the African American women, who preferred each other's company, spent their spare time playing bid whist.

'I never understood why they didn't just put us with the men at Tahoe,' sprinter Wyomia Tyus wondered: 'Separate-and-not-equal ruled the day.'[41]

By now it looked like the boycott was dead. At the end of August Edwards told the *New York Times* that the 'majority of athletes will participate in the Olympics'. He added ominously that athletes at the Olympics would 'demonstrate their support for the black power movement in some manner'.[42]

At the start of October the US Olympic team met in Denver to be fitted out for their uniforms. They would then board chartered planes to Mexico City. This was the last chance for African American athletes to see if they could agree on what form of protest they would make in Mexico City: a Plan B.

Various ideas were floated during a series of meetings. One suggested black armbands, but then someone complained that they cut off the circulation to his arms. Another suggested long black socks, but another said that it made his feet sweat. There were further suggestions, some quite wild. Why not refuse to stand on the victory platform during the playing of the national anthem or while the American flag was being raised? Maybe they should refuse to march during the opening ceremony, just as African Americans had been left out of the mainstream of American life? Or perhaps the African American athletes could march as a separate group? Someone proposed that during the competition they run full speed until the finishing line and then sit down without crossing it, or crawl out of the starting blocks, or deliberately come last: the position that blacks occupied in racist America.

As middle distance runner Larry James said, 'It boiled down to a clash between the goal – doing good for all mankind – and the gold: the individual's self-interest. There was, shall we say, counseling back and forth to sort out the two.'

In the end, they decided that each athlete would protest as he thought best. Smith then stood up and said: 'I have to do something. I don't know what I'll do.'[43]

Had the boycott gone ahead it would certainly have shaken up the American sports-loving public. A boycott would also have reduced America's haul of gold medals. This would probably have allowed the USSR to beat the US in the medal count, which would have been a disaster as the Olympics had become a proxy battleground in the Cold War. But the OPHR never had a chance of recruiting every African American athlete. Consequently, a multiracial US team would have still marched in the opening ceremony, even with a reduced number of African Americans. With the boycotters replaced by white athletes, their sacrifice would barely have been noticed – if it was at all – by spectators in Mexico or by the global media reporting on the Olympics.

# 5

# The Tlatelolco Massacre

Who? Whom? No one. The next day, no one.
Dawn found the plaza swept; the headline
in the newspapers
was the weather forecast.
And on TV, on the radio, at the movies
there was no change in the programming,
no newsflash, not even a
moment of silence at the banquet
(but the banquet went on)

> Rosario Castellanos, *Memorial de Tlatelolco* [trans. David Bowles]

Everyone remembers October 2 differently, which makes sense because we
all remember it from the place we lived it.

> Ana Ignacia 'La Nacha' Rodríguez

### BLANCO! BLANCO!

On the evening of 2 October 1968 glowering clouds over Mexico
City threatened rain. It was just ten days before the opening ceremony of the Olympics and Italian journalist Oriana Fallaci was
worried, with good reason. She was staring down the barrel of a .45
calibre pistol.

Fallaci had arrived in Tlatelolco,[1] a suburb of Mexico City, an
hour or so earlier to report on a student demonstration in Plaza
de las Tres Culturas (Plaza of the Three Cultures). The rally's organisers assured her that it would be peaceful. They could not have
been more wrong.

Despite fearing for her life, her journalist instincts kicked in as she
took in every detail of what was happening. What she saw did not

make sense. Before her, the young man holding the gun, was not wearing a uniform. He was in dark-blue slacks and a white shirt. What struck her as odd was that he wore a white glove on his left hand. It didn't help that she had been separated from her interpreter, fellow journalist Rojas Zea, and could only guess at what was happening.

With his gun in Fallaci's face and shrieking obscenities, he grabbed her by the hair and flung her against a wall. She crumpled to the ground, stunned.[2] Other men flooded onto the balcony where she crouched, some also wearing gloves, others with white handkerchiefs tied around their left hands.

A few minutes earlier, student leaders had stood on the third floor of the yellow-tiled Chihuahua building to address around 8,000 people in the plaza below. There were also journalists on the balcony.

Suddenly, gunshots erupted around them and her tormentor took cover. '*Blanco! Blanco!*' [White! White!] he called, like it was some sort of identifier. Next she heard, '*Somos Batallón Olimpia!*'[3] It was only later that she would learn that the '*blancos*'* were members of a paramilitary group secretly set up by the Mexican government to ensure that nothing disturbed the smooth running of the Olympic Games.

The gunman – the '*blanco*' – now looked frightened. And Fallaci knew that a frightened man with a gun was even more dangerous than one waving a gun around wishing to look dangerous.

◊

The Italian magazine *L'Europeo* had sent Fallaci to Mexico City to cover student protests. With the Olympics about to start, these protests might disrupt the Games. This made it international news, particularly as the government had signalled that it was determined to suppress further demonstrations.

On 1 September 1968, in his annual state of the nation speech, President Gustavo Díaz Ordaz accused the students of staging protests 'with the purpose of discrediting Mexico' and to 'prevent the celebration of the Olympic Games'. He also assured Mexicans that he and his government would 'do what we have to' in order to 'maintain internal order and tranquility'.[4]

---

* The term '*blanco*' was used as shorthand to identify members of the Batallón Olimpia, for the white glove or handkerchief they wore on their left hand.

The first student protest was staged in July and it was followed by others. They tapped into deep discontent harboured by young Mexicans from secondary schools, technical colleges, and universities.

After arriving in Mexico on 13 September, Fallaci interviewed students to discover what was behind their discontent. A common theme was that students were convinced that the government had betrayed the aspirations of the 1910–17 revolution, which had promised Mexicans democracy, economic, and social reform, and the end of corruption and privilege. Their anger was directed at the governing party – the Partido Revolucionario Institucional [Institutional Revolutionary Party], or PRI – which claimed to be the custodian of the revolution. It had ruled, under one name or another, since 1929. However, by 1968 the PRI's appetite for reform and social justice had long gone. According to Professor Alejandro Medina of the Universida Iberoamericana, 'The Mexican revolution has been paralyzed for a long time. Parliament and unions are pure government instruments, and the party rejects any dialogue because it believes it cannot reconcile opposition with its honour.'[5]

The Mexican students were not like the '68ers Fallaci had encountered in the US and Paris, who she described as a 'bunch of idiots with long hair who pretend to build barricades without knowing why'.[6] In Mexico City, Fallaci found students with a genuine cause to protest, and she liked them even more because they were the children of peasants and workers, radiating sincerity.

Poverty was one of the issues that the students railed against, which they believed would be made worse by the obscene number of pesos spent on the Games. 'We weren't against the Olympics as a sports event, but we were against what the games represented economically,' explained Gustavo Gordillo, one of the student leaders. 'We're a very poor country, and the Olympics meant an irreparable drain on Mexico's economic resources.'[7] Other students were proud that the Games were coming to their country and volunteered as *edecanes* to help athletes and visitors.

While student leaders were ambivalent about the Olympics, they saw it as an opportunity to have their voices heard. Since the start of the protest movement in late July, local newspapers and television stations had generally accepted the government's line that the students had no reason to complain and were being manipulated by communist provocateurs. Many of the protests had ended in violence, which the media blamed on the students, even though it was often provoked by the blue-helmeted *granaderos* [riot police]. This was unsurprising as the tame Mexican media was largely in the thrall of the government. The protesters hoped that the foreign correspondents, photojournalists, and international television networks in Mexico for the Olympics would objectively report their grievances to a global audience and shame the Mexican government.

The stakes were high for the government. If violent clashes continued, the IOC could call off the Olympics. For President Ordaz Díaz, this would undermine the authority of his government and the stability of his regime, which was already unpopular.

When Fallaci was told that there would be a protest on 2 October in the Plaza de las Tres Culturas, she made sure she arrived early to report what she saw for *L'Europeo*.

### ANATOMY OF A MASSACRE

On her way to the Tlatelolco rally, Fallaci heard people singing and laughing; some chanted '*México Libertad*' [free Mexico]. One child, no more than nine years old, held up a placard in one hand that announced: 'The violence is against us, not by us.' In the other hand he held an ice cream. He marched with his mother and grandmother.[8] Others held up two fingers, much like a Churchillian victory sign, except in Mexico it stood for *venceremos*: 'we will overcome'.

Fallaci has been a journalist for over two decades, covering war and revolutions, and her interviews with world leaders were often brutal as she took delight from vivisecting her interviewees. A petite woman, she wore her hair long and her grey-blue eyes took in everything.

As Fallaci approached the plaza she saw a large number of *granaderos*, policemen, and soldiers, all armed. She also saw tanks and two Huey helicopters hovering overhead. Having been in Vietnam, the presence of the military worried her, but for the protesters this was not abnormal.

The plaza had been named after the three cultures represented in it. In its centre was an Aztec archaeological site. Next to it, on the eastern side, was the seventeenth-century Santiago de Tlatelolco church, which represented the country's Spanish heritage. The rest of the plaza was bounded by buildings that represented modern Mexico: apartment blocks, shops, schools, a

cinema, and government buildings. On its southern flank, dominating the plaza, was an imposing twenty-four-storey building with
a white marble facade, which, at the time, was occupied by the
Department of Foreign Affairs. The whole plaza was two to three
metres higher than the surrounding streets, with steps leading up
to it, while the Aztec ruins near its centre, next to the Santiago de
Tlatelolco church, were a metre or so below the level of the plaza,
and were not fenced off.

Fallaci headed to the Chihuahua building, a fourteen-storey
apartment block on the eastern edge of the plaza overlooking the
church and ruins. On the third-floor balcony she met student leaders who would be addressing the rally. The open-air balcony ran
flush along the face of the building. It was around twenty-five metres
long and was supported by a series of rectangular columns. Its low
concrete balustrade had two large loudspeakers hanging from it.
There were stairs on each side and two elevators on the back wall.
Students guarded the entrances, and Fallaci had to show her press
card to gain entry.

In the plaza the mood was festive. Mingling with protesters were
quite a few curious residents, who lived in surrounding buildings
and who had come out to watch.

A little before 6 p.m. the speeches commenced. At the same time,
the helicopters that were hovering over the plaza descended, to be
were greeted with whistles and jeers.

◊

Around 6.10 p.m. Fallaci saw two green flares light up the sky, five
metres above the bell tower of the church. Others saw three flares:
two green and one red.[9] On seeing the flares Fallaci warned those
around her that in Vietnam flares signalled an attack. Before they
could respond, they heard shots.

Everyone on the balcony panicked except for student leader
Sócrates Amado Campos Lemus, who grabbed the microphone
and announced: 'Don't run, all of you, don't run, they're just shooting into the air ... stay right where you are, stay where you are,
don't panic.'[10]

Fallaci darted to the front of the balcony and saw military vehicles
below, entering the plaza from the northwest and advancing past
the archaeological site towards the church. Then there were gunshots, soon followed by the rattle of machine guns.

'I've been to Vietnam and I can assure you that there are barricades, foxholes, trenches, holes, and things like that you can take cover in during machine-gun barrages and bombings,' Fallaci explained. 'But here there was absolutely nowhere to take cover.'[11]

◊

The flares that Fallaci saw explode over the church signalled the start of Operation Galeana.

Earlier that day, at 7 a.m., General Marcelino Garcia Barragán was in his office putting the finishing touches to his plan. Its primary objective was to put an 'end to the [student] movement'[12] by arresting its leaders. The government did not want to be embarrassed by protests disrupting the Olympics when the world's eyes would be on Mexico.

With foreign journalists reporting the protest, General Barragán wanted to avoid violence. By closely coordinating the army, the *granaderos*, and the paramilitary Batallón Olimpia he hoped to 'apprehend the leaders of the movement, without dead or injured'.[13]

The plan was that armed members of the Batallón Olimpia, in plain clothes, would arrest student leaders on the balcony of the Chihuahua building. Prisons had been emptied of petty criminals in readiness. Soldiers and *granaderos* were charged with sealing off the plaza and detaining, identifying, and photographing protesters. This was designed to intimidate supporters of the student movement.

By mid afternoon, members of the Batallón Olimpia were in position, occupying empty apartments on the second floor of the Chihuahua building and guarding its exits. At about the same time, 300 tanks, assault units, jeeps, and military transports, and some 8,000 troops, were deployed around the plaza.

A control centre was established on the fifteenth floor of the building that housed the Department of Foreign Affairs, run by six men, all in plainclothes. Four scanned the plaza with binoculars and the other two operated a two-way radio. Once all the student leaders were on the balcony of the Chihuahua building, one of the men in the control centre took out a nickel-plated short-barrelled shotgun, loaded it with a cartridge, and then fired out of a window. He repeated this, firing off green and red flares that burst over the church. This signalled the commencement of Operation Galeana.

What followed was not part of the plan. The shooting and chaos in the plaza, which Fallaci witnessed, was an operation gone wrong. Horribly wrong.

◊

When Captain Ernesto Morales Soto, who headed two units of the Batallón Olimpia, saw the flares burst over the church, he ordered one unit to seal the doors into the Chihuahua building to prevent anyone from entering or leaving. The elevators were shut down and he ordered fifty of his men to climb the stairs and arrest the student leaders.

◊

Almost immediately after the flares had exploded over the plaza, Fallaci heard boots on the metal stairs. Hoping to escape, she ran towards the elevators. She was stopped by two *blancos*, who snarled, 'Now we are going to give you your revolution, you *hijueputa* [sons of whores]!'[14]

More *blancos* entered the balcony. '*Detenidos, detenidos, detenidos!*' [arrested, arrested, arrested], they yelled. A young boy, no more than fifteen years old, tried to get to the microphone to warn the people below. One of the *blancos* shot him. Then the *blancos* ordered everyone on the balcony to line up against the back wall with their hands behind their heads. 'Nobody move!' one shouted. 'Traitors! Communists! Bastards!' another *blanco* screamed. 'Don't raise your heads! Anyone who moves gets fucked over!'[15] Those who resisted copped a blow to the head or ribs with a pistol butt. Lined up against the wall, feelings of helplessness – mingled with hatred – washed over the student leaders.

Fallaci was standing near the back wall when one of the *blancos* held his .45 calibre pistol to her head.

Another *blanco*, a large burly man, his blond hair cut very short and wearing a raincoat, raced to the guardrail. Below him he saw protesters surging towards the Chihuahua building. Perhaps thinking they were going to storm the building to free their leaders, he started to fire into the crowd.

At the same time, soldiers were entering the plaza. Seeing gunfire coming from the third floor of the Chihuahua building, they fired back. High-calibre bullets hit the front balustrade, the ceiling, and the walls of the balcony. They may well have believed that the Batallón Olimpia had not succeeded in arresting the leaders and it was armed students who were shooting at them.

The *blancos* panicked when they realised they were being attacked by the soldiers below: their own comrades. This was not part of the plan. Something was going terribly wrong with the execution of Operation Galeana.

Realising they were in trouble, the *blancos* started to yell wildly: 'Don't shoot; we're wearing white gloves!'[16] What was extraordinary was that none of the *blancos* on the balcony had a walkie-talkie, so they were unable to contact the control centre to call off the attack.

They were under attack not only from soldiers below but also from unidentified snipers who were shooting at them from the upper floors of surrounding buildings.

Standing against the back wall, Fallaci was totally exposed. Alarmed, she pleaded with her captor, who still had his pistol trained on her, to be able to take cover behind one of the concrete pillars. It would offer some protection as bullets ricocheted around the balcony.

Certain that she'd be hit sooner or later, Fallaci fell to the ground like a rag doll, hoping the *blancos* would think she had fainted. Where she fell was still exposed: bullets bouncing off the ceiling were hitting the ground near her. When she thought the *blancos* were distracted, she slid across the floor to where there was better cover.

During another burst of gunfire, Fallaci felt pain, like a knife going into her back. A red stain was spreading on her jacket, and when she touched her leg she saw there was more blood. She had been hit by shrapnel. One fragment missed her spine by millimetres. Another embedded in her left knee. A third went clean through her thigh. As her cries of pain were ignored by the *blancos*, she cursed them: '*Asesinos! Asesinos!*' [Murderers! Murderers!].[17]

After about fifteen minutes of intense gunfire, a tank entered the plaza and fired its cannon at the Chihuahua building. One of its shells broke a gas pipe, causing a fire. Flames lapped the building between the tenth and thirteenth floors. Resident ran down the stairs, some carrying small children, dodging gunfire as they fled. Another shell burst water pipes, and the lower floors of the Chihuahua building were inundated with water.

After around half an hour, the shooting at the balcony subsided and the *blancos* were able to attend to their prisoners.

Shooting below continued, although it was nowhere near as intense.

Seeing the well-heeled Italian journalist lying prone, one of the *blancos* relieved her of her gold watch, money, and handbag. He then grabbed Fallaci by the hair and dragged her down the stairs. Her head banged against the banisters, the steps, and the wall, causing her to scream out in pain. He then dumped her in a room on the second floor of the Chihuahua building where they were holding other prisoners.

◊

At 6.10 p.m., General José Hernández Toledo was in a truck on the northeast corner of the plaza. He looked up and saw a green flare explode over the church. This signalled the start of Operation Galeana. Then a red flare seared the sky. This may have been a warning to be careful because some students might be armed.

His truck entered the plaza, stopping near the north side of the church. When it stopped, Toledo jumped up on the tray and, using a loudhailer, he told the students to leave the plaza peacefully. He'd only been speaking for a couple of minutes when he was hit by a bullet. With Toledo unconscious and losing blood, two members of his unit commandeered a car parked nearby and took their wounded comrade to the Central Military Hospital.

With their commander down, his troops were uncertain how to react. Were there armed students in the plaza? Perhaps there were snipers in the nearby buildings, or even on the roof of the church? They panicked. Not knowing where the hostile fire was coming from, soldiers shot upwards at surrounding buildings and across the plaza, creating mayhem.

When they saw shots coming from the Chihuahua building they returned fire. This, in all likelihood, was the source of gunfire that so unnerved the *blancos* on the balcony and wounded Fallaci.

◊

Having seen the flares blossom over the church, other army units entered from the northwest and southern ends of the plaza. They moved through the archways of high-rise apartment buildings, around the sides of those buildings, along roads that skirted the plaza, and then advanced through open areas between the buildings.

As they entered the plaza, they saw that Toledo's unit was under attack. Assuming the gunfire came from armed students, they fired at the Chihuahua building and into the crowd. They too came under fire from snipers. They panicked and fired indiscriminately, believing that the enemy was everywhere.

Still the helicopters hovered overhead. When they saw their troops under attack they joined the fray, unleashing grey streaks of semiautomatic fire into the crowd as they descended in tighter and tighter circles to get a better fix on their targets. One of the helicopters left after its co-pilot was wounded by return gunfire, probably from an armed student.

◊

Caught in the crossfire, some students encountered soldiers who were just as horrified as they were by the carnage. 'Get down stupid, can't you see that they're shooting?' said one soldier. 'And who is shooting,' asked one of the students? 'Your friends,' was the reply from a soldier who believed it was student militants who had started the firefight. 'Go that way, but take cover on this low wall.'[18]

◊

When the flares exploded over the plaza, Roberta Avendaño Martínez, better known by her nom de guerre 'La Tita', was sitting on steps in the Plaza de las Tres Culturas with her good friend Ana Ignacia 'La Nacha' Rodríguez. They were holding up a blanket on which they had painted the word '*libertad*' [freedom]. La Tita and La Nacha were leaders in the student movement, yet neither woman had been invited onto the balcony of the Chihuahua building to address the rally. That was the preserve of men.

There were few women in leadership positions in the student movement because, in Mexico's strongly patriarchal society, they were expected to do the shopping, cleaning, and cooking, and to take other traditional female roles. Not La Tita and La Nacha, though. They had been on the front lines of earlier protests, shoulder to shoulder with the men, and had spent time in jail.

When the shooting started, La Nacha was stunned: 'I couldn't believe what I was seeing.' She was still holding the blanket. 'Leave it,' La Tita screamed at her, and they ran for cover in the Aztec ruins near the centre of the plaza.[19] During a lull in the shooting they ran out of the plaza and were picked up by a white Volkswagen full of students. As they made their escape, they saw military vehicles heading towards the plaza and ambulances heading away from it.

◊

Around two hours before the protest commenced, a wedding was held at the Santiago de Tlatelolco church. It was interrupted at around 5 p.m. by a number of *blancos* bursting into the church. While some of them stood guard at the entrance, three others passed through the choir stalls and climbed up the stairs to the roof. They carried semiautomatic rifles.

When the flare exploded over the plaza and the women in the church heard gunfire, they screamed and children cried. 'Be still and remain silent,' ordered one of the *blancos*. 'You'll be safe.'

Soon after, five young men, probably students, ran into the church and were immediately detained by the *blancos*, who then closed and barred the church doors. As the intensity of gunfire increased, there was banging on the enormous doors of the church as people outside desperately sought sanctuary. The *blancos* refused to let them in.

Located near the front of the Chihuahua building, the roof of the church provided a good vantage point for the *blancos*, who started shooting at students in the plaza, heedless of the risk of hitting soldiers who were pursuing fleeing students.

After the shooting had subsided, the *blancos* left and were replaced by soldiers.

After hours detained in the church, the priest felt he needed to do something about the wedding. He approached the young couple and solemnly, but also speedily, declared them husband and wife.

After five or six hours, troops marched the wedding party out of a back door, located near the altar. They were led to a military bus that took them away from Tlatelolco. Before getting off the bus they were warned not to say anything about what they had seen.[20] But what had they seen? None of it made sense.

What was obvious was that the *blancos* in the church were following orders. Was this part of Operation Galeana or something else?

◊

When the flares detonated over the plaza, nineteen-year-old Ana María Regina Teuscher – Marietta to her family and friends – was standing in front of the Chihuahua building listening to the speeches.

Marietta was not supposed to be at the demonstration. Her father had forbidden her to attend. 'All those unruly people should be locked up,' he declared.[21] As an excuse to get out of the house and attend the protest, she told her father that her friend Guillermina had invited her to see a movie at the Metropolitan cinema.

Marietta was a bright, bubbly nineteen year old, with a pale complexion and long brown hair. She was studying medicine at university, where she had become infected by the fervour of the student movement. She also had a talent for languages and had secured a position as an *edecane* to the Swiss Olympic team. She was so proud of her connection with the Games that she wore her Olympic striped jacket, with the five rings emblazoned on the front, to the plaza.

When the shooting started, Marietta and Guillermina ran towards the church. Then they encountered fire from that direction. Nowhere seemed to be safe. The girls dropped to the ground, hoping to escape the bullets.

As they lay there, the heavens opened and the girls were drenched by heavy rain. For a while, the rain scrubbed the smell of cordite, laced with the stench of shit, that had fouled the air. The noise of the rain, however, barely masked the unnerving sounds: the thuds of dumdum bullets, the shattering of glass windows, and the desperate prayers of the people around them. Other people cursed: 'Murderers! Cowards! Killers!' The freshly flowing blood, however, made no sound.

During the shooting, Marietta had run off while Guillermina lay on the ground, hit in the leg by a bullet. Soon after, soldiers escorted Guillermina to the side of the Department of Foreign Affairs building, where she joined hundreds of protesters waiting to be processed. Guillermina, like the others, was asked to show her identity papers; otherwise she would be arrested. This exercise provided the government with a handy list of all the demonstrators, who they could deal with at their leisure, should they so wish. She was then taken to hospital, from where she rang Marietta's father: 'I'm at the Red Cross with a bullet wound to my leg,' she explained through a stream of tears. 'I lost Marietta. You need to look for her.'[22]

Members of the Teuscher family spread out, visiting first aid stations, hospitals, and everywhere else there was a remote possibility that Marietta might be. In the early hours of the morning, her brother Pablo found his sister's body in a makeshift morgue in the police station on Rayón Street. She had been shot in the back six times with a .45 calibre pistol: the sort of automatic pistol that was standard army issue.

General Gutiérrez Gómez Tagle, commander of the Batallón Olimpia, saw what happened to Marietta. After a flurry of shots, he reported that a 'young hostess fell, she seemed to have stumbled while running, but when I tried to lift her, my left hand with the [white] glove was soaked with blood and I could only drag her to one of the posts where the doctor ... declared her dead'.[23]

Unlike many other victims who remained anonymous, Marietta's father was able to have her body immediately released, using his contacts in the government. She was buried the next day at the Panteón Civil de Dolores, the largest cemetery in Mexico City.

◊

José Ramón Fernández and Gilberto Ibarra saw the results of the massacre first hand. At the time, they were young medical students who assisted with post-mortems.

During the night, military trucks and ambulances delivered bodies, which were left on tables in the corridors of the morgue. As Fernández and Ibarra examined the victims, they discovered that dumdum bullets had drilled into bodies and then exploded, leaving gruesome wounds. Some had been hit more than once. It was obvious that soldiers had not aimed at arms or legs but at torsos, hitting the heart and other vital organs. They were out to kill.

'They were people of my age, students, with gunshots, with bayonet wounds,' recalls Fernández. 'It was the first time I had seen so many bodies together.' One image that still haunts him is of a young woman who had the right side of her face blown off.[24]

Army trucks arrived the next morning to collect the bodies that had no identification.

◊

Fallaci did not witness the slaughter that was going on in the plaza. During the most intense shooting she was lying on the floor of the third-floor balcony of the Chihuahua building, and then in an apartment on the floor below.

In that apartment, the *blancos* were replaced by soldiers, who went about interrogating prisoners.

Badly wounded, Fallaci kept crying out that she was a journalist, demanding that they call an ambulance as she was losing blood and was in excruciating pain. Ignoring her pleas, her guards accused her of being an 'agitator' and a 'guerrilla'.[25]

Drifting in and out of consciousness, she didn't see the rough justice the soldiers were dishing out to their captives. In the next room a boy was being brutally beaten. Then a girl was shoved into the room. 'Why the violence?' she defiantly challenged her tormentors. To teach her a lesson, two soldiers dragged her into a bathroom where they stripped and probably raped her. Eventually she returned, half-naked. This time, through her sobs, she meekly answered every question she was asked by her interrogators.[26]

Finally, an ambulance arrived and Fallaci was taken to Hospital Rubén Leñero. Pale from loss of blood, she was having difficulty breathing. She was also cold, having been stripped of her wet clothes. All she had was a thin sheet covering her dignity. She was placed on a gurney and left to wait as doctors treated others with more serious wounds. Nearby, she saw a woman with a baby girl in her arms. A baby with a gaping wound in her tiny head.

In one of her lucid moments, Fallaci begged a nurse to call the Italian Embassy. Dr Giovanni Viale soon arrived as a result of this call, and after examining his patient he took her in his car to his private clinic.

As she was leaving, one of the Spanish doctors came up to her: 'Can I ask you a big favour?' he pleaded. 'Tell all that you have seen.'[27]

At his clinic, Viale operated to remove a piece of shrapnel that was lodged between two discs of Fallaci's spine. Thankfully, the operation was a success, otherwise she might have been paralysed.

That night in Tlatelolco left a deep mental scar on Fallaci: 'The physical pain was tolerable but the nightmare was not.'[28]

◊

Back in the plaza, once the shooting had subsided, the *blancos* and the soldiers rounded up the student leaders and marched them, hands behind their heads, to the south wall of the Santiago de Tlatelolco church. Soldiers then forced their prisoners to strip to their loose underwear. Many were wet from the burst water main and were shivering. Lined up against the wall, they looked like a row of ragged white flags of surrender. Some had been fully strip searched, and stood against the wall naked. Government photographers captured their humiliation, though some students looked defiantly into the camera, a small gesture of rebelliousness in the face of overwhelming intimidation.

At around 11.30 p.m. soldiers started to escort their captives to waiting military trucks and buses. At 5 a.m. the next day the final group of prisoners was evacuated.

That night, according to the government, a total of 1,043 arrests were made.[29] The protest's leaders were taken to Military Camp No 1, where they were interrogated. Many were beaten with blackjacks: socks filled with ball bearings. Others were tortured with cattle prods, and some men had electrodes attached to their testicles. Some of the women had their breasts burned with cigarettes. Others were raped.

◊

In the early hours of the morning, soldiers guarded the entry points to the plaza. They allowed access only to cleaners, who started to arrive at 7 a.m. to find the plaza littered with shards of glass, umbrellas, bloodstained clothes, and high-heeled shoes. It's hard to run in high heels. The cleaners swept and hosed down material evidence of what had happened the night before.

◊

Having heard that all the dead and wounded had been evacuated from the plaza, the distressed parents of the missing waited outside hospitals, police stations, and the morgue, trying to get news.

◊

After attending the rally in the Plaza de las Tres Cultura, Italian hurdler Eddy Ottaz returned to the Olympic Village and told his teammates about the horrors he had witnessed. If another student was shot, he told the Italian newspaper *l'Unità*, he would not compete: 'The Olympics are not worth a single human life.'[30]

◊

The next day, Maria Elena was at the Panteón Jardín – a cemetery located in the southwest of Mexico City – for her brother Julio's funeral.

Julio, who was just fifteen years old, had attended the Tlatelolco rally, where he had been hit by three bullets: once in the leg, once in the stomach, and once in the neck. He died in hospital.

Figure 5.1   Street poster calling for the freeing of political prisoners.

As the funeral procession walked behind the hearse, Julio's schoolmates held their hands up high, making the sign of the 'V', for *venceremos* [we will overcome]. Some bystanders also made the 'V' sign, in solidarity.

◊

In the months following the massacre, the government arrested student leaders who had escaped the Plaza de las Tres Culturas on the night of 2 October 1968. La Nacha and La Tita, the most prominent female leaders, were among those arrested. They were incarcerated in Cárcel de Mujeres, the women's prison on the outskirts of Mexico City.

While they were in jail, posters bearing the slogan '*Libertad a los presos políticos*' [Free political prisoners] appeared on the streets of Mexican towns and cities. On them were drawings of men behind prison bars. No women. La Nacha and La Tita had already been forgotten. This was a great injustice, complained La Nacha: 'Without us women, the movement would not have been as effective.'[31]

The reason for this omission from the history of the student movement is that while numerous accounts from male leaders were published, describing their suffering and heroism, there were precious few accounts by women.[32] The result, according to historians Lessie Jo Frazier and Deborah Cohen, is that women 'are written out of the story'.[33]

### WHAT WENT WRONG?

When the flares scorched the air above the Santiago de Tlatelolco church, it was a signal to members of the Presidential General Staff, under the command of General Gutiérrez Oropeza, to fire into the crowd. Like the *blancos*, they were not in uniform and wore white gloves or handkerchiefs on their left hands. However, they were not part of Operation Galeana. Instead, they inserted themselves into that operation without the knowledge of its commander, General Barragán.

It is quite possible that General Toledo was hit by a bullet fired by a member of Oropeza's rogue unit of *blancos*, who had positioned themselves on the upper floors of buildings surrounding the plaza.

As for the regular soldiers in the plaza, they naturally assumed that they were under attack from armed students, and they panicked and indiscriminately returned fire. It was this rogue unit that transformed Operation Galeana into a massacre.

Almost thirty years later information has come to light on who might have been behind the rogue operation. Care should be taken with this new evidence as it is based on interviews with some of the principal protagonists, who have good reason to deflect blame away from themselves.

After his death, a letter from General Barragán was discovered that revealed that ten military agents from the Presidential General Staff had been deployed in upper-floor apartments surrounding the plaza. This information came from General Oropeza, who rang Barragán at around 7:30 p.m. on the night of 2 October. 'My general, I have deployed officers armed with machine guns to shoot on the students,' he said. 'All of them succeeded in getting out of there; only two were unable to get away. They're in civilian clothes and I'm afraid for their lives.' He asked Barragán to protect them. Barragán then asked Oropeza: 'Why didn't you inform me about the officers you're referring to?' Oropeza replied: 'Because those were my orders, my general.'[34] He did not reveal who gave him those orders, however.

Most likely, the orders came from President Díaz Ordaz or Luis Echeverría, his Minister of the Interior. It is possible, although less likely, that this was a private escapade: solely the work of General Oropeza.

Many Mexicans blamed President Díaz Ordaz. He was desperate for the Olympics to succeed and he had already announced in his State of the Nation speech that he would do whatever it took to end student protests. As General Oropeza was the president's Chief of Staff, and was fanatically loyal, he may well have been carrying out secret orders from his boss. There is evidence to the contrary, however. According to Cuauhtémoc García Pineda, the official government photographer, when President Díaz Ordaz handed over the flag to the Mexican Olympic team a few days after the Tlatelolco massacre, he overheard the president muttering to himself: 'They fooled me! They fooled me!'[35] Student leader Luís González de Alba also didn't believe that Díaz Ordaz ordered the rogue operations because he was a stickler for detail and would have ensured that the operation was effectively coordinated and executed.[36]

The other candidate was the Minister for Interior, Luis Echeverría, who would succeed Díaz Ordaz as president in 1970. Echeverría defended himself in an interview he gave to CNN, in which he pointed the finger at Díaz Ordaz: 'The army is obligated to respond to only one man,'[37] he said. If he was implying that he had been sidelined from major decisions, this is untrue. On 26 July 1968, within days of the first political protest, Echeverría created and led a committee of key government officials who implemented tactics to stop further student protests. He was most definitely a major player within the government.

On 30 June 2006 Judge José Ángel Mattar Oliva placed eighty-four-year-old Echeverría under house arrest for his role in the Tlatelolco massacre, concluding that 'Echeverría must surely have knowledge of it'.[38]

Although unlikely, General Oropeza may have planned the rogue operation without telling the president or Echeverría. If so, perhaps he had been motivated by his obsessive hatred of communism, as he explained in his memoirs: 'The radical left ... received precise orders from international communism to take advantage of the preparation for the Olympics in order to carry out in Mexico the part that the country had been assigned in the Worldwide Revolution.'[39]

The IOC may, inadvertently, have set the stage for the massacre. A message from IOC president Avery Brundage that was delivered to President Díaz Ordaz in mid September warned that the Games would be called off should there be more trouble. According to John Rodda, a journalist for *The Guardian*, 'when the big rally was held on 2 October that was the time to smash them. From the government's point of view, it was a successful outcome; the brutality of that night snuffed out any possible further action.'[40]

## AND THE BANQUET CONTINUED

Even as the bodies were being carted to the morgue and student leaders taken to prison, the government called a press conference. Just before 1 a.m. on the day after the massacre, around sixty journalists were briefed for about an hour by Fernando Garza, the Director of Press and Public Relations, who was attached to President Díaz Ordaz's office.

Garza reported that about twenty people had been killed, seventy-five injured, and more than 400 detained. He also reported that Oriana Fallaci had been wounded. Nothing serious, just 'a slight bullet scratch'. She was recuperating at home.[41] He assured the foreign correspondents that 'peace would be guaranteed during the Olympic Games, there is and there will be sufficient vigilance to avoid problems'.[42]

The government was desperate to downplay the number of deaths. Otherwise, the IOC might call off the Olympics.

As many of the journalists in the room had witnessed the massacre, Garza's account of events was greeted by incredulity. Uli Schmetzer from the *Chicago Tribune* reported seeing the 'dying and the dead scattered like molehills across the vast square. Some still moved, others lay inert, some curled up, others were spread-eagled as if crucified.'[43] Heinrich Jaenecke from *Die Zeit* wrote: 'The whole thing was a major military attack on a peaceful group of people who were exercising their constitutional right of assembly.'[44] John Rodda from *The Guardian* estimated that up to 500 people may have been killed (a number he later revised down to 325).[45] Most worrisome for the Mexican government was an article that appeared in the *New York Times* that argued that 'the night's events cast into serious question the prospects for the Olympic Games'.[46]

Brundage's response to Tlatelolco appeared in a Mexican newspaper the next morning: 'I was at the ballet last night and we heard nothing of the riots,' he said. He ended the interview with the verbal equivalent of a shrug, when he heard that students had died: 'We live in that kind of world.'[47]

Executive members of the IOC were less blasé than their president, and at 8 a.m. the next day they summoned Pedro Ramírez Vázquez, the president of the Mexican Olympic Organising Committee, to an urgent meeting.

At the start of the meeting Lord Killanin banged the table as he confronted Ramírez Vázquez: 'What are you going to do to save your Olympiad?' The Mexican told him not to become 'hysterical about a police action that has nothing to do with the Olympic Games'. With this assurance, Brundage ended the debate, telling IOC members: 'If you, as host have confidence that this is not serious, then we trust the host.' As soon as he left the meeting, Ramírez Vázquez rang President Díaz Ordaz and told him: 'There is no problem; the Olympiad will go ahead.'[48]

Three hours later, Brundage made an announcement to the media: 'We have consulted with the Mexican authorities, who have assured us that there will be no interference upon the entry of the Olympic flame into the stadium on October 12, nor in any of the events until the closing of the Games.'[49]

Despite the assurances coming from the IOC, some teams in the Olympic Village were ordered not to venture out. It was too dangerous. Others received telegrams from worried parents insisting they

Figure 5.2    Street posters that appeared in Mexico City after the Tlatelolco massacre.

return home. With little accurate information, athletes didn't know what to think. A day after the massacre, the British hurdler Dave Hemery saw a young man with dark curly hair – eighteen, perhaps a little older – at the wire fence that surrounded the Olympic Village, waving him over. 'We are not against you and the Olympics,' the student explained. 'What we want is the world's press to notice our protests.'[50]

A day before the opening ceremony, and a scant nine days after the massacre, Dick Beddoes, a sportswriter for the *Globe and Mail*, casually remarked that 'shots from rebellious students will not be heard, apparently because revolution has been scrubbed from the Olympic program'.[51] He was right. The outrage over the massacre was short lived. Rather than being seen as an assault on Olympic values, it was, ironically, the razzmatazz of the Olympic Games that diverted the world's attention away from the massacre.

Fallaci well understood how the emotions of the Olympics swept all other news off the front pages of the newspapers. Recovering in the comfort of her hotel room, but still in pain, she wryly remarked: 'We talk about records, stopwatches, athletes, dives, medals. There are many cocktail parties to celebrate the participants, to toast sport and the athletes. How uncomfortable the dead are: you get rid of them too soon.'[52]

# 6

## Let the Fiesta Begin

We Mexicans are by character great *fiesteros*, so our Olympics will be a big party for the world.

Pedro Ramírez Vázquez, president of the
Mexican Olympic Organising Committee

Look at the Olympics and you'll see all of life in microcosm. You'll see pain and struggle, perseverance, failure, triumph. You'll see principle in action; you'll see man in his splendor, as we want him to be. Look closely, and you'll see what we ourselves can be.

Bob Richards, US Olympian

### A MOOD FOR FORGETTING

'The whole world loves a fiesta – and now that the whole world will be converging on Mexico, a fiesta is what they are going to get,' promised Pedro Ramírez Vázquez, two months before the Games were due to open.[1]

An architect by profession, Ramírez Vázquez had been applying his refined aesthetic sensibilities to the presentation of the Games since being appointed president of the Mexican Olympic Organising Committee. He orchestrated the cityscape, with bright pinks, oranges, and blues used in concentric circles on pavements around sporting venues. Along La Ruta de la Amistad, a major thoroughfare south of the main stadium, there were nineteen modernist sculptures in vibrant colours, creating the largest sculpture corridor in the world, seventeen kilometres in length. The main thoroughfares were dressed with flowerbeds of dahlias in the Olympic colours.

Impressed by what he saw, a journalist from *Time* magazine wrote: 'Mexico City scrubbed, brash, vital, is as bright and gay as a *piñata* party.'[2] At Olympic venues, *edecanes* helped overseas athletes and visitors. Wearing dresses featuring an Op Art design, they were described by Ruben Salazar from the *Los Angeles Times* as 'pretty girls in psychedelic miniskirts'.[3]

Perhaps the single most watched event at every Olympic is the opening ceremony. For Ramírez Vázquez it was an opportunity to demonstrate that Mexico could put on a show just as spectacular as any previous host city.

On the morning of 12 October 1968 people walked or drove to the main stadium along the broad Avenue Insurgentes. They passed scores of lamp posts on its median strip, on which hung brightly coloured banners depicting a silhouetted white dove of peace against yellow, green, blue, and rose backgrounds. The symbol complemented the motto of the Games: *'Todo es posible en la paz'* [Everything is possible in peace].

An unfortunate counterpoint to these symbols of peace was the presence of police and armed soldiers, who guarded the routes to the stadium. After Tlatelolco, the government was worried that student protesters might disrupt the Games. Around the stadium most of the soldiers were out of sight, so as not to alarm visitors. They slouched behind trees and crouched in bushes. Inside the stadium plainclothes members of the Batallón Olimpia mingled with spectators, using walkie-talkies to keep in touch with one another. It was a cruel irony that this festival of peace opened just ten days after the massacre in Tlatelolco.

Yet people with tickets to the opening ceremony were in a mood for forgetting. Perhaps they believed what they read in the mainstream Mexican newspapers: that the massacre had been initiated by armed communist provocateurs, and, in any case, the number of dead was small. Perhaps they believed IOC president Avery Brundage, who stated after the massacre that the Olympics would be 'a veritable oasis in a troubled world'.[4] Spectators were looking forward to the pomp and pageantry of the opening ceremony, which would kick off a sporting fiesta the likes of which Mexicans had never seen before. It was an opportunity to showcase Mexico to the world.

### A FESTIVAL OF HUMAN UNITY

As a spectacular, the opening ceremony that Ramírez Vázquez organised did not disappoint. However, it was more than a piece of entertainment. This ceremony, like all the other Olympic rituals, symbolically promoted Olympism. Internationalist in its ambition, it advocated 'the love for concord and a respect for life'[5] as a path towards 'moral betterment and social peace', according to Pierre de Coubertin, the father of the modern Olympic Games.[6]

For much of his life de Coubertin wrote extensively about Olympism, seeking inspiration from ancient Hellenic Olympics, medieval chivalry, and Thomas Arnold's ideas on physical education.

While secular, de Coubertin was keen to infuse the Olympic Games with 'religious feeling'.[7] To this end, he consciously appropriated the form and functions of religious ceremonies to promote the sacred mission of Olympism.

Cultural anthropologist John MacAloon wrote that the Olympic Games, populated with impressive ceremonies redolent with meaning, presents 'alluring, consistent, and powerful rites, [which are] the closest we have been able to come to true world rituals'. He went on to argue that Olympic rituals are 'designed to render [Olympic ideology] emotionally veridical',[8] which makes its rituals so affecting for spectators and athletes alike. Taken together, Olympic ceremonies create a 'rite of passage, in which millions and millions of persons are, so to speak, taken on a voyage: away from their routine, daily lives; through a special time and space; and then returned,' explained MacAloon.[9]

With varying success, its ceremonies also served to initiate athletes into the cult of Olympism, in which they are expected to epitomise physical and ethical strength.

A few minutes before 11 a.m., President Díaz Ordaz and his wife arrived at the entrance of the stadium, where they were met by their hosts: Pedro Ramírez Vázquez and IOC president Avery Brundage. Díaz Ordaz and his wife were led to the Tribune of Honour (the VIP box), where they were welcomed by a twenty-one-gun salute. From the start, the show belonged to the IOC. The Mexican president was an honoured guest, even though the Games were in his country and his government was footing the bill: a bill that would add up to 2.2 billion pesos (equivalent to US$765 million in 2020) by the end of the Olympics.[10]

The government was willing to spend lavishly to promote Mexico as an emerging economy. Commonly known as the 'Mexican miracle', growth had increased at an impressive seven per cent a year since the mid 1950s.[11] The government intended to use the

Olympics to dispel the image of the typical Mexican, asleep against a cactus, wearing a poncho, with his face shaded by a sombrero; a citizen of the land of *mañana*.

There was another reason why Díaz Ordaz needed the Olympics to be a success. He was desperate to restore his authority in the face of student protests that had challenged the government during the second half of 1968. The governing party, the Partido Revolucionario Institucional [the Institutional Revolutionary Party], presided over a *dictablanda* (soft authoritarian) regime, and the country was a democracy in name only.[12]

While Mexico was becoming wealthier, poverty remained endemic, and human rights abuses were commonplace. By 1968 the government, and particularly Ordaz Díaz, were disliked among the younger generations, the '68ers. The president hoped that staging the Olympics would both confer a de facto moral legitimacy on his government and raise his popularity among the populace.

While ordinary Mexicans were proud that the Games were being held in their country, and those in the stadium for the opening ceremony were looking forward to a memorable fiesta, not everyone was in a mood to forget. As President Díaz Ordaz entered the Tribune of Honour, a black kite in the shape of a dove flew above the stadium. It was not part of the official ceremony, though: it was a protest to draw attention to the massacre in Tlatelolco. The kite did not stay in the air long; presumably, the students flying it were apprehended by soldiers surrounding the stadium.

While the opening ceremony had a strong Mexican flavour, it nevertheless followed rigid Olympic protocols that ensured the integrity of its rituals.

After the arrival of the official party there was a fanfare of forty trumpets followed by the Mexican national anthem. Five huge Olympic rings, filled with helium and looking like plump donuts, then lumbered skyward. According to de Coubertin, the five interlinked rings 'represent the five parts of the world won over by Olympism'.[13] They visually announce the consummation of nation-states into an international marriage. Participating countries were now part of the Olympic family.

One of the most popular and colourful parts of the opening ceremony was the Parade of Nations. The first such parade was staged in 1906, at what are called the 'Olympic Intercalated Games', held in Athens to celebrate the tenth anniversary of the revival of the Olympics.

As each team entered the Estadio Olímpico Universitario they were greeted by a welcoming roar from 80,000 spectators. While there were 7,226 Olympic competitors, the number who marched was smaller. Athletes whose events were early in the programme didn't want to tire themselves out by participating in the march. Instead, they either sat in the stadium or watched the opening ceremony on television in the Olympic Village.

For over an hour athletes marched into the stadium behind their national flags. Each team was led by a cadet from the Colegio Militar who wore a black kepi ringed by a gold band and who held up a placard with the name of the country on it. A steady drumbeat helped marchers keep time.

What followed was as much a fashion show as a pageant. Members of the Indian team wore white turbans called *pagri*, duck egg blue sports jackets, and patent leather shoes. Nigerians wore lime green *agbadas*: flowing wide-sleeved robes. High fashion was also in evidence when the women in the French team appeared in pleated turquoise skirts and navy blue shoes, with chic hats completing the ensemble. It looked like their outfits had come straight from an exclusive Parisian atelier. There were gasps of surprise, followed by enthusiastic cheering, when Mongolian flag bearer Jigjidiin Mönkhbat appeared. He was dressed like he was on furlough from Genghis Khan's hordes. He wore knee-length leather boots, a red loincloth, and a light pink cape that flowed back from his broad shoulders.

As athletes marched behind their country's flag, each wearing different parade uniforms to distinguish one from another, the ceremony seemed to celebrate national differences rather than participants' common humanity, a core value of the Olympic movement. National flags adorned the top tier of the stadium. Rather than negating Olympic internationalism, de Coubertin had devised a formula by which the two comfortably coexisted. He advocated an internationalism that 'should be the state of mind of those who love their country above all, who seek to draw to it the friendship of foreigners by professing for the countries of those foreigners an intelligent and enlightened sympathy'.[14] His genius was not to repudiate nation-states, but to temper patriotism. He went on to argue that 'true internationalism certainly involved the discovery and experience of social and cultural differences. However, far from dividing and repelling men from one another, national differences were to be celebrated as different ways of being human; their recognition was the first step toward peace, friendliness and mutual respect.'[15] By promoting rivalry tempered by amity, the Olympics avoided 'the lamentable atmosphere of jealousy, envy, vanity and mistrust' of unbridled competition.[16]

From his detailed study of Olympic rituals, John MacAloon concluded that national flags were carefully downplayed so that 'the symbols of the Olympic community are positioned hierarchically above those of nation-states, but without contravening them'.[17]

There were other ways in which the IOC undermined the existing political order. In the Parade of Nations, Olympic internationalism was on show. For example, the lone competitor from Malta, Louis Grasso, dressed in a neat business suit and wearing serious-looking spectacles, was given equal prominence to the 357-member US team. Whether they are a small nation-state or a superpower, all member countries are treated the same, and, with two exceptions, each team marched into the stadium in strict alphabetical order. The two exceptions were Greece, which came first to honour the country that founded the Olympic Games, and Mexico, as the team for the host always comes last.

The ceremony has a profound emotional impact on athletes, as US weightlifter Bob Bartholomew explained: 'You looked at each other, and you didn't see religion, color or national origin. You saw only athletes. I became more aware of the need for cooperation in all aspects of life. Olympic sport changed my way of thinking.'[18] For US middle-distance runner Francie Kraker (now Goodridge): 'coming into the stadium was a deeply emotional experience. As an American, I took great pride in my country, but I was also now an Olympian and part of the wider world.'[19]

After teams completed their circuit of the track, they gathered in the centre of the stadium, behind a sign bearing the name of their country. They no longer stood behind their flags, and the flag bearers now stood in a semicircle below a raised dais, on which Olympic officials stood. Visually, this communicated de Coubertin's hope that 'Olympism is a destroyer of dividing walls'.[20]

Brundage then went to the microphone and, in excruciating Spanish, spoke a few words of welcome. He then invited President Díaz Ordaz to recite the words: 'I declare the games of the XIX Olympiad of the modern era are opened.' The Olympic flag was then raised above the stadium, in prime position, significantly higher than the flags that had been carried in by the competing teams. Olympic flags also flew in the same exalted position over the other venues.

The programme then turned to the athletes' oath. This ritual would transform competitors into Olympians. For de Coubertin, the oath was important: 'The individual who takes part in the games had to be purified, in some sense, through professing and practicing these virtues [nobility and selflessness]. In this way, the moral beauty and the profound consequence of physical culture were revealed.'[21]

Belgian fencer Victor Boin was the first to swear the Olympic oath, during the 1920 Olympic Games in Antwerp. Wearing his white fencing uniform, his right arm upraised, Boin swore fidelity to Olympic rules on behalf of all participants and committed them 'to show a spirit of chivalry' during the Games.[22] The words of the oath have changed since then, but its intent is unchanged.

Mexican marathon runner Pablo Lugo Garrido stepped onto a platform, with flag bearers standing below him in a semicircle. Facing the athletes and the Tribune of Honour, he swore the sacred oath.

Now formally welcomed into the Olympic Family, athletes were transformed, according to John MacAloon: 'The suite of Olympic symbols – the five-ringed emblem and flag, the Olympic anthem, the Olympic flame, the IOC – are likewise layered on, over and around the Olympian, adding the third identity of a transpersonal, transnational human being.'[23] They were now global citizens, as US rower Paul Hoffman explained: 'The creed seems to have become: "Once an Olympian, Always an Olympian", even if you never compete in another Olympic Games. Indeed, you are expected to spread the faith.'[24]

At precisely 12.52 p.m. Norma Enriqueta Basilio de Sotelo (known affectionately by Mexicans as 'Queta') entered the Estadio Olímpico Universitario carrying the Olympic torch. As she ran around the stadium's track she was accompanied by music played on traditional instruments: teponaztli, huēhuētls, and chirimias.

Queta's arrival was like a fresh breeze. She sported a white headband – more a fashion accessory than a necessity for keeping her short black hair in place – and was wearing elfin shorts and top, which looked startlingly white against her bronzed skin.

It was a historic occasion: for the first time, a woman would light the Olympic cauldron. Spectators greeted her with enthusiasm: 'Mex-hee-co, Mex-hee-co, ra-ra-ra!' Clap, clap, clap.

After completing a circuit of the track she headed towards white steps that led up, through the tiers of the stadium, to the Olympic cauldron.

Like many Olympic rituals, the lighting of the cauldron was a recent innovation, first seen at the 1928 Summer Olympics. On that occasion, rather than an athlete lighting the cauldron, an employee of the Electric Utility of Amsterdam lit the first modern Olympic flame. On witnessing it, Frederick W. Rubien, Secretary of the American Olympic Committee, remarked that the flame would 'announce to all people of the world that peace, harmony and understanding must now reign, and thoughts of discord, discontent and misunderstanding must be put aside and that every one must concentrate on this as the attitude to be assumed'.[25]

As Queta approached the steps, athletes who had previously formed neat columns on the infield broke ranks and invaded the track to photograph the historic moment.

Having weaved her way through the throng, and now quite nervous, all Queta could think of was that she must not stumble. 'The noise was hellish, but as I stepped on the first of the 93 steps to the cauldron I stopped listening to the screams,' she recalled. 'I stopped seeing people.'[26] She need not have worried. Queta ascended with the grace of a gazelle.

Silhouetted against the sky, Queta stood on a platform at the top of the stadium and raised the torch in a salute towards the people sitting in the stadium. She then pressed a button on the floor with her right foot to turn on the gas and lowered the torch to light the cauldron – to a roar of delight from spectators. The flame shone brightly against a pale blue sky, mottled with clouds.

The flame had started its journey in Olympia, Greece. There, on 23 August 1968, Maria Mosxoliou, wearing the white flowing dress of a priestess, placed a small amount of resin in a vessel containing a concave metal mirror. Reflected rays of intense sunlight heated the vessel, containing flammable resin, to incandescence and the Olympic flame flared into existence. This ceremony imbued the flame with faux divine authority. A torch relay followed, bringing the sacred flame from Olympia to Mexico City: a journey of 13,620 kilometres.

When Queta lit the cauldron it represented the sanctification of the main stadium and the other Olympic sites. It also marked the start of sacred time that would end when the flame was extinguished during the closing ceremony.

With the Olympic flag fluttering and the sacred flame burning in the cauldron, the stadium was now consecrated. In this way, the sacred space carved out by the Olympics would be ritually separated from the profane. Olympic venues were no longer part of Mexico: they had been symbolically transformed into the 'island of the blessed' for the duration of the Games, governed by the rules of the IOC, where the tenets of Olympism reigned.

After the cauldron had been lit, 6,200 homing pigeons were released, symbolising peace. They circled a number of times as they struggled to find their way out of the stadium. Whether due to nervousness or just out of pique, having been kept in cages for three days, they released a fusillade of droppings onto the athletes below. The British were ready, having brought raincoats with them. Others suffered direct hits, including US heavyweight boxer George Foreman. Finally, the flock grew smaller and smaller until they disappeared over the rim of the stadium.

The giant electronic board at the northern end of the stadium then lit up: 'We offer and wish friendship with all the peoples of the Earth', written in English, French, and Spanish.

The official ceremony ended a little after 1 p.m., when athletes marched out of the main arena. They congregated in a large space under the stadium, waiting for buses to take them back to the Olympic Village.

Teams now totally broke from their national formations and the area became a barter market. The men from Bermuda stripped down to their running shorts, which had been covered by several pairs of Bermuda pants during the ceremony. Those pants were now in high demand, and they were able to do some very good deals. Swimmer Kaye Hall was able to swap her Thom McAn shoulder bag, part of the female uniform for the US team, for a handmade snakeskin bag from one of the Nigerian women. This swap meet further disaggregated athletes of their national identities, as they found they had much in common with fellow athletes who had gone through the same rigours and sacrifices that they had to reach the pinnacle of their sport.

The Olympic experience nurtured camaraderie among athletes. In the recreation hall, athletes from West Germany and Poland, without being able to speak a word of each other's languages, happily played table tennis together. On the training track, Latvian Jānis Lūsis, the hot favourite for the javelin gold medal, offered to help female javelin throwers with their technique, showing that hormones were not in the least nationalistic. There were also moments of fun and high jinks. When sixteen-year-old US swimmer Gary Hall mistakenly went into the Soviet dormitory and entered the lift, he encountered weight-lifter Leonid Zhabotinsky, who stood 6' 4" (194 centimetres) tall and weighed 163 kilograms (359 pounds). Hall's trepidation turned to delight when the large Russian spread his arms and, rocking to and fro, burst into song: 'My baby does the hanky panky'. A popular song in the US, and apparently in the USSR as well.

## UP CLOSE AND PERSONAL

Early risers in Sydney started watching the opening ceremony at 4 a.m. Viewers in San Francisco turned on their television sets at the more civilized time of 9 a.m. In Toronto the opening ceremony commenced at noon; in Paris at 6 p.m.; in Nairobi at 8 p.m.; and in Tokyo at 2 a.m. An estimated 500 million viewers watched from the comfort of their couches, in bars and pubs, or around communal television sets in their village stores. A further 100 million who couldn't be bothered getting up in the middle of the night watched it on replay.

It was hard to ignore the presence of ABC television cameras during the opening ceremony. A camera was suspended 246 feet (75 metres) above the stadium, hanging from a crane for a bird's eye view, and an ABC helicopter flew overhead, filming panoramic scenes of Mexico City and the main stadium.

No expense was spared: production costs came in at around US$15 million (equivalent to US$112 million in 2020). This budget covered a 450-member crew and fifty cameras, which were spread over sixteen different locations. Equipment alone weighed 50 tonnes. Sixty-five kilometres of cable snaked around playing fields, swimming pools, the sports hall, and the main stadium, and camera operators and sound technicians were an annoyance to officials and athletes alike as they looked for the best angle from which to film events.

ABC's production was overseen by Roone Arledge, who wanted to immerse viewers in the spectacle so as to 'add show business to sport'.[27] To deliver on his promise, the network combined live, taped, slow-motion, stop-action, close-up, and split-screen coverage of events. Arledge also ensured that microphones were placed just about everywhere: there was even one on the sacred Olympic cauldron so that viewers could hear the whoosh when Queta lit it. Technology brought the Games alive in so many different ways. The ripple of muscles, the grunt of a shot-putter, the grace of a gymnast in the floor exercises in slow motion, the agony on the face of a boxer as he took a sharp jab to the midriff, beads of sweat glistening off a weightlifter. This was sports television at its best; up close and personal. Immediately after events, athletes were ambushed as they came off the track. For example, after the 4 × 100 metres relay, ABC's Howard Cosell interviewed the medallists, some still out of breath from their race. In these ways, television revealed aspects of the Games that spectators in the stadium were not privy to.

As well as creatively employing technology to enhance the show, Arledge breathed warmth into ABC's coverage by profiling athletes in two-minute segments called 'Up Close and Personal', which he used to tell the stories of athletes who had triumphed over adversity and to recount tales of heroic struggles by those who did not prevail. Television viewers got to see the special qualities that made an Olympian.

Arledge knew that ABC had to deliver a great show to attract advertisers: advertisers who paid for ABC's lavish production.

For the IOC members, the commercial motives of television companies were suspect, and Brundage in particular was worried about their influence on the nobility and integrity of the Games. Brundage claimed that Baron de Coubertin 'did not revive the Games for the counting house, for the journalists or for the cinema'.[28] For cinema, read television. During the 1960s, however, and facing insolvency, the IOC became a reluctant party to selling off television rights.

Brundage was right to be worried about the intrusion of commercial interests into the Games, which would become more pronounced in the coming decades to the point where the Olympics would become a television event rather than a sporting one. On the other hand, what television did, particularly under the approach taken by Arledge, was to bring Olympic rituals 'up close and personal' to a vast audience. The Olympic movement's global ambitions were finally matched by its global reach. To this end, television provided a powerful medium for communicating the core values of Olympism to the world.

For Arledge, the opening ceremony had a good story to tell, and it served the commercial interests of ABC to highlight the idealism and majesty of the Olympics. The ceremony was so unlike any other international sporting event. Over the course of two hours, Arledge's cameras did an outstanding job, and the commentary by Jim McKay did justice to explaining Olympism's commitment to peace and the betterment of mankind. For *Sports Illustrated* journalists, television elevated the Olympics: 'The cameras' scrutiny deprived the Games of a purely athletic appearance and made them a deeper ceremony.'[29]

Through the magic of television, viewers had the best seats in the house and were transported out of their national space and into a global one. A space that was now delineated by Olympic rituals, symbols, and ceremonies.

Within this global space, viewers are linked by Olympic *communitas*, 'a plurality of people without boundaries', which anthropologist Edith Turner argues 'warms people toward their fellow human beings' during the Games.[30] As competitors from around the world competed in the Olympic Games, feelings of *communitas* are strengthened by linking the local with the global.

It was these features that attracted discontents to the Mexico Olympics, particularly athletes. Being seen on television was important. In addition, the humanitarian ideals of Olympism appealed to '68ers, who held similar values. The Olympic Games were therefore a natural platform to highlight injustices – as they saw them. In addition, as recently sanctified Olympians, the athletes believed that calling out injustices, inequality, and intolerance made concrete the rather amorphous moral objectives of Olympism.

# 7

# The Salute

People recognize me as a fast nigger but that still means I'm a nigger.

Tommie Smith

The athlete who triumphs is a picture of divinity.

Paul Souchon, *Les Chants du Stade* (1943)

## HOW IMPORTANT IS WINNING?

The media descended on the US team with questions as soon as they arrived in Mexico City. Journalists had heard about the decision by African American athletes, before they left the States, that many were committed to protesting in Mexico City. Are you going to demonstrate? What are you going to do on the victory podium? Will you accept your medal from Avery Brundage? Are you running? What are you going to wear? These questions were shrugged off as athletes got on with their training. They had worked so hard to get to the Olympics, dedicating much of their young lives to the dream of taking home a gold medal, that they could think of little else.

As two of the more vocal African American discontents before the Games, sprinters Tommie Smith and John Carlos came in for particular media attention. Even the usually garrulous Carlos was taciturn, as was Smith. What journalists did not know is that they had not yet discussed what sort of protest they would stage. Even in their own minds they were undecided.

The main spokesman for the OPHR, Harry Edwards, who would normally be ready to provide a colourful quote for the newspapers, was not in Mexico City. Edwards had gone to Montreal after he was told that there were credible threats to his life. He was a speaker at the Congress of Black Writers, held between 11 and 14 October at McGill University.[1] Smith and Carlos resented his absence: they too had received death threats, yet here they were in Mexico City.

Now that Smith and Carlos were at the Olympics and so close to realising their dreams of a gold medal, they knew what was at stake, having been forewarned by Brundage that protesters would be severely punished. Might this include taking their medals away from them? On the other hand, growing up they had suffered from poverty and racism, which had driven them to become activists. It was these experiences that would undoubtedly shape their decision on whether to protest.

### THE ROAD TO MEXICO CITY

Tommie Smith's family were sharecroppers: a form of quasi-slavery based on indentured labour to a white landowner. As Smith later recounted: 'My father worked the land for The Man. Our entire livelihood depended upon The Man and the wages he wanted to pay. We never owned our own house or land.'[2] The family's shack was on the farm, well away from any town. 'I saw more snakes and alligators than humans.'[3]

The family lived in Clarksville, a small segregated town in Texas, so he had little experience mixing with white kids.

Despite being poor, his family life was rich. During the day he played with his eleven brothers and sisters, and at night the family gathered round the piano – one of the few luxuries in the Smith household – for a singalong. Then, on Sunday mornings, Tommie and his family would give full vent to their musical talent singing hymns in the humble wooden church that served the black community. Religion would remain important throughout his life.

Outside the black community he noticed that his father was called 'boy' by whites, and he in turn called them 'sir' or 'ma'am', even if they were children. Such was the etiquette in the Jim Crow South.

One night, Tommie's father forgot to show the deference expected of a black man, and a farm supervisor nearly killed him in a fight. After this incident the family packed their belongings and headed to southern California. Tommie was just seven.

There was little improvement in the family's fortunes, though, and when Tommie was not at school he had to help his father with picking cotton and sorghum. Nevertheless, education was important. 'I didn't want to go back to the fields, picking cotton, cutting grapes, milking cows,' he recalled. 'I had to rise above where my daddy had been stopped by lack of schooling.'[4]

His new school was integrated, but Tommie was very shy. He wasn't used to having white kids around. It was there that he discovered that racism was not confined to the Jim Crow South. One hot summer's day Tommie bought a chocolate ice cream in a cone with a nickel from his meagre savings. He was leaning against a wall at school enjoying his treat when a white kid knocked the cone out of his hand: 'Niggers don't eat ice cream,' he said.[5] Tommie walked away, frightened.

At thirteen Tommie was over six feet tall and weighed around 155 pounds. His height and speed let him dominate in basketball. A year later, wearing his first pair of spikes, he covered 100 yards in 9.9 seconds. Here was his way out of poverty: 'From then on, every time I got on the starting line, even when I was in college, I thought I'd be in the cotton fields if I got second place. That's where I got the impetus to beat folks – not just beat them, to positively destroy them.'[6]

His performances at high school earned him an athletic scholarship to San José State College, where he excelled at sprints. Compared with his previous life, there was much to like about college. The dorm had running water, the mattress was firm, and he was doing what he loved and did best: running. However, trying to live on an athletic scholarship was difficult, particularly after he married Denise Paschal, a pentathlete. With his wife five months pregnant, they had to find an apartment. Everyone in San José recognised Smith as a world class athlete. Nevertheless, his reputation counted for naught when he went looking for a rental, and he was rejected on every occasion: 'One woman ran out when she saw us coming, pulled down the "vacancy" sign, slammed the door and pulled the blinds,' he remembers.[7]

Despite these problems, Smith stuck it out. He loved running, and by 1967 he was breaking world records. The ultimate prize was now within reach: a gold medal at the Olympics.

Tommie Smith met John Carlos, who moved from East Texas State University to San José, at the end of 1967. They were drawn together by their activism, but they were quite different personalities and were not close friends. Whereas Smith was thoughtful, but shy in public, Carlos was impulsive: a whirlwind of words rich with street slang. This was not surprising as he was the product of the Harlem ghetto, where you needed to be tough to survive.

Johnny, as Carlos was known as a kid, lived with his family in a two-bedroom apartment. His father ran a shoe repair shop and Johnny helped out, stacking boxes and shining shoes. He also worked the neighbourhood hustling. He earned extra cash running errands for local bartenders, petty thieving, and running numbers. He also earned a few dollars busking outside the Savoy Ballroom.

Johnny lived in a rough neighbourhood and his talent with his fists, as well as his skills at hustling, saw him attract a gang of five to six buddies (he called them his 'crew'). On one occasion, when he and his crew went to a movie theatre in the Bronx, they were confronted by a white gang, who told them that blacks were not welcome in their neighbourhood. That was an invitation to fight. Carlos knocked out the white gang leader and proceeded to empty his bladder all over him: 'When he wakes up, tell him that John Carlos pissed in his face and I will be back again.'[8] It was this bravado that drew people to him throughout his life. As a child of the ghetto, though, Johnny's future was bleak.

His life turned around when he was thirteen years old and discovered sport. His first choice was swimming: 'Daddy, I'm going to be the first black swimmer for America at the Olympics.' His father didn't wish to discourage his son, but he decided Johnny needed to be told the facts of life: 'It's not about you being good. Where would you train?' Swimming clubs were not an option as they did not allow in African Americans. 'The colour of the skin is going to prevent you from going to the Olympics,' his father told him.[9]

Not easily discouraged, Johnny turned to running as his route to the Olympics. The Pioneer Club was nearby, and mainly catered to young African Americans, so he joined. 'Being good at sports meant status, it meant style, and it meant you were noticed.'[10] Johnny craved being noticed.

After training, Johnny would challenge the other kids to a race along 168th Street. He liked to run the 100 yard dash, but with no tape measure they marked out the course length by the number of cars. It might be a seven-car race or a nine-car race depending on whether there were Volkswagens or Cadillacs parked there. He would challenge all-comers: 'Man, I'm going to give you four car lengths. I'm gonna beat you by three.'[11] Always looking for an angle, Johnny had friends take bets on him. He didn't like losing, and he seldom did. For example, on one occasion when Johnny slipped on the ice, he called for a rematch, doubling the bet. And then won.

On a chilly February day in 1965, while still at school, Carlos married Karen 'Kim' Benjamin Groce, and their first child, Kimmie, was born in November. Now a family man, Carlos worried. How would he provide for them? Athletics provided the answer when, in 1966, he was offered a scholarship to East Texas State University. Coach Delmer Brown was keen to acquire this promising prospect, so he told Carlos: 'It's nice down here, and there's no prejudice or anything.'[12] A major plus for Carlos was that Brown had worked as a trainer with the US Track and Field Olympic Team in 1964; Carlos already had his mind set on competing in the Olympics.

When Carlos arrived in East Texas, Coach Brown greeted him as 'boy'. Carlos shot back: 'Coach, my name is John Carlos. My name ain't Boy.' The message didn't get through, and next he found the coach referring to African Americans as 'nig-gras'.[13] Then, at meets, Coach Brown's idea of a pep talk was to tell his athletes: 'Okay slaves, get the cotton harvest in quick.'[14]

Unwilling to tolerate the raw racism at East Texas, Carlos transferred to San José State, where he quickly attracted attention – and not just for his athletic prowess. 'He is like a rattle,' one of his teammates, Sam Davis, remarked. 'He is a constant noise. I don't even listen. The noise goes on from morning to night.' The track was his stage and his teammates his audience: 'And in order to win that Emmy, he has to be smooth. So he keeps practicing.'[15] Carlos could be charming, funny, and entertainingly insolent, with ghetto slang flowing off his tongue like warm molasses. On the track he was an exponent of junk talk, which he used to psyche out his rivals.

### YES, WINNING MATTERS

Soon after arriving in Mexico City, Carlos encountered Peter Norman, who was also competing in the 200 metres. The Australian had run some very quick times during some unofficial races held just before the Games. He was a real threat. Norman found Carlos physically imposing, describing him as 'being built like a brick shithouse'.[16] Norman was slightly built, 5' 10" (178 centimetres) tall. Carlos was 6' 4" (193 centimetres) and weighed 26 pounds (12 kilograms) more. As a rival in the 200 metres race, Norman soon sampled Carlos's junk talk when he referred to the Australian as the 'white boy'. What Carlos soon found out was that Norman could not only take it, he was no slouch at dishing it out too.

By comparison, Norman's relationship with Smith was cordial. They had met in Melbourne in December 1967 when Smith had visited Australia to compete in some local meets. Smith was also attracted to the Australian for his deep-seated sense of decency; he believed in giving 'everyone a fair go'. Moreover, Norman sympathised with the plight of African Americans: 'I couldn't see why anyone would dislike or hate someone simply because they were a different colour,' said Norman.[17] Smith also saw that Norman was a devout Christian, like himself. On Sundays, at home, Norman would put on his navy blue twill uniform and join the Thornbury Salvation Army band and march around the inner suburbs of Melbourne banging his kettle drum with great gusto. During competitions, Norman wore a tracksuit on which were sown the words: 'Jesus Saves'.

The qualifying heats and the quarter-finals for the 200 metres were held on 15 October, with the semi-finals and final taking place the next day. Carlos won the first heat in a relatively slow time of 20.54 seconds. When Norman saw that Carlos was within earshot, he remarked to a teammate: 'That guy must be the third string American.'[18] Carlos was left in no doubt that Norman could play psychological games too. When Norman won his heat in a time of 20.17 seconds – an Olympic record – Carlos realised that the Australian was a real threat. In the quarter-finals, Norman's time was again better than that Carlos's, but not faster than Smith's, who took back the Olympic record. 'I'm going to spank your ass tomorrow,' Carlos told Norman after the quarter-final.[19] The next day, when they ran head-to-head in the semi-final, Carlos finally bested Norman. 'You ain't nothing,' he told the Australian, with a dismissive wave of his hand. Copying the gesture, Norman retorted, 'you ain't nothing'. This surprised Carlos who was not used to 'white boys' talking back to him.[20]

Norman was performing better than he ever had in Australia, where he ran on poor-quality cinder tracks held together by sump oil. On the synthetic track in Mexico City he 'blossomed like a Cactus flower,' according to Ray Weinberg, the Australian team coach.[21]

While everybody assumed that the contest for gold would be between Smith and Carlos, Norman was now a threat to the two African Americans.

### ANATOMY OF A PROTEST

During the heats it was clear that Smith and Carlos had come to Mexico City to run. Carlos told *Newsweek* before the race: 'We've worked all year for our cause. Now we've got to concentrate on winning.'[22] Smith was equally singled minded about his preparations, and neither man wanted to think about a protest.

The issue of a protest, however, could no longer be avoided when Linda Evans, the wife of the 400 metres sprinter Lee Evans, and Tommie Smith's wife Denise arrived in Mexico City just before the final. Along with Kim Carlos, they demanded to know how their husbands intended to protest on the victory podium. The three women were not happy with the answer. Their husbands were ambivalent. There had been death threats; Brundage warned that the IOC would punish them, perhaps taking their medals off them should they win; and they knew that any protest would overshadow their athletic performances and their moment in the Olympic sun.

Frustrated by the lack of a plan, the day before the 200 metres final the women caught a cab to downtown Mexico City and went to a large department store. They shopped for anything black: socks, scarves, berets, and leather gloves.

The night before the final, Denise showed Tommie what she had bought and put in it his kit bag, making it clear that she expected him to stage a protest should he make it onto the winner's podium.

The final was the last race of the day, and Linda, Denise, and Kim took their seats in the stands. On the track they saw that the men were wearing calf-length black dress socks, as they had worn in the heats. As a protest, it had been downplayed by Stan Wright, an assistant coach, who said: 'As far as I know, they wore high stockings because it was cold, but they may have intended it to be a demonstration. If they did, it is their business.'[23] Carlos had also pinned a small green and white Olympic Project for Human Rights badge on his chest, but it wasn't possible to see what it said from the stands.

As a protest, these gestures were underwhelming, and Denise and Kim hoped that their husbands would make a more emphatic gesture on the victory stand, should they win medals.

In the late afternoon of 16 October, the men lined up behind their blocks for the 200 metres final; the sun had dipped over the rim of the stadium. Spectators noticed that Smith's upper thigh was heavily strapped. In the semi-final he had pulled up too soon after crossing the finish line, straining his left adductor muscles. Smith made a relatively slow start, perhaps worried about putting too much strain on his injured leg. To his relief, he was moving freely, and at the curve he was just one and a half metres behind Carlos, who had taken the lead early in the race. Going into the straight, Smith's stride began to lengthen, as his famed 'Tommie-jet gear' kicked in; he flew past Carlos at the 100-metre mark, who was feeling his upper thighs starting to tighten. Eating up the track, Smith knew no one could catch him, and 12 metres from the finishing line he raised his arms in triumph, a huge grin spread across his face. This might have added a tenth of a second or two to his time but he didn't care. He was an Olympic champion. For the first half of the race, Norman had been well back, but the Australian had come on like a rocket down the straight. With 45 metres to go Carlos was shocked when the Australian passed him. Norman could almost hear Carlos say: 'Oh shit, the white boy!'[24] Norman took the silver and Carlos had to content himself with bronze.

After the race Carlos embraced Smith and then shook hands with Norman. The race was over and the friction between the two men was forgotten.

An Olympic official ushered the three medallists to the Athletes' Lounge, under the stadium, where he then spent a few minutes explaining the medal ceremony.

After the official left, the athletes combed their hair, readying themselves for the medal presentation ceremony. They would have to wait a little, as the pole vaulting had gone on longer than expected. Smith and Carlos then sat down on a wooden bench to decide what they would do on the victory podium. 'It wasn't as if they were having a secret huddle,' recalled Norman. 'They were letting me know.'[25]

Having talked so much about a protest before they came to Mexico, and with their wives insisting they make a dramatic gesture on the victory stand, they now had less than an hour before they returned to the stadium to receive their medals. Under time pressure, they were forced to improvise. Smith pulled out the items that Denise had packed in his bag. Holding up the black gloves, he suggested he would execute a salute during the rendition of the national anthem.[26] Would Carlos do the same? That was a problem as Carlos had not packed gloves. Smith insisted he'd go ahead alone, if necessary. 'I'm not going to stand there like a stale bottle,' replied Carlos.[27] Norman suggested that they wear one glove each as they were only going to hold up one fist. Smith kept the right glove and handed the left to Carlos.[28]

Norman noticed that Smith and Carlos were wearing OPHR badges. He wanted to show his support by wearing one during the ceremony but they didn't have a spare one. 'I couldn't see why a black man wasn't allowed to drink out of the same water fountain or sit in the same bus or go to the same schools as a white guy,' Norman remarked.[29] Offended by racism, the least he could do was express his support by wearing the badge.

As they returned to the stadium, they passed Paul Hoffman, a white rower who supported the protests by black athletes back in the US. 'Hey mate,' asked Norman, 'do you have another one of those badges?' Hoffman was puzzled: why would an Australian athlete want his badge? After all, Australia still had an immigration policy that excluded people of colour, as far as Hoffman knew. 'Are you going to wear it?' he asked. When Norman said he would, Hoffman took off his badge and gave it to him.[30]

### SOLEMN GLORIFICATION

Unlike the opening ceremony with its razzmatazz, the victory ceremony is solemn and emotionally charged. By being repeated, unvaryingly, during the Games, spectators and television viewers know what to expect and how to behave. Like other Olympic rituals, it is rich with meaning.

Trumpets heralded the start of the ceremony, and Smith, Carlos, and Norman were ushered to the three-tiered victory podium by officials. The two African American athletes felt exposed as they walked into the stadium. Carlos was worried and whispered to Smith: 'Look, man, if someone has a rifle and they're going to shoot us, remember as sprinters we are trained to listen to the gun. So you keep that foremost in your mind.'[31] Smith was well aware of the threat to his life: 'I was much more frightened on that stand than I had ever been on the starting blocks.'[32]

Normally, Brundage would have officiated at the victory ceremony. However, when he got wind of a rumour that Smith and Carlos might either refuse to shake his hand or wear black gloves when they shook his hand, Brundage, showing uncharacteristic tact, decided to avoid provoking an incident. Instead, he went to Acapulco to watch the sailing.

Instead, the medal ceremony was conducted by Lord Killanin and the Marquess of Exeter, the vice-president of the IOC and the president of the International Amateur Athletic Federation (and an IOC Executive Board member), respectively.

Smith's name was called first and he stepped onto the podium's top step. He bent his 6' 3" (191-centimetre) frame to receive his gold medal. He was also given a box that contained an olive tree sapling – an emblem of peace. The other two medallists then stepped onto the lower tiers of the podium in turn, to receive their medals.

This is one of the few rituals when Olympic officials do not stand in a commanding position, although the athletes do have to bend down to receive their medals, in effect being anointed by the Olympic movement.

The athletes were surrounded by Olympic symbols that acted as counterpoints to the national symbols: the US flag and its anthem. The podium on which the athletes stood was emblazoned with the Olympic rings. The ceremony took place in the stadium that the opening ceremony had transformed into a 'sacred Fortress', as described by de Coubertin,[33] where the Olympic flag flew and the sacred Olympic flame glowed in the cauldron. And finally, the design of the medals worn by recipients showed Nike, the Greek goddess of victory, holding a palm in her left hand and a winner's crown in her right. On the reverse, an Olympic champion is carried in triumph by spectators. The coexistence of national and international symbols reflected Olympic internationalism.

As they stood on the podium, an announcement came over the public address system: 'Ladies and gentlemen, please stand for the national anthem of the United States.' Only the anthem of the gold medallist is played. In line with Olympic internationalism, all spectators, whatever their nationalities, are expected to show respect for the national anthem of the victor.

The three athletes then turned to their right to face their national flags; Norman had his back to Smith and Carlos. According to Olympic protocol, athletes stand erect, in sombre reverie, as their bodies are presented in all their athletic majesty. They are expected to show none of the emotion or exuberance that one might expect, but rather to play their assigned role in creating a static tableau. At this point in the ritual they lose their individuality, their agency. Instead they are the symbolic embodiment of Olympism – virtuous heroes. Virtuous because they dedicate themselves to their sport,

Figure 7.1   Tommie Smith and John Carlos staging their protest on the victory podium.

and as amateurs they practice self-sacrifice, not profiting from their talents. And also virtuous because they possess 'moral nobility and moral purity as well as physical fortitude and dynamism', according to de Coubertin.[34] Another virtue is their commitment to fair play and *esprit sportif.* Their mission is heroic because, by their example, they contribute to 'moral betterment and social peace'.[35] De Coubertin imagined the Olympian as a modern version of the chivalrous knight: honourable, admired, an inspiration.

According to cultural anthropologist John MacAloon, at various times during this ceremony each of the athletes on the podium exhibits the identities of 'an individual, a national and a human body each constituted through a set of marked symbols and symbolic practices'. They also present themselves as the epitome of an Olympian: a 'transpersonal, transnational human being'.[36]

This ceremony is designed to engage athletes and spectators and make them feel part of the Olympic movement. To this end, 'ceremonies should never convey messages of doubt or interrogation but messages of conviction,' argued François Carrard, former Director General of the IOC. For that reason they need to follow 'impeccable observance of predefined forms'.[37] No variations; no room for improvisation.

But on this occasion, nothing was predictable. Nothing was normal.

When *The Star-Spangled Banner* started to play over the PA system, Norman heard a man, a baritone, who was sitting in the second tier of the grandstand, sing along. After about six bars, Norman noticed the baritone hesitate and stop singing: 'They've done it,' he thought. 'Good on 'em!'[38]

Behind Norman, Tommie Smith had raised his clenched right fist, sheathed in a black glove. His arm was ramrod straight, his head was bowed, and his eyes were closed. John Carlos followed his lead and raised his left fist, his arm casually bent at the elbow.

In this way, through their bodies, they imposed their own views and values rather than play their assigned role as the epitome of the Olympic champion. And as transnational human beings, citizens of the world, performing in a sanctified global space – 'the isle of the blessed' – their protest was global in a way never seen before.

The rituals of the victory ceremony added layers of meaning to their protest. For sociologist Douglas Hartmann, 'Rarely is human expression as focused, elegant and eloquent as Smith and Carlos's was that day.' It was, he continued, 'an act of inspiration, passion and originality, of sheer expressive genius – truly, by these standards or any others, a work of art.'[39]

The spectators' role in this ceremony is crucial because they were silent witnesses to what Kathryn McClymond, Professor of Religious Studies at Georgia State University, described as a 'kind of consecration'. It is 'through their act of witnessing' that they transform the athlete, who, 'once "medalled," holds new status in Olympic mythology'.[40]

In the past, sanctifying each medallist as being worthy of assuming the mantle of being an Olympic hero was automatic; unconsciously, spectators played their assigned role. Now that was not possible because Smith and Carlos had imposed their own meaning on the victory ceremony. They had given a symbolic voice to their discontent, to the injustices, poverty, and denial of human dignity suffered by African Americans. All spectators now had to decide whether they were still willing to consecrate Smith and Carlos as paragons of Olympism. In response, spectators also departed from the script. Their reactions ranged from anger to confusion, and there were even a few cheers. Others were disquieted by the intrusion of politics into sport. The protest was so unexpected that many sat in stunned silence, wondering what they had just seen. 'And then there were the catcalls, the boos, the hisses and the whistles and the cheers,' recalled Norman. 'Every single human emotion that you can imagine came down out of those stands. And it was directed at those two guys.'[41] It was the naked racism that was worst, with one spectator yelling: 'Them fuckin' niggers.'[42]

After the ceremony, fifty to sixty journalists squeezed into a small room under the stadium for a press conference, where they hoped to hear more from the athletes. Smith sat in the centre, Carlos to his left, and Norman to his right.

As a blue fug of cigarette smoke enveloped the room, Smith started the press conference with a brief, dignified statement: 'We are black and proud to be black. White America will say an American won, not a black American won. If we had done something bad, they would have said "a Negro".'[43] He then went on to explain the significance of the props that they had used; the scarf, the badge, the beads, and the black socks. The press were more interested in the salute and the fact that it was executed during the playing of the national anthem.

Carlos took over next, speaking for about ten minutes. His words erupted like a belligerent volcano, full of barely contained fury. It was Carlos the street fighter on display: 'They look upon us as nothing but animals. Low animals, roaches and ants.' He went on to add: 'We are sort of show horses out there for the white people. They give us peanuts, pat us on the back and say, "Boy, you did fine".'[44]

While the foreign journalists took down what Smith and Carlos said, many of the American journalists were furious. Here were two African American athletes trashing the US in front of the world.

Norman said nothing until near the end of the press conference. Would racist Australia approve of his protest, he was asked. 'I think you'll find that a majority of Australians would favour what I did.' However, he qualified his support of the protest by pointing out that he was not totally comfortable with 'black power methods'. He ended by saying: 'It takes a fair bit of guts when you back up your opinions with actions like that.'[45]

The day after the protest Smith was interviewed by Howard Cosell on ABC television: 'My raised right hand stood for the power within black America. Carlos's left hand stood for the unity of black America. Together, they formed an arch of unity and power.'[46] Here, Smith was thinking on his feet. The real reason they wore one glove each was not to make a symbolic gesture – an arch of unity and power – but because they only had one pair and had to share. Regardless of the improvisations that went into explaining the elements of their protest, it was a courageous gesture – and one that would cost the participants dearly.

But the story, as Smith and Carlos told it, was incomplete. The men's autobiographies failed to mention that it was Denise and Kim who had helped them overcome their indecision about protesting on the victory podium.[47] This was not unusual. According to Carole Boyce Davies, Professor of Africana Studies at Cornell University, African American women 'were too often written out of history'.[48] Smith and Carlos minimised their wives' role because 'our militancy and leadership challenged their masculinity,' posited Linda Evans, who had been on the shopping trip with Kim and Denise. 'Racist white society was constantly putting down black men, making them feel emasculated, and the protest was one way they could reclaim their manhood. Perhaps they thought that crediting us – the women – as an integral part of the protest would somehow diminish them.'[49]

Linda Evans's observations are borne out by Richard Majors and Janet Mancini Billson, authors of Cool Pose, a classic study of black

manhood in the US. They argue that African American men felt oppressed by the dominant white society: 'Being male and black has
meant being psychologically castrated – rendered impotent in the
economic, political, and social arenas that whites have historically
dominated.'[50] By taking all the credit for the protest, Smith and Carlos were perhaps unconsciously asserting control in a world where
they had little of it.

NO TRIAL, JUST PUNISHMENT

In Acapulco, Brundage watched the protest on the local television
network Telesistema (now Televisa), which took its feed from US
network ABC.

He was appalled by what he saw. The protest was inexcusable.
Smith and Carlos, and to a lesser degree Peter Norman, had introduced politics into the Olympics. In addition, they had defiled one
of its sacred rituals by not following its rigid protocols. The athletes
were apostates, challenging Olympism, with its quasi-religious affec-
tations. This was sufficient reason for Brundage, who saw himself
as a staunch defender of the faith, to banish them from the 'isle of
the blessed'.

Brundage was not a man to cross. He was first elected as IOC president in 1952, and he'd come to dominate the organisation like no
one had before him. In *The Official History of the Olympic Games and
the IOC*, David Miller wrote that 'Avery Brundage was despotic, a
moralistic bulldozer, fanatical defender of de Coubertin's legacy'.[51]
William Johnson of *Sports Illustrated* observed that he 'strode the
earth as if he were a crowned monarch, and he ruled the Olympic
movement as if it were a fiefdom'.[52]

As much as Brundage would have liked the IOC to punish the
athletes, its rules left Olympic justice in the hands of each nation's
Olympic committee. Returning to Mexico City that night, Brundage confronted members of the US Olympic Committee (USOC).
He wanted the athletes severely punished.

The USOC executive held an emergency meeting. The hawks supported Brundage. They wanted Smith and Carlos suspended from
the team and tossed out of Mexico for disrespecting the American
flag. The doves hoped to resolve the situation peacefully and avoid
provoking other US athletes to protest in sympathy. After four hours
of heated debate, they decided to censure Smith and Carlos.

Brundage was furious with what he saw as a tepid reprimand. At 6 a.m. the next morning the president of the USOC, Douglas Roby, was woken and ordered to attend a 9 a.m. meeting of the IOC's nine-member Executive Board. At the meeting Brundage issued an ultimatum. Expel Smith and Carlos from the Olympic Village and send them home or the IOC would ban the entire US track and field team.

At 9.30 p.m. Roby called together the members of the USOC to consider Brundage's ultimatum. After almost three hours of debate they decided to eject Smith and Carlos from the Olympic Village. Their decision was more symbolic than it was a real punishment: both athletes had no more events to run and had already moved out and were staying in hotels downtown.

Did the punishment fit the crime? And what was the crime? The USOC had issued a statement charging Smith and Carlos with 'immature behavior' and 'untypical exhibitionism [that] ... violates the basic standards of good manners and sportsmanship'.[53] What sort of offense was *untypical* exhibitionism? How did it differ from *typical* exhibitionism, which was presumably acceptable? And was immature behaviour such a heinous crime that it called for the public humiliation of Smith and Carlos?

Peter Norman's part in the protest was not forgotten either. The day after the race, Norman was summoned to the office of Julius 'Judy' Patching, the general manager of the Australian team, who was also under pressure to mete out punishment. Norman explained that he supported human rights and saw nothing wrong with wearing an OPHR badge. 'I've got to take action here,' said Patching. 'I've got no choice, so consider yourself severely reprimanded, and do you have tickets to the hockey today or do you want some?'[54]

On the morning of 18 October Roby gave a press conference outside the US dormitories in the Olympic Village. Standing on a table and surrounded by around a hundred journalists, he read a statement from the USOC announcing its decision to expel Smith and Carlos. He warned any other athlete who was thinking of staging a protest that they would suffer the 'severest penalties at the disposal of the United States Olympic Committee'.[55] As Roby read his statement he was interrupted with questions from journalists: 'How many Blacks on the committee [USOC]?' Roby ignored the interjection and continued to read. Another shouted question: 'What rule did they break?'[56] Again, Roby refused to respond; he could not respond, because clearly no rule had been broken.

There was one more hurrah for Olympic justice.

On the same day as Smith and Carlos were expelled, the USOC turned its attention to Paul Hoffman. It was the evening before the final and the Harvard crew were due to row in the men's eight. Hoffman was their coxswain, and he knew that if he were suspended the whole team would refuse to compete.

The Harvard crew were known as the 'shaggies', although, by the standards of the day, their hair was perhaps only a couple of inches longer than regulation cut. They also liked to wear very wide, flowery neckties. Hardly 'wild hippies', another term Olympic officials liked to use to describe them. Hoffman was the least flamboyant of the crew, and his 'shagginess' went only so far as slightly longer than normal sideburns. To confound expectations, he turned up to his hearing dressed in an Olympic blazer and wearing a conservative tie.

Hoffman was not particularly interested in student politics, but racism offended him. 'This was 1968; the country was in revolution,' Hoffman explained. 'With the civil rights movement, it would have been immoral to be silent.'[57]

As soon as Hoffman sat down, USOC members said that he had 'conspired to aid a demonstration'.[58] When Hoffman gave Peter Norman his OPHR protest button he was sitting with Denise Smith and Kim Carlos. The implication was that they had put Hoffman up to drawing the Australian into the protest by their husbands.

The evidence presented was circumstantial and flimsy, and USOC members soon gave up trying to extract a confession out of Hoffman. They moved on to ask him whether he thought that Smith and Carlos had dishonoured the Olympics. It was more an accusation than a question. But men from Harvard are not easily intimidated. 'It struck me as pretty clear that the Olympic ideals were represented by people who were talking about equality and brotherhood,' he replied.[59] Other than this lapse, which infuriated some USOC members, Hoffman played it cool. 'I did my best to not provoke any of the Committee as there was no chance of a meeting of the minds,' he recalled: 'The best outcome was that they would find a face-saving way to back away from the apparent allegation that I had somehow aided or abetted the demonstration, a charge I could in all honesty deny.'[60]

Before he was excused Hoffman had to promise that, whether his crew won a medal or not, they would not demonstrate. Hoffman had no problems giving them his word as the Harvard crew had no intention of staging a protest. After thirty minutes Hoffman was told that he was clear to compete.

So while the *black* athletes, Smith and Carlos, had been given no opportunity to defend themselves and had been tried *in absentia*, judged guilty, and punished by the USOC, a member of the *white* rowing crew was given the opportunity to defend himself. This was hardly an example of Olympic fair play. Norman, also *white*, had likewise been afforded due process (albeit in a laid-back Australian manner). Stan Wright, the African American coach of the track and field team, was convinced that the treatment by the 'Good Old Boy' system 'was about the color of Tommie and John's skin'.[61] There is little doubt that Olympic justice was not colour-blind.

Smith and Carlos didn't have to contend only with Olympic officials: great swaths of the white press pack were baying for blood too. They were also ready to act as judge and jury.

A few columnists were supportive, with Red Smith declaring that the IOC considered 'children's games more sacred than human decency'.[62] He was in the minority.

In the *Detroit News*, Pete Waldmeir ridiculed Smith and Carlos's protest as 'a little childish and more than a trifling disgusting', which was a 'slap in the face to all Americans'.[63] The *Chicago Sunday American* accused the athletes of acting like 'boors and brats'.[64] The *Chicago Tribune* called their act 'contemptuous of the United States' and an 'insult to their countrymen'.[65] Editors at the *Los Angeles Times* attacked Smith and Carlos for their 'anti-United States nonsense' and for using the victory podium at the Olympic Games 'to denigrate their homeland'.[66] In the same newspaper, columnist John Hall, referring to Smith and Carlos as 'black racists', wrote that they 'did no favour for themselves, their cause or their country with an act which appeared to be rooted only in hatred and bitterness'.[67]

Some of the attacks were positively vile. Associated Press, syndicated around the world, accused the athletes of executing a 'Nazi-like salute'.[68] Along similar lines, Brent Musburger of the *Chicago American* called them 'black skinned storm troopers'.[69] Perhaps the most loathsome attack came from sportswriter Jim Murray in the *Los Angeles Times*. He suggested that 'if you've got something to get off your chest, start practising the 200. We may get our next Hitler out of lane 4.'[70] Lane 4 was the lane in which John Carlos ran the 200 metres final.

Smith and Carlos arrived back home on 21 October. In San José they were ambushed by journalists, who questioned their patriotism. Carlos responded: 'The National Anthem is not for me, it's for white people.' Emotionally exhausted, Smith said was that he was 'sick of all this being hounded'. They then pushed their way through a throng of journalists and cameramen to a waiting car.[71]

# 8

# Take the Money and Run

The Negro has the keener desire to excel in sports because it is more mandatory for his future opportunities than it is for a white boy.

Jack Olsen

## THE UNNOTICED PROTEST

As Smith and Carlos returned to the infield of the Estadio Olímpico Universitario for the medal ceremony, they were tailed by an ABC cameraman. First he captured a close-up of their hands. Each man was wearing a black glove on one hand. Panning down revealed that their tracksuit pants were rolled up and they were wearing calf-length black socks. Behind their backs each man clasped a single running shoe in their hands.

For Smith and Carlos, the shoes were an integral, yet overlooked, part of their protest. Shoes did not have the obvious symbolism of the gloved fists, the black socks, the beads, and the other props that have been much commented on. Also, the display of the shoes came at the start of the ceremony, which has been ignored by commentators, who have focussed on the end of the medal ceremony when Smith and Carlos stood with their fists raised high during the playing of the national anthem.

When the medallists reached the three-tiered podium, they stood behind it. Then there was an announcement: 'Presenting the winner of the 200 metres in a new world record time of 19.83 seconds, from the United States – Tommie Smith.' This was the cue for Smith to mount the top tier of the podium. He towered over the Marquess of Exeter, who was officiating. Wearing a fire-engine-red jacket and white slacks, Exeter was the president of the International Amateur Athletic Federation and vice-president of the IOC.

In all other medal ceremonies in which Exeter had officiated, as soon as he held up the ribbon on which the gold medal hung, winners were quick to bend down to receive their prize. Not Smith. Instead, he raised both arms in the air. On the right hand he wore a black glove, which he made into a fist. In his left he held up the shoe he had carried to the podium. For a few excruciating seconds Exeter stood waiting, his arms outstretched in front of him, holding the ribbon. He looked upset. Before Smith finally bent down to receive his gold medal, he carefully placed the shoe down to his left.

When it was John Carlos's turn, he too raised both arms into the air. His stance was more nonchalant, arms bent at the elbows, but like Smith he clenched one fist, his left, on which he wore a black glove, and held his Puma shoe in the air in his right hand. Afterwards he placed his shoe down to his left before receiving his bronze medal.

The shoes were black with white soles and flat white laces. They were made of soft suede, and on their sides was the Puma form-strip logo, which was also white: 'They [the Puma shoes] were as important as the black glove and the black sock,' explained Smith afterwards. 'I have them on the stand, because they helped me get there during the race and long before.'[1]

Carlos also acknowledged that the presence of the shoes on the podium was premeditated: 'If you look at the way the shoes were placed on the victory stand, Mr. Smith took his shoes and placed them behind him. I took my shoes [sic] and put it where everybody could clearly see the Puma logo.'[2] They had purposely placed the shoes at right angles to each other so that the logo would be picked up regardless of where a photographer stood.

It should come as no surprise that Smith and Carlos were grateful for the generous help they had received from Puma. They were often desperately short of money, as they struggled to support themselves and, later, their wives and children on athletic scholarships that paid a miserable stipend of US$85 a month. When they were at interstate or overseas meets they had to make do without income from part-time jobs at home, too, and they received a miserly per diem of just US$2 a day.

But it wasn't only Puma that was willing to pay athletes to wear its shoes as a marketing strategy: so was Adidas, Puma's larger rival. In 1968 the two shoe companies fiercely competed against one another to sign up the best athletes to wear their brand.

Smith and Carlos believed that Puma treated African Americans much better than did Adidas, hence their choice of shoes.

Smith had worn Adidas throughout his college career. He had heard that white athletes were getting between US$150 and US$500 from Adidas for an exceptional performance at a meet.[3] 'I couldn't understand why the shoe companies didn't give me some of the loot, too,' he complained. 'After all, I held more world records than anyone else in the world.' Yet no under-the-table payments had come his way. 'And while I was flat broke, white athletes were cashing in on the sport. Jesus, I could have used that money!'[4]

In 1966 Smith switched to Puma: 'There I was again, a living advertisement for a shoe company,' he said. 'Only this time, by God, I was getting paid for it.'[5]

Carlos also chose Puma because he believed the company was a good friend to African American athletes: 'With Adidas, if you weren't a superstar athlete, a known athlete, you couldn't get their product. Puma would give their product to anybody that needed it and a lot of black athletes – girls and guys – needed that. I've never forgotten the fact that they supported those black kids.'[6]

While Carlos claimed he received no cash-in-hand from Puma, the company gave him a job at its Elmsford warehouse whenever he returned home to New York.

Amateur athletes were not allowed to accept money or other gifts. Athletes knew that if the IOC discovered they were accepting money from the shoe companies, they would lose their medals and never be allowed to compete again as amateurs.

Nevertheless, many athletes felt justified flouting the rules of amateur sport when they saw Olympic officials staying in top hotels, flying first class, and eating in fine restaurants while they struggled to get by on a pittance. Their resentment was heightened when, in 1968, they watched the Olympic movement earn millions of dollars through the sale of television rights, while they – the talent – received nothing.

To avoid scrutiny from the IOC, both the shoe companies and the athletes were discrete in their dealings, and it was a running joke that a true amateur never accepted cheques.

What is surprising is that Smith and Carlos were willing to make such a public display of their gratitude – one that entailed considerable risks.

## WAR BY OTHER MEANS

The ruthlessness with which Puma and Adidas competed against one another had a personal edge to it.

In 1924 Adi Dassler and his older brother Rudi established Gebrüder Dassler Schuhfabrik (Dassler Brothers Shoe Factory) in the thirteenth-century southern German town of Herzogenaurach.

The brothers fell out after the war and started Adidas and Puma, respectively. Following the breakup, the brothers never spoke to one another again, despite their factories being just across the river from one another. In their battle for market supremacy, low blows were not uncommon.

The fierce enmity between the families was taken up by their sons: Horst, who represented Adidas, and Armin, Puma. The two cousins were just as keen to beat each other as their fathers had been. The result was that in 1968 a fierce bidding war erupted for the feet of possible medal winners.

Promoting shoes at the Olympics was good business. Now, for the first time, the Games were telecast live around the world, meaning that winning athletes wearing Adidas or Puma would be seen by an audience of up to 600 million potential customers. In this way, television turned the feet of medal winners into walking, running, and jumping billboards, exposure for which the shoe companies did not have to pay the television networks a cent. Athletes were quick to appreciate that what brand they wore on their feet had become valuable to the shoe companies.

The shoe companies regarded the Olympics as a global showroom where they could promote their shoes. They didn't care that doing so flew in the face of Olympic ideals that eschewed the intrusion of commerce, which was seen as fouling the 'isle of the blessed'.[7]

Of the two cousins, Horst was the more formidable. According to his former business partner, Patrick Nally, 'Horst was out to do whatever he could to the enemy – and he was very good at it.'[8]

As far as both market share and the number of Olympic hopefuls who wore their shoes, Adidas was well ahead of Puma.

The competition for the feet of athletes started well before the Mexico Olympics. The first skirmish occurred in a run-up meet used by athletes to prepare for the Games. The meet was held at Mt. San Antonio College in April 1968. When Horst arrived we was shocked. 'I couldn't believe my eyes,' he told *Sports Illustrated*: 'Fifty percent of the athletes were wearing Puma shoes.' As Armin was paying athletes to defect, Adidas had no choice but to follow: 'I realized 80% of the American team would have been in Puma shoes had we not done something.'[9] And so the bidding war started in earnest.

A few months later, a number of US athletes travelled to Europe to attend Olympic warm-up meets. Afterwards, they were invited by Adidas to stay in Landersheim, where the company ran its French manufacturing operations. Beside the factory was the Auberge du Kochersberg, a private hotel where guests were treated to the company's lavish hospitality: luxury suites, excellent cuisine in its Michelin starred restaurant, and, for those who liked wine, the choicest vintages.

After dinner, all the athletes agreed to sign contracts that they would wear Adidas shoes in Mexico City, and each was handed US$500 in cash.

After leaving, the athletes went straight to the Puma offices in Herzogenaurach, a four-hour drive across the border into Germany, where they were offered more money. The only condition was that they hand over copies of the contracts they had signed with Adidas. Making the most of this situation, Puma leaked the contracts to the German tabloid BILD-*Zeitung*, which published an exposé on how Adidas was bribing athletes.[10]

The next major confrontation between the shoe companies occurred at Echo Summit, where the US track and field team gathered for trials at high altitude.

All the talk among athletes was about Puma's brush shoe, *Der Bürstenschuh*, with sixty-eight tiny 3 mm needles on its sole instead of spikes. The new shoe had been specially designed for the synthetic Tartan surface on which most track and field events would be held in Mexico City.[11]

Two weeks before the Echo Summit trials, Vince Mathews had run 44.4 seconds, breaking the 400 metres world record. At the trials, Lee Evans smashed the record just set by Matthews, and John Carlos ran a 200 metres world-best time. They were all wearing Puma's brush shoes.

As soon as athletes saw world records falling they wanted a pair of brush shoes for themselves. Understandably, Adidas was worried. If these shoes were legal then it would lose most of its athletes to Puma, and no amount of money would arrest the haemorrhaging.

Horst decided it was time to tap into his network within the International Amateur Athletic Federation (IAAF) to see if he could have Puma's brush shoe declared illegal. He commissioned a report that concluded that the brush shoe would damage the Tartan track. The report was technically suspect as long spikes were more likely to damage the synthetic surface than tiny brush needles. Nevertheless, the report was considered by the Council and Technical Committee of the IAAF, which subsequently declared the brush shoes illegal. Puma alleged that the decision to ban its shoes occurred after Adidas distributed 75,000 deutschmarks (equivalent to US$128,000 in 2020) to IAAF officials.[12]

Following the ban, the records set by Matthews, Carlos, and Evans were struck from the record book.

The shoe companies continued their bidding war in Denver, where the US team met to receive their uniforms.

Tommie Smith witnessed this rivalry first hand. An Adidas representative came to his hotel room and, without saying a word, placed fifty $100 bills on his bed. This was more than double what Puma had given him. However, Puma had also offered to market a 'Tommie Smith' running shoe after the Olympics, from which he would receive US$0.50 for every pair sold.[13] He stayed with Puma.

While the shoe men were busy trying to buy the loyalty of athletes, African Americans competitors met to decide how they might protest in Mexico City. When one athlete suggested that they dye their shoes black, others disagreed. Painting over the shoe's logo would see them lose promised payments from the shoe companies.

Ready to engage in battle once more, the Dassler cousins arrived in Mexico City with a small army of aggressive salesmen; less men in plaid jackets and slicked back hair than ruthless commandos who would do what was needed to win. They were helped by a handful of athletes who were on retainers from one brand or the other and were happy to act as shills among their teammates.

In the Olympic Village, the Adidas store became a popular hub for athletes. They could get their shoes repaired or be given a free pair – a pair that, for medal hopefuls, might be stuffed with a roll of banknotes.

Puma, though, had no store because it had no shoes. In a deft move by Horst, he had obtained an exclusive licence to supply shoes to Mexico, duty free.[14] To import shoes into Mexico, Puma was charged US$10 per pair (equivalent to US$75 in 2020).

On the eve of the Olympics, Puma imported 3,000 pairs of shoes with 'AD-Mexico' stamped on each box. This looked to officials like the code prefix used by Adidas to identify its shipments.

When Horst discovered what his cousin was up to he notified customs, who impounded the whole shipment. Mexican officials then stormed into Armin's hotel room in the middle of the night and charged him with forging customs papers. During his interrogation, which lasted several hours, Armin explained: 'They are my initials. I am sorry, I can't help it. "Armin Dassler, A.D.".'[15]

The Mexico Olympics were turning into a disaster for Armin because he had no shoes to hand out. All he had to offer were cheap straw sombreros emblazoned with Puma's name.

With few options left, Armin sent Art Simburg, one of his US representatives, into the Olympic Village to circulate a petition among athletes. It asked the Mexican Organising Olympic Committee to pressure customs into freeing the impounded Puma shipment.[16]

But Simburg was intercepted by two officials while at the Village. The Mexicans took him to an immigration detention centre and kept him incommunicado.

Simburg's disappearance was a serious setback for Puma. He was good friends with a number of almost-certain medal winners, including Bob Beamon, Tommie Smith, and John Carlos, who he had signed up to Puma. With Simburg out of the way, might Horst convince them to defect?

In the detention centre, Simburg lived on a monotonous diet of stale bread, beans, and rice. Three meals a day: stale bread, beans, and rice. He slept on a thin mattress and shared a filthy toilet with six others. After four days Puma discovered where Simburg was being held and had him released. Simburg never found out who was behind his incarceration, but he suspected it was Horst's handiwork.

Simburg's detention did, however, affect his work. Once the Games commenced, he shared his time between meeting athletes, watching events, and making lightning dashes to the bathroom; a reminder of his days dining on stale bread, beans, and rice.

### PAYDAY

Even before the opening ceremony, medal prospects fielded offers and counter bids from the warring camps. And in the Olympic

Village the conversation often turned to shoes: 'What did they offer you?' 'What did you get?' 'What are you going to do?'

According to sources within the shoe companies, a gold medal could be worth up to US$10,000. Athletes were also offered cars, future jobs, plane fares to bring their wives and girlfriends to Mexico City, and expensive baubles to entice them to change brands. What athletes received depended on whether they had a chance of winning a gold medal and how hard they played one company off against the other. Those who had no chance of a medal received a pair of free shoes.

One athlete who was intrigued to find out how much he was worth was Tom Farrell. Soon after qualifying for the US Olympic team in the 800 metres, he was invited to dinner by Armin. 'Is there anything we can do for you?' Farrell was asked. Surprised at the directness of the approach, Farrell replied: 'I intend to stop running soon and would like to take up skiing.' Armin replied: 'Not a problem, we'll give you all the ski equipment you need.' Farrell continued to negotiate, obtaining ski equipment for his wife as well as airfares to the skiing fields of Europe. This was a nice little package thought Farrell, but he wanted to hear what Adidas would offer him so he went to see Horst. He had always worn Adidas and he was not about to change, so he wasn't going to be too greedy: 'If you give me $3,000 I'll wear your shoes,' Farrell told Horst. Horst nodded and sent one of his minions out to the bank, who returned with twenty crisp $100 bills and twenty $50 bills.[17]

But not everyone had the shoe companies come knocking on their door: 'There was always a lot of talk about people slipping money into your shoes,' said long jumper Martha Watson. 'Well, I left my shoes everywhere and they were always empty when I came back.'[18] Having won two gold medals in Mexico City, Wyomia Tyus also complained that while money was being splashed around to the male athletes, 'the women were really excluded'. Well almost. She collected a paltry US$600 from Adidas, which was top money among the female athletes.[19]

Other athletes weren't interested in accepting payments, fearful that they could be thrown out of the Olympics for breaching their amateur status. One of them was US sprinter Larry Questad. When he picked up his spikes from the Adidas store, where he had dropped them off for repairs, he found US$500 stuffed inside: 'I was terrified,' he said. 'If I was caught with the money it would mean disqualification.'[20] Questad handed the money over to Payton Jordan, his coach, who did not alert the IOC. Had he done so, and there was a serious inquiry into payments, he knew that many US athletes who were taking money from the shoe companies would be disqualified. It was better not to shake that tree.

Another athlete that Adidas was keen to wrench away from Puma was Bob Beamon, who was a good prospect for a gold medal in the long jump.

While attending the University of Texas at El Paso, Beamon was always short of cash – a problem made worse because he was black: 'I have a 4-year-old car that needs $300 worth of repairs. I don't know where I'm gonna get the money to fix it. If I were a white long jump champion that car would be fixed like magic.' He had seen how mechanics in El Paso fixed the cars of white athletics stars for free, something they wouldn't do for him. This problem was exacerbated by the fact it was impossible to find a rental close to campus that did not discriminate against African Americans: 'My wife and I lived two miles away, and I have to have a car,' he explained. 'I go around borrowing money, practically begging people for money, and I wind up in debt.' He was also aggrieved that the best job his wife could find was stacking boxes at US$1.35 an hour, even though she was a qualified secretary, bilingual in English and Spanish. By contrast, campus counsellors had no trouble placing the wives of white athletes into good jobs.[21]

Beamon had worn Puma in the qualifiers, so Armin was looking forward to the final. When the athletes came onto the field, though, Armin was dismayed to see that Beamon was no longer wearing Puma: he was wearing white shoes with three stripes on the side. What was behind Beamon's defection to Adidas? Hadn't Puma been generous to Beamon throughout his athletic career? What had Horst offered him to wear Adidas? Armin was upset but not surprised. Such dirty tricks had become commonplace in Mexico City.

Beamon jumped 8.90 metres, beating the world record by 55 centimetres. 'I was in the Twilight Zone, between time and space,' he recalled. 'I did not believe I had jumped that far.'[22] It was an astonishing jump that stood in the record books until 1991.

During the victory ceremony Beamon wore Puma. Was he trying to collect cash from both companies? Quite possibly. For the Dassler cousins, a more important question was: which company could claim Beamon as their own? The Adidas-wearing Beamon in mid-flight, creating the world record, or the Puma-wearing Beamon on the victory stand with a gold medal round his neck? The question was settled by Tony Duffy, an amateur photographer, who was fortunate to be in the right place at the right time to capture Beamon at the apex of his jump, with his outstretched left foot closest to the lens and the three Adidas stripes clearly visible. It was dramatic – much more memorable than any shot of Beamon standing on the victory podium – and it is one of the photographs closely associated with the Mexico Olympics.

When Duffy's photograph was published, Horst quickly appropriated it and produced an advertising poster bearing the words: 'adidas on the threshold of the 21st century'. For Horst, such advertising was the reason his company had invested so much in convincing Olympic athletes to wear their shoes. Whatever Adidas paid Beamon, it was well worth it.

The IOC was well aware that athletes were taking money from the shoe companies: there had been an exposé in *Der Spiegel* three months before the 1964 Olympics. The magazine had reported that the 'Dasslers throw out considerable sums of money to secure title-holders and record-breaking stars to wear their shoes or to replace their rivals' with their own'.[23] Yet the IOC did nothing, perhaps worried that the practice was so widespread that if they acted they might have to take medals off scores of athletes. Doing so would damage the reputation of the IOC, so they chose to look the other way.

In any case, after the protest by Smith and Carlos, the minds of IOC members were focussed on whether other competitors would also protest.

After witnessing the salute close up, the Marquess of Exeter knew what he would do if faced with a recurrence: 'I will not countenance such actions again. I'll refuse to hold a victory ceremony if any such attempt is made again.'[24]

The question now, in the wake of the expulsion of Smith and Carlos, was whether other athletes would take the risk.

# Berets, Smiles, and Fear and Loathing in Mexico

I've dreamed about participating in the Olympics ever since I learned to run.

Lee Evans

## FALLOUT

On 18 October, after the USOC announced the expulsion of Smith and Carlos, sprinter Vincent Matthews was furious. While he should have been concentrating on his event – he was due to compete in the semi-final of the 4 × 400 metres relay the next day – he wanted to tell the world who was responsible for the unjust persecution of his teammates. Matthews pulled the sheet off his bed and, using liquid black shoe polish, he scrawled the words 'Down with Brundage'. He then hung the sheet from his window on the sixth floor of the building housing the American athletes.

This was but one story reported by the journalists who descended on the Olympic Village, where American athletes found themselves under siege. Television crews set up bright klieg lights that ripped through the thin curtains of their bedrooms, making it difficult for them to sleep. Black cables snaked along the corridors of the US dormitories, while hopeful reporters knocked on doors looking for a quote or buttonholed athletes on the training track or in dining halls in the Village.

There were athletes who were willing to tell journalists they supported the protest, and some of them threatened to quit if Smith and Carlos were expelled. Others criticised the sprinters for mixing sport and politics and were upset that the controversy was drawing attention away from their achievements in the stadium. Most did not want to be distracted: they were at the Olympics to win a medal and so when reporters approached they fled.

Not everyone had the luxury of responding to questions from the media on what they thought of the protest. Athletes who were members of the armed forces or the Reserve Officers' Training Corps (ROTC) were constrained by military discipline.

To ensure no member of the armed services breached their oath of service, Colonel Don Miller, the military liaison to US Olympians, met with Captain Mel Pender, a sprinter, who was a leader among the African American athletes. Knowing that Pender was sympathetic to the protest movement, Miller warned: 'Mel, you could really ruin your career. You could be court-martialled, you could even go to Fort Leavenworth [the notorious military brig].'[1] A career soldier – he had joined the 82nd Airborne Division as a seventeen year old – Pender had no desire to risk a dishonourable discharge. Having been warned, Pender advised other members of the armed forces and the ROTC that they would be punished if they embarrassed the Army in any way. It was sage advice: athletes who protested could quickly find themselves in a dank jungle somewhere in Vietnam.

Pender nevertheless found a small way to signal his solidarity with his black brothers. Before leaving for Mexico City he had asked Adidas to make him a special pair of black track shoes with gold trim. He had worn them in the 100 metres race and he would do so again in the 4 × 100 metres relay. Such was the subtlety of his protest, though, that it was not even noticed.

One of the athlete-soldiers who ignored the warnings was Captain Tom Waddell, a white athlete. As he was heading for the stadium to compete in the decathlon, Waddell was questioned by a journalist, who asked whether he thought that Smith and Carlos had dishonoured the flag: 'I think they have been discredited by the flag more often than they have discredited it.' When asked whether the protest had tarnished America's image before the world, he replied: 'Our image is so bad it can't get any worse. Maybe this will help.'[2]

The Army was not amused. Just as Waddell was about to begin the second day of decathlon competition, Colonel Don Miller sent a subordinate to warn Waddell that he would be court-martialled for his comments, which had been reported in a number of US newspapers.[3] 'Talk to me tomorrow,' Waddell told him and went off to run in the 110 metres hurdles.[4]

After the competition, in which Waddell came sixth, he had time to reflect. He was six weeks away from being discharged and desperately wanted to avoid a court martial. With the help of rower Paul Hoffman, who was studying law at Harvard, he penned a tactful letter – 'a non-retraction retraction'.[5] The missive worked, allowing Waddell to leave the Army on good terms and enabling the Army to save face.

Many of the African American athletes were so upset at the shabby way Smith and Carlos had been treated that they met to discuss whether they would protest. On the evening of 17 October, around twenty-five black athletes, and a few white ones, all male, attended the meeting. None of the fourteen black female athletes were there: they hadn't been invited. This was not unusual. The men just assumed that their black sisters would fall in with whatever they decided, as they had over the previous twelve months during which the men held numerous meetings to discuss a possible boycott.

Jesse Owens arrived late. Out of respect, the meeting did not start until he appeared. Owens had been brought to Mexico City by the United States Olympic Committee (USOC) as part of its Consultants Committee.[6] His role was to handle political problems that arose among discontented African American athletes. Owens badly misread the mood, taking the side of the USOC against Smith and Carlos. According to Lee Evans, 'he came and talked to us like he was Avery Brundage or the King of England or somebody, and really talking stupid to us, and we just shouted him out of the room'.[7] Before he left, Owens begged the athletes to find a less confrontational way to express their discontent. But by this stage, few were listening.

## BLACK BERETS AND SMILES

On 18 October, when the USOC announced the expulsion of Smith and Carlos, it also made clear to other athletes thinking of protesting that 'a willful disregard of Olympic principles ... would warrant the imposition of the severest penalties'.[8] The threat was deliberately vague. Would they have their medals taken away from them? Would they be slapped with a lifetime ban, meaning they could never compete again? For athletes who had dedicated their lives to their sport, such a ban would be devastating.

Now the athletes knew that they could be severely punished, the question was: who else might protest and how?

All eyes turned to the sprinter Lee Evans, who, together with Tommie Smith, had been a leading member of the Olympic Project for Human Rights (OPHR).

Evans won his 400 metres semi-final, but he hadn't decided how he would protest, or even if he would. He had broken the Olympic record and was the favourite for the race. He was now tantalisingly close to achieving a long-held ambition: Olympic gold.

The night before the final, Linda Evans worried that her husband might not protest, should he win. She was more militant than Lee, who was easy going: more an athlete than an activist. 'Please don't embarrass me,' she reproached him. 'You have to do something; you must do something!'[9]

Lee was in the canteen at the Olympic Village the next day. He was a mess, emotionally, after hearing that Smith and Carlos had been expelled. In a few hours he was due to line up for the greatest race of his life. Sitting alone, Evans pushed his food aside, unable to eat. When a USOC official gave him a friendly wave, Evans got up and grabbed the man: 'Mother, don't even speak to me after what you have done to my partners!'[10] The poor man fled, slamming the door behind him. Evans then left, and as the elevator descended to the ground floor he started to cry: 'There was so much pressure, I was dizzy all over.'[11]

Bud Winter, Evans's coach at San José State, was in Mexico City as a spectator. That morning he caught up with Evans, who told Winter that he didn't know what to do. Worried that Evans might drop out of the race, Winter asked Smith and Carlos to speak to him. Carlos told Evans: 'You run, win and then do your thing, man.' Smith nodded agreement.[12] Now that he didn't feel like he was betraying his black brothers by competing, he said: 'I was never more determined to win a race.'[13]

Before the race, Lee caught up with Linda, who was in the stand with Denise Smith, Tommie's wife. He told her that he was still thinking of not protesting as it could jeopardise their future. 'If you want to do something for me,' she told him, 'then stand up to those devils.'[14]

Feeling the pressure, Evans got together with his teammates Larry James and Ron Freeman, who agreed to join him to stage a demonstration should they win medals.

It was a wet afternoon when Coach Stan Wright escorted Evans, James, and Freeman into the stadium from the warmup track. Five

minutes before the race, as they approached the track, Douglas
Roby, president of the USOC, confronted them: 'What are you going
to do?' he asked fiercely. Without waiting for an answer, Roby threatened to expel them from the Games and told them they wouldn't
compete in another Olympics if they protested. Normally a placid
man, James yelled: 'Listen! You better get this son-of-a-bitch out of
here, or I'll punch him in the mouth.' Wright did not want the athletes upset and yelled at Roby: 'Get out of here!' Without saying
another word Roby stomped off.[15]

Thankfully, the long jump contest was running late and their
race had been delayed, giving the athletes time to settle down
and refocus.

Despite the worry of the past 24 hours, Evans ran like a man possessed. As usual, he made a fast start. He liked to tell the story of
how he had become so good off the blocks: 'One day my brother
and I were walking through a sheep field. A guy thought we were
stealing his sheep and started shooting at us. I outran my brother
and kept going – and after that, don't think my adrenalin doesn't
get going every time I hear the starter's gun.'[16] James's start was even
better and he led the field. As they entered the straight, Evans shot
ahead and won in a world record time of 43.86 seconds. James was
a close second and Freeman third.

Rain had fallen after the race but had stopped by the time the
medallists approached the victory podium. Evans wore the black
beret bought for him by his wife Linda, and he had pinned an OPHR
protest button to his jacket. The others also wore berets, which they
had bought in Denver. They all wore long black socks.

Recalling the accusations hurled at Smith and Carlos for disrespecting the flag, they took off their berets and stood respectfully
to attention as the anthem was played. They wanted their protest to
be noticed, but they didn't want it to provoke their expulsion: 'If we
were thrown out, there'd be no US 1,600-meter [4 × 400 metres]
relay team,' explained Evans.[17]

Afterwards, with their berets back on, laughing, and with fists
raised in a wave rather than a salute – they were not wearing black
gloves – they left the podium. Having received death threats in the
days leading up to the race, Evans joked: 'It is harder to shoot a guy
who is smiling.'[18]

Unlike Smith and Carlos, who appropriated the victory ritual, imposing their own meanings on it, Evans and his teammates worked

within its protocols – although the berets, with their association with the Black Panther Party, was a statement of sorts. Afterwards, Evans was asked about the berets: 'It was rainin,' he replied, with a grin. 'We didn't want to get wet.'[19] When asked whether his performance on the victory podium was a protest, he dodged the question, responding that he had won the race 'for all the black people in America'.[20]

That night, Linda Evans tore into her husband: 'Why did you show such deference to the flag, when, in the land of the free, we are not free?'[21] She was furious that Lee had taken a light-hearted approach to his protest. The next day she packed her bags and flew home.

Evans was back on the track on 20 October for the 4 × 400 metres relay final. He ran anchor, with the other legs run by Vince Matthews, Ron Freeman, and Larry James. The American team won in a world record time of 2 minutes 56.1 seconds.

The medal ceremony was conducted at the end of the day and the four gold medallists appeared wearing black berets. The mood of spectators changed from festive to hostile as soon as they realised there may be another black power salute. After receiving their medals, the athletes gave a bent-arm salute with their fists; no gloves. Only Evans was wearing an OPHR protest button. When the anthem was played they removed their berets and stood to attention.

On the podium, support for their protest came from an unexpected quarter. West Germany had taken the bronze medal, and one of their team, Martin Jellinghaus, wore an OPHR protest button on his track suit, just as the Australian Peter Norman had done during the 200 metres medal ceremony: 'I am wearing this badge because I feel solidarity not only for them as athletes, but as a fierce opponent of racism.'[22] Jellinghaus was not punished or even reprimanded by German Olympic officials.

We don't know why Lee failed to execute a more emphatic protest. Looking back on his motives and those of teammates, Vince Matthews explained that 'all of us harboured some type of fear over possible reprisals. ... We were all young and felt that we might be jeopardizing our future careers in sport, at a time when no one seemed supportive.'[23]

By nature, Evans avoided confrontation. He was horrified when he saw the intense attention – not to mention hatred – rained down on Smith and Carlos. Evans was an athlete first – an athlete who was a dreamer. His waking dreams, and those when he was asleep, were dominated by athletics: he dreamt about tactics, about records, and about victories. And he had no more intense dream than that of winning gold medals in Mexico City. While in his heart he was upset at the racial injustices that plagued the US, his activism took a back seat to his dreams. And those dreams including winning further gold medals at the next Olympic Games in Munich.

Harry Edwards, who had been the driving force behind the OPHR and who was a mentor and friend of Evans, felt betrayed by his half-hearted protests on the victory podium: 'He attempted to stand up and be counted on both sides of the fence at once,' Edwards argued. 'Because this is a struggle for black survival in which there is no middle ground, he failed on both accounts.'[24] While the criticism was probably valid, it should be noted that Edwards did not travel to Mexico following death threats. By comparison, Evans was in Mexico even though he too had received death threats.

## OTHER PROTESTS

After the emphatic protest by Smith and Carlos, the protests that followed were, by comparison, restrained. Understated.

Ten minutes before the start of the 400 metres race, long jumper Bob Beamon had smashed the existing world record by 55 centimetres: an astonishing jump. When he mounted the victory stand his sweatsuit legs were rolled up to reveal black socks. He later told the *New York Times* that he too was 'protesting what's happening in the USA'.[25] Ralph Boston, who finished third, went barefoot: 'They are going to have to send me home, too; because I protested on the victory stand.'[26]

Other African American athletes ran in long black socks, and their protests were diplomatically ignored by Olympic officials.

After the media frenzy over the expulsion of Smith and Carlos, Roby had no appetite for more controversy: 'We let a lot of little things go by, berets, black socks, hands up and down, even though there are specific rules against changes in uniform in the competitors' handbook. But we felt it would have been flyspecking.' As for the clenched fists raised in the 400 metres races, Roby rationalised that many athletes raised their fists in triumph, so nothing more should be read into that.[27]

Had Roby and the USOC punished these protests, they would certainly have attracted more unwelcome headlines and even a walkout.

One group of athletes from whom no protests were expected were the boxers. Keeping a close watch on his charges was Robert 'Pappy' Gault, the first African American head coach of a US Olympic boxing team. 'None of my fighters have been involved in any of this demonstration stuff,' Pappy told the *New York Times*. 'We came here to fight. We're proud to be fighting for the United States. This is our country. We're all brothers aren't we?'[28] Nine of his eleven boxers were African Americans, and of the other two, one was born in Mexico and the other in Puerto Rico.

When Pappy ran into Paul Hoffman, he was worried that Hoffman might be looking to recruit boxers to the OPHR. He threw the diminutive coxswain against the wall and warned him to keep away from his charges.

One of his boxers was George Foreman, who dismissed athletes like Evans, Smith, and Carlos as 'college boys', and brushed aside the civil rights protests as 'a faddish statement of the times – like wearing a dashiki, long hair, faded blue jeans, an Afro'.[29]

As a kid, Foreman had joined a street gang, where he was known as 'Monkey' or 'Monk', and on the mean streets of Houston's Fifth Ward he stole, drank, and brawled. He described his younger self, in his autobiography, as a 'thug'.[30] His salvation from a life of crime came by way of the Job Corps: an anti-poverty programme established by President Lyndon Johnson, which Foreman joined in 1965. It was through the Job Corps that he met Coach Charles 'Doc' Broaddus, who encouraged Foreman to take up boxing.

Through his skill with his fists, America became the land of opportunity for Foreman. That opportunity led him to Mexico City, and should he win a gold medal, that opportunity would secure his future.

On 26 October Foreman stepped into the ring in the Arena México for the final against Jonas Čepulis, who was born in Soviet-occupied Lithuania. Čepulis was intensely disliked by the crowd because he had mauled Mexico's Joaquín Rocha in his previous bout. The partisan crowd were hoping that Foreman would beat his opponent to a pulp. Although much less experienced than Čepulis, Foreman was soon on top, with his left jab, more a battering ram, doing the damage. At the end of the first round Čepulis was bleeding from his nose and mouth, much to the satisfaction of spectators. Foreman continued to punish his opponent with vicious left hooks followed by punishing rights to the head and body before the referee stopped the fight.

After winning, Foreman took a small American flag out of his robe pocket, which was there for good luck. He paraded around the ring, grinning and holding up the flag: 'Everybody started cheering, so I started waving the flag.'[31]

Some journalists interpreted his gesture as a riposte to the unpatriotic behaviour by Smith and Carlos. John Hall, columnist for the *Los Angeles Times*, referred to Foreman's flag waving as 'American Power', in contrast to the black power protest by Smith and Carlos, which he argued was an excuse for 'black racism' and 'bigotry'.[32] Not so, claimed Foreman: 'It wasn't protest or anything. It was just a happy teenager wanting everyone to know where I was from.'[33]

When Foreman heard about the expulsion of Smith and Carlos he felt sorry for them: 'it's almost like grief,' he recalled.[34] But he spoke to neither man before they left Mexico.

Afterwards, Tommie Smith was unhappy with Foreman: 'When I saw that, I was very bitter, very angry; I thought he was doing it to minimize the effect of what we had just done on the victory stand, which is what it did. But I don't even know if he knew it at the time. I believe he realized it later and came up with an alibi for what he did.'[35] Carlos was more sympathetic: 'He was just a young guy from Texas that didn't really have an understanding as to what the real issues were at that time.'[36]

After the Games, when Foreman returned to Texas to visit his family, he discovered how African Americans viewed his flag waving in the ring. He was so proud of his achievement in Mexico that whenever he walked around his old stamping ground, Houston's Fifth Ward, he wore his gold medal. But African Americans who lived in the neighbourhood were not impressed, and they shot him hostile looks. On one occasion, when he met a friend, Foreman was asked: 'How could you lift up the flag that way when the brothers were doing their thing?' The 'brothers' were Smith and Carlos. Foreman also noticed that it was posters of their salute decorating the walls of African American houses. 'What a homecoming,' he recalled in his autobiography. 'Imagine – the Olympic heavyweight champion, an outcast.'[37]

What Foreman was witnessing was a seismic shift among African Americans, particularly the '68ers. They would no longer play the 'good Negro', in the hope that the white majority would improve their civil rights and address black disadvantage. Whereas 'good Negroes' like Jesse Owens and Joe Louis were once heroes to African American kids, this had changed. Now they had new heroes like Muhammad Ali, Smith, and Carlos, who refused to play the 'good Negro' and asserted their right to the American Dream.

# After Spring, Mexico

They may crush the flowers, but they cannot stop the Spring.

Alexander Dubček, 1968

## AN UNSEASONABLY EARLY SPRING

In the 1960s there was no more luminous and popular sporting hero in Czechoslovakia than gymnast Věra Čáslavská. Having won a silver medal at the 1960 Rome Olympics and a silver and three gold medals at the 1964 Tokyo Games, she was one of the greatest Olympic champions the country had produced. By 1968 she was expected to have reached her peak and to win many more medals in Mexico.

With her cotton candy hairdo piled high, Čáslavská was a sporting icon, having captured the hearts of ordinary Czechoslovaks with her grace and ethereal elegance. At home she was known simply as 'Věra', 'Věrka', or 'Věruška'; no surname was necessary.

On returning from Rome, Věra was approached by a government official with an offer that few had the courage to refuse. 'It will be an honour for you to represent the socialist system,' the official told her. At the time, the country was led by General Secretary Antonín Novotný, an unapologetic Stalinist. To soften its image, the Communist Party recruited promising athletes. After all, giant posters of grim political leaders in public buildings, and even larger statues, did little to endear them to the populace, so they hoped to co-opt the popularity of successful sportspeople for the regime. When Věra declined, she was threatened: 'Comrade, you might not be allowed to go overseas to compete.' Government officials tried twice more before giving up in the face of her steadfast refusal.[1]

Věra had no love for hard-line communism. In 1948, when the Komunistická strana Československa took over, the new communist government confiscated her father's delicatessen. While he took his changed circumstance stoically, he resented working for the food cooperative that replaced his business.

While the family learned to live on a much-reduced income, Věra's ambitious mother scraped together enough money for German, piano, and ballet lessons for her four children. Věra's first love was ballet, but as the family had little money her first ballet outfit was a hand-me-down swimsuit. This earned her the nickname 'orange', for its colour. Later, she wore her father's Sokol [sporting club] T-shirt, which her mother sewed into a makeshift outfit.

As well as learning to move gracefully, she also developed strength with generous help from her two older sisters. They bribed Věra to take their turns with the chores. Every day, she hauled two buckets of coal into their apartment, up four flights of stairs. As a result, she developed broad shoulders and muscular legs.

When she turned fourteen, Věra took up gymnastics, a sport she discovered she loved even more than ballet. Within two years she debuted internationally, in the 1958 World Artistic Gymnastics Championships, winning a silver medal in the team event. More victories followed at other international events.

During 1968 Věra's life was dominated by her preparations for the Mexico Olympics. Nevertheless, she also took a keen interest in the transformation in public life that was underway in Czechoslovakia: a period now known as the 'Prague Spring'.[2] The reform movement started soon after 5 January 1968, when Alexander Dubček became First Secretary of the Presidium of the Central Committee of the Communist Party. He and other liberals in his government developed the idea of creating 'socialism with a human face'.[3] It shocked the Stalinists who dominated the governments of Eastern Europe and alarmed the Kremlin. What would happen if it worked? Might their own citizens demand the same liberties?

These reforms flowed into the streets of Prague, as spring came early. Once-forbidden jazz and pop music were heard, *Časy se mění* (Bob Dylan's *The Times They Are a-Changin'*) became one of the unofficial anthems of the Prague Spring, and the Hippies Soul Club was rocking to its own peculiar beat.

On 5 March censorship was eased, and it was possible to read articles in newspapers and literary journals debating what a free

Czechoslovakia should look like. Much of the talk was about democracy, and liberals hoped for truly free and multiparty elections.

Věra's political views were strongly influenced by her much-loved brother, Vašek, who was three years younger than she was. She hung out with him and his student friends occasionally: they would sit around talking politics during the evening, or her brother would strum his guitar and sing anti-Soviet songs. And of course there was laughter. Much laughter.

The next morning, Věra would invariably be back at training – four hours in the morning and another four in the afternoon – happy to see others champion the Prague Spring.

Dubček was acutely aware that the Kremlin and Stalinist leaders in the Soviet bloc were determined to end the Prague Spring. He knew that if he did not back down they might invade.

By now, however, his reform programme was popular, and intellectuals and writers called for the programme to be expanded and accelerated. Worried that Dubček might retreat, liberals promoted the *2,000 Words* manifesto, as it came to be known. Written by Ludvík Vaculík, the manifesto urged their government to resist Soviet bullying and to press ahead with political and economic liberalisation, going beyond Dubček's original reform programme.

Before publishing the manifesto, its sponsors approached eminent figures asking them to publicly support it. This would give it credibility and make it difficult for Dubček to ignore. Particularly prized were signatures from sportspeople, and there was none more valuable to the manifesto's author than that of Věra Čáslavská.

On 27 June the *2,000 Words* manifesto was published in several newspapers and the literary weekly *Literarni listy*. At the end of the manifesto were the names of seventy prominent Czechoslovaks, including Věra, who endorsed its sentiments. Other sportspeople who supported the manifesto were Emil and Dana Zátopek, the heroes of the 1952 Helsinki Olympics, and Jiří Raška, who won a gold medal in the ski jumping competition at the 1968 Winter Olympics.

After the manifesto appeared, the Soviet leader Leonid Brezhnev saw that, even if he could bring Dubček to heel, the reform movement was gaining grassroots support. Moreover, the Kremlin was under pressure from the leaders of other Warsaw Pact countries to intervene. As a consequence, on 13 August plans were made to end the Prague Spring.

The Prague Spring was one of the bright spots of 1968. Unlike overseas protestors who shook up the political Establishment, Věra and other Czechoslovak '68ers did not oppose their government, although they did criticise its reform programme for being too timid. In this way, the supporters of the Prague Spring had little in common with, for example, the '68ers who occupied the streets of Paris in May, who were intent on overthrowing the government of President de Gaulle. Student demonstrations against the Vietnam War were also anti-government, as were attacks on the South Africa government over apartheid. In the case of the Prague Spring, the threat was not the Czechoslovak government but the Kremlin.

### THE RUSSKIS ARE COMING

Despite being worried about the threat of invasion, in August 1968 Věra travelled to a training camp in Šumperk, located in the foothills of the Jeseníky Mountains, 230 kilometres east of Prague.

On 21 August, in the early hours of the morning, she was awoken by shouts: 'The Russians are invading! The Russians have invaded!'[4] At first she thought it was a bad joke – but then she heard military jets roaring overhead.

It was not, in fact, the Russians who were invading Šumperk, though: it was Polish troops and tanks. They were part of Operation Danube and they had been sent in by the Warsaw Pact to put down the 'counter-revolution', which is how they viewed the Prague Spring. Estimates of troop numbers vary from 165,000 to half a million, and they were made up of the armed forces from the Soviet Union, Bulgaria, Poland, Hungary, and East Germany.

As the sun came up, Věra jumped on a bike and rode to the centre of Šumperk. Soldiers were already there, but their tanks could not reach the town centre because protesters had blockaded the boulevard with a dairy truck, which they had turned on its side.

Over the next few hours Věra and the townspeople tried to reason with the Polish troops gathered outside the Hotel Grand. The support of such a famous athlete gave everyone heart, but there was a risk that the troops might lose their patience and open fire. To calm the situation, someone brought out some glasses of beer for the troops: 'Drink, and come in as friends,' the soldiers were told. 'Leave your tanks at home and see how well we'll welcome you.'[5]

At 11.10 a.m. Radio Prague was silent. Věra couldn't get any reliable news about what was happening. What she did not know was that a unit of the Soviet airborne division had arrested Dubček and the other reformist leaders in his government and whisked them off to Moscow.

As the leaders were touching down in Moscow, sometime around midday, confrontations between the invaders and ordinary Czechoslovaks were starting, with both sides trying to avoid casualties. In Wenceslas Square, in the centre of Prague, people were protesting, yelling abuse, and impotently shaking their fists at the Russian soldiers. Loudspeakers warned that if the square was not cleared by 5 p.m., soldiers would open fire on 'counter-revolutionaries'.

There were other small acts of defiance. Patriots swapped street signs to confuse the invaders, or simply replaced the street signs with the word Москва (Moscow) and an arrow pointing north. Students painted graffiti on walls – "*Rusi domov!*" [Russians, go home] – while others chalked white swastikas on tanks. Girls in miniskirts flashed their breasts at Soviet troops and when they began to wolf whistle the girls spat in their faces.

Věra was in danger because she had signed the *2,000 Words* manifesto so she fled to an isolated cottage, fifty kilometres northeast of Šumperk, where she would be safe.

Věra was determined to continue her Olympic preparation in her hideaway. With no apparatus, Věra improvised, turning the forest into her gym. She used a fallen tree log as a balance beam. The mossy-surfaced meadow allowed her to work on her floor exercises. She used strong low-hanging branches as parallel bars. To build her strength and keep her hands calloused, which she needed for the uneven bars, Věra shovelled coal.

When she was too tired to exercise she sat by her transistor radio, hoping for news. 'What about Dubček?' she wanted to know. 'Is he still alive? Will the Russians let him and the others return home?'[6] No answers were forthcoming. Nevertheless, hoping that all would turn out for the best, she continued her training, with only the forest creatures for company.

Dubček returned to Prague on 27 August. He was only released after he and the other reformist leaders had signed the Moscow Protocol, renouncing most of their reform programme and legitimising the intervention of the Warsaw Pact.[7] Knowing nothing about Dubček's infidelity to the Prague Spring, Věra believed he would resume the reform process once the invaders had withdrawn.

But Věra was wrong. She would soon witness the start of a new stage in Czechoslovak history: one euphemistically referred to as 'normalisation'. It took several months for Czechoslovaks to understand that 'normalisation' meant the end of the reforms that had sought to give socialism a human face.

When Věra heard the news of Dubček's return, she decided it was safe to leave her forest refuge. Back in Prague she saw that the city was now devoid of the brightness and passion that had marked the Prague Spring. The music had gone. So had the laughter. In the street, people's faces were shrouded in the pallid colour of defeat.

When Věra heard that Czechoslovakia would be allowed to compete in the Olympic Games, she believed the decision had been taken by the Kremlin: 'Fortunately, it seems that the Soviet ruler Brezhnev decided that if he stopped us going to the Olympics, he would draw attention to the occupation.'[8] She was probably right.

The day before Věra left for Mexico City she made a pilgrimage to the statue of St Wenceslas, outside the Národní Muzeum [National Museum]. She stood before the statue, which was surrounded by a sea of flowers and candles. It had become a memorial to the Prague Spring. Bending down, she placed her Olympic team badge at the base of the monument, making a solemn promise not to disappoint her humbled country. An elderly lady approached her: 'Golden Věruška, you have to beat the Russkies and don't fall off the beam.' She then enveloped Věra in a hug that left her gasping for breath: 'We will be praying for you.'[9]

Věra returned to her apartment to pack. She had already decided that these would be her last Games. Four years earlier she had fallen in love with middle-distance runner Josef Odložil, and they now lived together in Prague. At twenty-six years of age, Věra was ready to settle down and start a family. Before leaving Prague, Věra and Josef had agreed that if she did well they would marry in Mexico City. She carefully packed her wedding dress in her luggage.

## CONQUISTADOR OF THE OLYMPICS

When Věra arrived at the Mexico City airport, she was met by around 400 well-wishers and *vaqueros* [Mexican cowboys] toting silver colts.

And the press. The first question from reporters was: 'Will you or Kuchinskaya win?'[10]

Natalia 'Natasha' Kuchinskaya was the star of the Soviet team and she'd beaten Věra at the Tokyo Olympics on the balance beam. Kuchinskaya had been just fifteen years old at the time. During the next four years their rivalry grew. At the 1966 Artistic Gymnastics World Championships in Dortmund, Kuchinskaya won three gold medals – the same number as Věra. But in 1967, at the European Championship in Amsterdam, Věra made a clean sweep of the gold medals, with Kuchinskaya picking up only two silvers.

Věra knew the Soviet gymnasts well. She had even struck up a friendship with Larisa Petrik; they would swap vinyl records when they were at the same competition and they enjoyed each another's company. Věra, however, loathed Kuchinskaya, who she thought was vainglorious.

By the time Věra arrived, Kuchinskaya had been in Mexico for two weeks and had already won the hearts of the Mexican people. She had even dated a Mexican student, and a rumour circulated that President Díaz Ordaz's son had proposed marriage.

Kuchinskaya's status as the popular favourite was confirmed when the Mexican press started to call her the *Novia de México* [Bride of Mexico]. This title, so the newspapers said, was given by the Aztecs to the most beautiful girl, who was sacrificed to the gods so that they would be merciful. No one, however, had proposed sacrificing Kuchinskaya. Taking a lead from the newspapers, on the first day of competition members of the Mexican organising committee visited Kuchinskaya in the Olympic Village, where they formally bestowed the title on the Soviet gymnast. With an impish grin, she thanked them for the honour and then explained that, as a citizen of the Soviet Union, she had nothing to sacrifice.[11]

Physically, the two women were quite different. Kuchinskaya was petite compared with the muscular Věra. They both sported bouffant hairdos: Kuchinskaya's brunette, Věra's blonde. But both women had outgoing and vibrant personalities, with the Russian's puppy-like vivacity and spontaneity defying the stereotype of the robot-like Soviet athlete.

While Kuchinskaya was known as the *Novia de México*, it did not take long for the press to also fall in love with Věra, showering her with affectionate nicknames: *La Reina de la Gymnasia* [the queen of the gymnasium], *La Věra Grandiosa* [Věra the magnificent] or simply *La Rubia* [the blonde].

Each country was given a daily three-hour block in the gym for workouts. These were open sessions and the stands were often full of spectators. When Věra attended her first official training session at the Centro Deportivo Olímpico Mexicano [Mexican Olympic Sports Centre], fans chanted 'Věra-Věra-ra-ra-ra'. As it turned out, during Kuchinskaya's training sessions, fans greeted her rival with chants of 'Natasha-Natasha-Natasha-ra-ra-ra'. There was no clear winner of the hearts of Mexicans.

The Soviet gymnasts avoided Věra and her teammates after being told by officials (in all likelihood KGB agents) that the Czechoslovaks might physically attack them. Now that Czechoslovak gymnasts had become 'counter-revolutionaries', they would evidently have no qualms about crippling peace-loving Soviet gymnasts.

A couple of days before the games began, the Czechoslovak team received a message from Dubček, which could be read as a political statement of hope for the future: 'I wish you much joy for every success, and if your hopes are not achieved, do not be discouraged; a failure today can be a success tomorrow.'[12]

At the opening ceremony the 122-member Czechoslovak team marched into the stadium wearing dark blue jackets and, for the women, cream Breton hats. They were greeted by clapping and chanting: 'Cheko, Cheko, Cheko. Ra! Ra! Ra!' On the other hand, when the Soviet team appeared, they were received with scattered jeers. 'There was such enormous sympathy,' recalled Věra. 'Everyone knew the Russians had occupied us.'[13]

The Auditorio Nacional at Chapultepec was filled to capacity with 12,800 spectators looking forward to the head-to-head contest between Věra and Kuchinskaya.

During the finals, each competitor was required to execute compulsory and optional exercises on each apparatus, with the composite score determining the final places.

Wearing an elegant black leotard with white buttons and piping on the collar, Věra was nervous and sensitive to the squeak of every seat and to every cough. Her throat tightened and she felt a cold tremor in the pit of her stomach. The stakes could not have been higher: a loss to the USSR would have dealt yet another blow to her blighted country.

As she approached the vault, in the first final, she looked chalk-pale. But the crowd was behind her, as they chanted 'Věra-ra-ra-ra'. In a series of near-perfect vaults she scored 19.875, easily taking the gold medal.

The next event was the uneven bars. Defying gravity, Věra soared, moving from bar to bar with effortless grace and peerless precision. Unfortunately for Kuchinskaya, she fell during her compulsory bars routine, putting her out of contention for a medal. For Věra, it was another gold.

For the balance beam, Věra completed her routine with a front handspring and cartwheel, then a full-twisting back somersault for a perfect dismount. Her performance was splendid. Spectators certainly thought so as they chanted 'Věra, Věra, Věra' for a good ten minutes. When she scored 9.60 on her optional exercise, after being penalised for being over time, spectators went wild, jeering and stamping their feet. Berthe Villancher, the president of the women's technical committee, hurried over to the judges' table. After a terse five-minute conversation, the judges changed Věra's score to 9.85, but it was not good enough to take gold, which went to Kuchinskaya. Věra felt she had been robbed: 'Kuchinskaya made two mistakes and my set was better, more demanding.'[14] Věra blamed biased judges from the Communist Bloc – East Germany, Romania, the Soviet Union, Bulgaria, and Poland – the very countries that had invaded her homeland. In a competition heavy with political significance, denying Czechoslovakia a victory over the Soviet Union was no surprise.

On the victory podium, knowing that she would be forced to listen to the Soviet national anthem, Věra decided to stage a protest. But what? Could she turn her back when the Soviet flag was raised? Clenching her right hand by her side, she considered raising her fist, as Tommie Smith and John Carlos had done. Perhaps, she could give a 'V for victory' salute. All these political gestures, she knew, were illegal under Olympic rules, and she would surely be punished: 'I didn't want to lose the medal, our nation needed it.'[15] As the Soviet anthem started and its flag was raised, Věra quietly turned her head away from the flag and looked down: 'I longed to humiliate the Soviet flag and raise my humble nation, at least for a moment.'[16]

The next event was the one everyone was eagerly anticipating: the optional floor exercises. For spectators, it was a moving confection of beauty and grace. Behind the artistry, each gymnast was minutely in control of her body as it moved through space and time.

Soviet gymnasts Larisa Petrik and Kuchinskaya put on dazzling displays that married gymnastics, choreography, and ballet. Věra would need an extraordinary performance to beat them.

She started brightly with a somersault with a double twist and then skipped across the floor like she hadn't a care in the world. She had chosen *Jarabe Tapatío* (better known as the 'Mexican Hat Dance'). Spectators clapped and roared their appreciation that she was using Mexican music – their music – for her routine. With her honey blonde hair tied in a chignon, she incorporated elements that she had seen Mexican street dancers perform. Her routine was full of fun as she flirted with the audience, totally seducing them. When the pianist accompanying her routine started to play *Alá En El Rancho Grande* [There's a Big Ranch], Věra upped the tempo, ending with a backwards somersault. Her performance attracted a standing ovation.

Věra scored 9.900, but expert commentators believed she deserved a 10. Regardless, it was enough to earn her another gold medal – or it should have been. In a surprise move, the judging panel upgraded the preliminary scores of Petrik. While the Russian's routine did well in originality, she lacked the flair and joyfulness of Věra's routine. Once the scores for the compulsory and optional exercises were tallied, Petrik tied with Věra for first place with combined scores of 19.675.

During the victory ceremony the Czechoslovak anthem was played first, and both women stood respectfully as the Czechoslovak flag was raised. Having seen her earlier protest, the Soviet team, standing nearby, turned their heads away.[17] Next, the Soviet anthem was played and once more Věra protested by lowering her head and looking away.

Afterwards, as Věra shook hands with Petrik, she said: 'I congratulate you as a gymnast, but not for your country's invasion of Czechoslovakia.'[18]

Compared with the reaction to the salutes given by Smith and Carlos, Věra's protests barely caused a ripple. Chris Brasher, reporting for the UK *Observer*, waxed lyrical about Věra's performance but said nothing about her protest.[19] The rest of the media gave fulsome reports of the gymnastics competition, but failed to recognise that Věra's gesture was a protest. Only the live commentary of ABC's Jim

McKay gave a hint that something was amiss: 'Now the Soviet anthem. And again she [Věra] has turned her head to the right and down, just as she did at the last ceremony. This does not appear to be an accident.'[20] He made no further comment, failing to recognise the significance of her gesture.

The medals were handed out by IOC officials, so they were close to Věra when she dropped her head. They could not have missed her gesture on the podium, but no action was taken to punish her. Věra's protest came nine days after the protest by Smith and Carlos, which Brundage had described as a 'nasty demonstration against the United States flag by negroes'.[21] The difference was that Věra had disrespected the flag of another country, which could have been seen as more offensive than disrespecting the flag of your own country, as Smith and Carlos had done.

While Smith and Carlos divided opinion, Věra was very popular and, had it been noticed, her protest would have undoubtedly been greeted with acclaim. The invasion of Czechoslovakia had outraged global opinion, so any decision to punish her protest would have been met with widespread condemnation.

In any case, legally, the IOC could not punish Věra. Doing so would have been the responsibility of Czechoslovak Olympic officials, and they quietly supported her protest. Before arriving in Mexico City they had staged their own protest. The head of the delegation, Emanuel Bosák, with the support of other officials, had sent a telegram to the IOC calling on them to ban the USSR from the Olympics.[22]

Had the IOC taken offence at Věra's protest, and had the Czechoslovak Olympic Committee still refused to act, as it certainly would have, the IOC would have had to retaliate by expelling the whole Czechoslovak team, as it had threatened to do to the US team. With the Soviets firmly in control in Czechoslovakia, had Věra been sent home she may well have been imprisoned or sent to the uranium mines (as salt mines were in short supply in Czechoslovakia). Věra's timidity saved the IOC from a number of invidious choices.

Having completed an outstanding series of performances, Věra was declared the individual all-round winner, ending her successful Olympic campaign with another gold medal. The team all-round medal, however, was won by the USSR by the slimmest of margins – 382.85 to 382.20 – aided by some dubious judging decisions. Věra was disappointed: a victory over the Soviet Union would have raised the morale of Czechoslovaks, who had not had much good news since the invasion.

At home, most Czechoslovaks had stayed up to listen to Věra's victory on the radio. One of those listening was Alexander Dubček, who rang Věra to congratulate her on her victories.

The Soviet team did not attend the press conference that followed the finals, claiming they were too tired. This was probably an excuse made in fear that Věra might denounce the Soviet invasion of Czechoslovakia. When it was Věra's turn to speak, she did not mention her protests. Instead she announced that she would marry her fiancé Josef Odložil in Mexico City the next day.

## NOVIA DE MÉXICO

Věra planned a small wedding in a modest wooden chapel in the Olympic Village, but the Mexicans had a different idea. When Pedro Ramírez Vázquez, president of the organising committee, found out about her plan to marry in Mexico City, he insisted she move the wedding to the Catedral Metropolitana on Zócalo Square.

Věra wore a rhinestone tiara for the wedding; a cascade of pearls ran down the back of her wedding dress, which was made of soft white lace that she described as feeling 'light, like a gentle breeze'.[23] Her face was covered by a white veil and in her hand she held a bouquet of orange orchids and white roses, tied with a ribbon. The groom wore a morning suit.

When the wedding party arrived at the cathedral, the scene was chaotic: between 20,000 and 50,000 enthusiastic Mexicans were there to greet them. There were around 200 local and international journalists and photographers present to report on the wedding, and TV networks had cameras at the cathedral. While none had noticed her silent protest, they were keen to capture the happy event.

Archbishop Miguel Darío Miranda used the PA system to remind the crowd that they were in a place of God. His exhortation had little impact. The nave was full of fans and they crowded the aisles. It was hot in the cathedral and at least ten women fainted. People stood on pews, hung over balconies, and clambered over the altar. One enterprising individual had set up a ladder next to the aisle from which he and six friends could better view the ceremony.

As Věra walked down the aisle her tiara was knocked off her head. She was in tears. Aggressive photographers crowded in, as did well-wishers. The church resembled a bubbling cauldron of people, with everyone desperate to get a glimpse of the bride. Věra and Josef were only able to reach the altar through the efforts of weight-lifters and a hammer thrower who cleared a path for them.

Before the archbishop could start the nuptial mass, he had to shoo cameramen off the altar. 'I didn't hear a single word,' recalled Věra, as the din in the cathedral did not abate during the service.[24] The archbishop rushed through the mass in just under forty minutes and then Věra and Josef exchanged wedding bands.

Věra recalled that the Czechoslovak ambassador had warned her before the ceremony that once the Mexicans have an idol, they will trample them to death out of love and then go to pray for them at their grave site. Hoping to escape this fate, the newlyweds made a hasty escape via a small door behind the altar that led down some stairs into the catacombs. While they waited for the crowd to clear, they were able to enjoy the company of mummified archbishops, some four centuries old, sitting in beautifully carved chairs.

The next day the Mexican press named her *La Novia de México*, her Soviet rival Kuchinskaya had been all but forgotten.

### A LONG WINTER NIGHT

Back home, Věra and Josef attended a reception in Prague Castle. With some ceremony, Dubček introduced Věra as '*paní* [Mrs] Odložilová', her newly minted married name. Such formalities did not last long and soon he was affectionately calling her 'Věrka'.

Present along with Dubček were other politicians closely associated with the Prague Spring: Ludvík Svoboda, Oldřich Černík, and Josef Smrkovský. Věra presented each of them replicas of her gold medals.

Věra and Josef were the toast of Czechoslovakia: a ray of sunlight in a country that was about to enter a long political winter.

As she settled into married life, Věra realised that Dubček and the other political leaders, who she had placed so much faith in, were now under the thumb of the Kremlin.

In January 1969 Věra was upset when she heard that a student, Jan Palach, had set himself on fire in Prague's Wenceslas Square to protest the invasion five months earlier. To show solidarity, she courageously penned an open letter to Palach's mother, which was published on page 1 of *Československý Sport* [Czechoslovak sport].

After passing on her condolences, she wrote: 'It is now the duty of all of us Czechs and Slovaks to fight for basic human rights not only to be proclaimed in our beautiful homeland, but to be implemented as soon as possible.'[25]

Then, during a four-week tour of the US that started on 21 January 1969, Věra was asked about the invasion by a Radio Free Europe reporter. She defiantly responded: 'We all tried harder to win in Mexico because it would turn the eyes of the world on our unfortunate country.'[26]

The Soviets eventually tired of Dubček, even though he offered little resistance to their occupation, and on 17 April 1969 they installed Gustáv Husák as the new General Secretary, because he was willing to obliterate the last traces of the Prague Spring.

With a new hardline government installed in Prague, Věra began to suffer the consequences of her defiance. On 21 October 1969 the Federation of Physical Culture publicly denounced the 'unhealthy influence' of Věra and the other sportspeople who had signed the 2,000 Words manifesto.[27] Věra was at home with her newborn daughter, Radka, at the time, and she decided to stop publicly criticising the government.

After two years at home, Věra started to look for a job. On 22 February 1971 she met officials from her sporting club, Rudá hvězda [Red star]. She hoped to obtain a position coaching children, but instead she was met with hostility: 'Comrade Čáslavská, because you are hard-headed and stubborn and because you won't cooperate we've decided to expel you from Rudá hvězda.'[28] Shocked, she left, dizzy and distressed.

Věra knew why she was being shunned. She had on a number of occasions refused demands by communist officials to renounce her support of 2,000 Words. Other sportspeople who had signed the manifesto had, but Věra stubbornly refused.

In 1972 she was summoned to a meeting with General Secretary Husák. He too asked her to withdraw her signature from the manifesto: 'Be reasonable and nothing will happen to you,' Husák said. 'You'll get nowhere being stubborn.'[29] Rather than being cowed, she attacked the invasion by the Warsaw Pact forces: 'If they came without tanks and not at night, under the cover of darkness like thieves, then I might think about it.'[30]

For the next five years she could not find a job nor take up offers to coach overseas because officials refused her a visa. Instead, she cleaned houses, wearing a disguise so no one would recognise her. 'I went from the mountain top to the abyss,' she recalled.[31]

She was eventually allowed to coach children at Sparty Praha, a sporting club. She had to conduct her classes in secret, though, out the back of the gymnasium, and if anyone important visited, Věra would hide in the changing room.

It was not until 1979 that Věra was allowed to take a coaching position. Mexicans had not forgotten *La Věra Grandiosa* and the job was in Mexico.[32]

It is significant that during the period when she was a pariah, Věra's 'crime' was that she had signed the *2,000 Words* manifesto. She was not being shunned for her silent protest on the victory stand in Mexico City. Her gesture had been too subtle to be noticed. Yet, with the passage of time, her courageous protest is now appreciated in the Czech Republic, where she has become a national hero.

# 11

## Adiós, Hasta la Vista

I thought that was just so cool, that you could show a unified whole, all
mixed up, the whole world together.

Tom Lough, US modern pentathlete

### FRUSTRATED

Chris Brasher, a reporter for the British newspaper *The Observer*,
was knowledgeable and abrasive in equal measure. He was in Mexico City to report on the Olympics, as he had done for the previous
two Games.

When he heard about an alteration the IOC had made to the closing ceremony, he was incensed. It was an event that should end the
Games on a high note, but now the IOC was determined to spoil the
ceremony for most athletes.

A gold medallist in the 3,000 metres steeplechase at the 1956
Olympics in Melbourne, Brasher was impressed by a major innovation to the closing ceremony at those Games. Rather than
entering the stadium in national teams, athletes arrived as an amorphous mass, representing the amity between them forged during
those Olympics.

The change was suggested by seventeen-year-old Melbourne
schoolboy John Wing in a letter to the organising committee. By
allowing athletes to mingle, he argued, there would be 'only one
nation. War, politics and nationality will all be forgotten. What
more could anybody want, if the whole world could be made as one
nation?'[1] His proposal was quickly adopted, with little if any con-
sultation with the IOC, who as a matter of principle resisted ideas
from outside its ranks – particular if they promised to be popular
with athletes.

As a competitor, on 8 December 1956 Brasher entered the stadium with other athletes, eight abreast, arms linked, grinning, and waving as they half-marched, half-strolled around the cinder track to thunderous applause. The Melbourne experience was much more satisfying for athletes than the dreary closing ceremony that had been part of the Olympics since it was first performed at the 1924 Paris Games. Over the decades, the IOC had added pomp and solemnity to the ceremony, but it had a natural aversion to spontaneity and fun.

The Melbourne innovation, according to sports historian Daryl Adair, 'is one of the few occasions when representative parochialism is broken down to emphasize the common humanity of athletes – taking the participants and audience beyond group depictions of marching for country behind a national flag'.[2] Athletes mingle indiscriminately with one another, symbolising the *esprit de corps* nurtured during the Games, giving rise to a joyful display of Olympic internationalism.

The next two Olympiads followed Melbourne's example and were popular with athletes and spectators alike. But now the IOC intended to upend this innovation, for the worse.

After an incident that occurred in Tokyo, Brundage regretted the freedom the IOC had given athletes. As competitors strolled around the stadium, a group of six grinning New Zealanders bowed three times and then performed an abbreviated version of the *haka*, a Maori war dance, before the royal box. Greying, bespectacled, and nattily attired in a morning suit, Emperor Hirohito, a living god among his subjects, did not appear to be offended. Nevertheless, Brundage was upset on his behalf and was determined to prevent a recurrence.

On 9 October 1965, at an IOC meeting in Madrid, Brundage told his executive that he was 'not too happy with the closing ceremony [in Tokyo]. It was disorderly and undignified, in my opinion.'[3] At its next meeting the IOC decided to limit participants to six from each country, plus the flag bearer, which the IOC hoped would reduce the possibility of similar outbursts of youthful high jinx. They would still allow athletes to march into the stadium arm in arm, not in national groups, thereby maintaining an important symbolic part of the ceremony.

Back in Mexico, it was just five days before the end of the Olympics when Brasher heard of the change. Incensed, he went on the attack, arguing that 'all competitors should mix freely in one vast throng of humanity', which he explained had been 'the poignant highlight of everything the Olympics stands for: one huge family, striving, failing, succeeding together'.[4] Brasher was not alone in criticising the IOC. Journalist John Rodda wrote in *The Guardian* that the IOC would 'strip this emotional occasion to a rattling skeleton'.[5]

Understandably, many athletes were upset at not being allowed to take part. US discus thrower Olga Connolly complained: 'All the athletes go to the Olympics, hoping to win, but there is also the other side – making friends and demonstrating to a trouble-filled world that we, as athletes, have a particular love for each other. The closing ceremony proves our point to the world.'[6] US decathlon gold medallist Bill Toomey was also upset: 'I think it stinks.' Had he known, he would have returned home after his event ended: 'I'm 29 years old and I may never get a chance to be in another Olympics, but now there won't be anything about the closing of this one to remember.'[7]

## NOT QUITE THE FINAL ACT

On the evening of 27 October the Estadio Olímpico Universitario was at full capacity. Tickets were at a premium, having sold out, but they could be purchased outside the stadium from scalpers for 1,000 pesos (equivalent to US$380 in 2020). And while some athletes had already left Mexico City, the athletes' area in the stands was still well populated.

The start of the closing ceremony was delayed for thirty minutes because of television schedules; it commenced at 6.30 p.m. International networks had paid US$9.5 million for the rights, and the IOC had little choice. Having flirted with Mammon, the IOC discovered that it no longer had the same freedom over its programming.

The last event of the Olympics was the Grand Prix equestrian event, and once it finished, all the jump obstacles were removed. Afterwards, as a curtain raiser, spectators were entertained by Danish gymnasts.

The day had been hot, and spectators were able to quench their thirst with Coca-Cola, sold by vendors dressed in red and white outfits, with insulated white tanks on their backs and a hose to dispense cold drinks into disposable cups. It was a year before the moon landing, and they were soon nicknamed *astronautas* [astronauts] by Mexicans.

Through its arrangement with the IOC, Coca-Cola had been quenching the thirst of athletes, Olympic officials, and spectators since 1928. In 1968 the relationship deepened, with the company paying US$3 million to become an official sponsor of ABC's television coverage; its advertisements featured 1960 swimming gold medallist Lynn Burke. The IOC had resisted direct sponsorship, but this kind of tryst was inevitable: by the 1960s the IOC was teetering on the edge of insolvency, even with its increased income from television.

As it was getting late in the evening, spectators sated their hunger with local delicacies: *cacahuates* (peanuts coated with salt, chilli powder, and lime juice) and *muéganos* (cubes of fried dough covered with caramel syrup). As night fell, a soft wind cooled the air and spectators reached for their *jorongos* (called 'ponchos' outside Mexico) to keep warm.

The ceremony began with the Parade of Flags. Entering from a ramp on the southern gate of the stadium, flag bearers – 112 of them in all – marched in single file into the stadium, separated by cadets carrying signs bearing the name of each country.

On the electronic scoreboard, 'Mexico 68' appeared in huge letters, and then a fanfare welcomed the athletes into the stadium. Spectators waved sombreros, programmes, and handkerchiefs as the athletes trooped in – six from each country – not by country but in rows of five, more or less. Grinning, they entered arm in arm.

All the flag bearers then gathered in a semi-circle around a temporary podium on which Brundage stood. While there was no noise from spectators, as they anticipated the next part of the ceremony, the rotors of the ABC helicopter hovering overhead disturbed the silence. Even at this most solemn moment, the demands of the network's producer were allowed to intrude on the ceremony so that television viewers could have a bird's-eye view of the final hurrah.

In insufferable Spanish, Brundage formally announced: 'I declare the Games of the XIX Olympiad over and I invite the youth of the world to meet, in four years, in Munich, for the celebration of the Games of the XX Olympiad.' The mainly Mexican crowd were in a forgiving mood – at least he had tried – and politely clapped. Some had tears in their eyes, as did some athletes: after sixteen days the sporting fiesta was coming to an end.

The Olympic flag was lowered next, and then twelve cadets from the Heroica Escuela Naval Militar, a naval school located in

Veracruz, carried it for a circuit of the track. They then folded the flag and handed it to Ramírez Vázquez, president of the Mexican Olympic Committee. Four years later he would present the flag to the new host city, Munich, at its opening ceremony.

At 7.21 p.m. the floodlights were turned off and all that could be seen was the sacred Olympic flame. By now there was a breeze blowing and the flame danced merrily in the cauldron, but not for much longer as the gas was turned off and the cauldron disappeared into the blackness.

Fireworks exploded over the stadium for fifteen minutes and then the scoreboard, which had read 'Mexico 68', changed to 'Munich 72'.

As the floodlights were turned back on, 800 mariachis emerged out of the darkness. They were wearing black outfits with silver trim. Carrying guitars, violins, and trumpets, they played traditional Mexican folksongs, ending with *Las Golondrinas*, a soft wistful song about a migrating swallow who longs to return home.

At around 8 p.m. the flag bearers, followed by the athletes, should have left the stadium, ending the ceremony. They didn't.

## AND THE MARIACHIS PLAYED ON

Deviating from Olympic protocol, participants remained in the stadium and started to seriously party.

Instead of packing up and leaving, the mariachi musicians were infected by the spontaneous display of youthful exuberance and continued playing cheerful Mexican songs. In the stands, spectators put matches to newspapers and programmes, turning them into makeshift torches – faux Olympic torches. Mexico had never been in the global spotlight like this and they didn't want their moment to end.

Athletes in the stands wanted to join in. The only thing stopping them was a low fence around the infield, a narrow ditch, and some scouts, who did not look particularly fearsome. The first attempt by a few athletes to get onto the field was frustrated by the scouts. There was a second attempt in another part of the stadium. This time the athletes were more determined, and with numbers behind them they reached the infield. Some say it was the Americans who jumped the fence first; other gave credit to some Australians. Soon the trickle became a flood.

Athletes sang or just ran around the infield, shaking hands with spectators, who presented them with sombreros. What followed was joyous anarchy. Mexican gold medallist Felipe Muñoz was carried on the shoulders of his teammates, like a victorious bullfighter, as was a hapless naval cadet who had officiated earlier in the ceremony. A competitor from Chad ran towards the crowd, spreading the sleeves of his robes like a great white bird. Columbian athletes broke into a salsa, while other athletes formed circles and danced hand in hand. There were hugs and kisses between new friends who might never see one another again. Smiles and joy mixed with sadness, as many knew they would never participate in another Olympics.

Madeline Manning, an American who had won gold in the 800 metres, had jumped the fence to join the festivities: 'It was that one unique unity of fellowship of athletes that are swarming the stadium and having a party.'⁸ For British flag bearer Dave Hemery, Olympism was epitomised by this closing ceremony: 'Following days integrating fierce competition and cooperation this was a joyful celebration, intermingling different nationalities, by the members of a unique global family.'⁹

Enjoying the show, spectators' chants of 'Mex-hee-co, rah, rah, rah' and 'Viva México' shook the stadium, and the colourful but chaotic scene was soaked up by the television cameras and newspaper journalists.

Now much happier at the turn of events, Chris Brasher described the scene in his Olympics diary. Uplifted by the spontaneity of the moment, he concluded that: 'Humanity has saved me from my depression. Whatever the IOC decree, they cannot stop the youth of the world from mingling in one vast polyglot throng.'¹⁰

If all that television viewers had seen was the unofficial part of the closing ceremony, they could have witnessed no better display of the youth of the world enjoying one another's company, spiritually united by the universal language of sport. It was a spontaneous demonstration by the temporary citizens of the 'isle of the blessed' of Olympic internationalism, and it did more than the solemn rituals that preceded it or words could convey.

The genuine emotion, sincerity, and impromptu revelry certainly impressed journalists. US columnist Al Cartwright wrote that the parade 'soon disintegrated into a merry melange of fellowship. It was a beautiful sight, but apparently not to some of the Olympic daddies.'¹¹ Arthur Daley wrote in the *New York Times* that the 'kids showed Brundage and the other elders what fraternization really means'.[12] For US syndicated columnist John Griffin, the mingling of athletes was a 'carefree, poignant symbol of the international goodwill Games like these are supposed to foster'.[13] And the author of an editorial in the *Decatur Daily Review* was captivated: 'The camaraderie and intense feelings of emotion that were expressed among the hundreds of athletes, some of whom could not even understand each other when they spoke, was unmistakable. With. the world broken into so many bitter powers and factions today, such spontaneous expressions are the stuff of which hope is made.'[14]

After fifteen days of wonderful athletic performances on the fields and in the sporting halls and swimming pools of Mexico City – ending in a chaotic but unforgettable party at the closing ceremony – Mexicans wondered how the world would judge their city as a host. By the records broken or by the protests of Smith and Carlos? By the friendliness of Mexican spectators or by the massacre in Tlatelolco?

Each Olympic Games adopts a sobriquet or has one foisted upon it through a judgement of history. For example, there were the Sunshine Games (Stockholm, 1912), the Nazi Games (Berlin, 1936), the Austerity Games (London, 1948), and the Cold War Games (Melbourne, 1956). Would Mexico be remembered as the 'Peace Games', as the organisers hoped? The spontaneous explosion of amity at the closing ceremony gave Mexicans hope, but as it turned out it was a vain hope.

# Bearing Witness

The pictures talk to us. And they say plenty.

William Carlos Williams

### O SAY CAN YOU SEE

On the evening of 16 October 1968 Marjorie Margolies was on the infield of the Estadio Olímpico Universitario. She was on the lookout for talent: athletes to interview. On her return home, her interviews were packaged into *Marjorie at the Olympics*, which was later shown on WCAU-TV, a CBS station in Philadelphia.[1]

Twenty-six-year-old Margolies, who had been a reporter-at-large for WCAU for just two years, was living her dream. A keen athlete in her younger days, she could not believe she was being paid to rub shoulders with Olympic royalty.

Margolies was just a stone's throw away from where Tommie Smith and John Carlos were to receive their medals. It was getting late and she should have been back in the media centre editing that day's footage, but, on a whim, she decided to stay to watch the medal ceremony.

As the American national anthem started, she mouthed the words: 'O say can you see.' After the first line of the anthem, she stopped. 'Oh my,' was Margolies's immediate reaction when Smith and Carlos's fists shot up in the air and the booing started. 'It jarred because it was not part of the carefully scripted medal ceremony,' she recalled. 'It caught me by surprise and I didn't know what to make of what I was witnessing.'

Most of the audience following the Olympic Games would have first seen the protest on television or in newspapers: more than 600 million around the world, compared with around 50,000 spectators present in the stadium that evening. While watching it live may seem to be preferable, few in the stadium were close enough to clearly see the protest. Even Margolies, who was nearby, did not immediately appreciate its import: 'Did I think it was a historic moment and that I'd be talking about it fifty years later? Honestly, I'd have to say no.'[2]

A number of photographers captured the protest. The next day, a photograph taken by an anonymous photographer from Associated Press was syndicated around the world. The other photographers who captured the moment were John Dominis (*Life* magazine), Neil Leifer (*Sports Illustrated*), and Angelo Cozzi (Moroldo Portfolio).[3] It is the photograph by John Dominis that is the best composed because the athletes are in the centre of the frame. It is this image that is most closely associated with what has become known as the 'Black Power Salute'.[4]

When the photograph appeared in newspapers the next day, it was usually accompanied by an account of the day's sporting news. It was small and could easily be missed. It was only after Smith and Carlos were punished and their action became much discussed by commentators that their protest went from a sports story to a news story. These stories were accompanied by larger photographs of the protest, and it was at this point that the image took on a life of its own.

Eight months later Brundage received some most unwelcome news. The protest was about to be cemented into the official record of the Mexico Games by Alberto Isaac, the director of a documentary on the XIX Olympiad, who planned to include footage of the salute in his film. The documentary had been commissioned by the Mexican Olympic Organising Committee. Brundage wanted history to remember the Mexico Games for its sporting achievements and its solemn ceremonies – and certainly not for its political protests. On 19 August 1969 Brundage wrote to the head of the organising committee, Pedro Ramírez Vázquez, insisting that footage of the protest be removed. Brundage also wanted changes to the official poster for the film, which prominently featured the photograph of the salute. To his credit, Ramírez Vázquez refused to censor history. Piqued, Brundage publicly snubbed the film by refusing to attend its premiere.

Brundage was right to be worried that the photograph of the salute would become indelibly linked to the 1968 Olympics, and in the years that followed it almost always accompanied retrospectives of those Games.

Its historic importance is that it was the first overtly political protest by athletes performed during an Olympic Games. By staging their salute in this global space – 'the isle of the blessed' – Smith and Carlos fulfilled the aspirations of many '68ers: finding a stage where they could globalise their discontent.

### THE MAKING OF AN ICONIC IMAGE

As Smith and Carlos hastily planned their protest before returning to the stadium to receive their medals, their aim was to attract the attention of the world's media: 'We put out a message to be seen not heard,' explained Smith in his autobiography. 'We said nothing, but as they say, a picture is worth a thousand words.'[5] Aiming to speak to a global audience, Smith and Carlos choreographed an image that would be understood everywhere: through visual language, the lingua franca of an increasingly globalised world. They succeeded, and according to art historian Mike O'Mahony, their protest has become an 'icon within the pantheon of Olympic imagery'.[6]

What is it about the photographs of the salute, specifically – and particularly the one taken by Dominis – that has made them iconic?

As the first bars of *The Star-Spangled Banner* rang out over the stadium, Smith and Carlos turned to their right to face the American flag, and so their protest began.

This should have been a moment of triumph, yet their heads are bowed; Smith's eyes are closed, Carlos's half-closed. Their faces radiate sincerity and deep feelings – perhaps they are inviting viewers to join them in reflecting on issues of racism. As their heads were bowed in thought, their hands shot up into the air, gloved fists clenched. The gesture is visually accentuated by both men having rolled up the sleeves of their track jackets: their bare arms draw the eye to their fists. This is an unmistakable call to action; an assertive demand for change.

It is the juxtaposition of these elements that creates an aesthetically arresting image with the capacity to produce complex emotions in viewers. The image commands attention because it engages, provokes reflection, and demands a reaction. Its quiet eloquence is deafening in its rhetorical power and sincerity.

The photograph created anxiety among many white Americans. When they 'saw that raised fist … [they] were afraid,' remarked Smith many years later.[7] Why? As Smith and Carlos stood to attention, they represented the epitome of physical prowess and strength. If black bodies turn their athletic talents to the great glory of the US, they are admired by white America. This was the case with heavyweight boxer George Foreman, who waved an American flag after his victory. It was for this reason that Harry Edwards disparaged Foreman as a 'good Negro' or, more cruelly, 'the white man's nigger'.[8] Aggression was acceptable in the pursuit of sporting victories. However, away from sport, the 'good Negro' needed to meld 'black manliness … and gentlemanliness',[9] and, above all, he needed to know his place. By disrespecting the American flag, Smith and Carlos were, according to many whites, 'bad Negroes'. The image conjured up a racist trope: the powerful black male body as a threat through its 'combination of physicality over intellectual ability, a lack of restraint associated with incomplete socialization, and a predilection for violence,' according to sociologist Patricia Hill Collins.[10]

The timing of the protest was critical in how it was received. The Olympic Games came just after the 1967 Newark riots and the violent protests seen in many parts of the US following the assassination of Dr Martin Luther King Jr. Images of strong black bodies wreaking havoc aroused fear among many white Americans. And this fear was heightened by Richard Nixon, who alluded to black lawlessness in the law and order scare campaign he used to attract white votes.[11]

By contrast, African Americans responded to the physicality of Smith and Carlos with pride. They were winners, 'champions of the best of the best', as they were described in the African American newspaper the *New York Amsterdam News*.[12] What appealed to African Americans was that Smith and Carlos represented fine specimens of manhood – black manhood – who refused to be intimidated by racists; they refused to meekly fulfil the role of 'good Negroes'.

The photograph of their Olympic protest was so very different from other civil rights iconography, with black victimhood its mainstay: African American protesters being beaten by police and savaged by their dogs; white racists harassing African Americans as they confronted segregation in diners, schools, and polling stations, and on buses. Within the African American community these images evoked a range of emotions: anger, indignation, frustration, resentment, hopelessness, and even resignation. What they saw in these images was the brutal exercise of white power, with too many defeats and humiliations. Nevertheless, these pictures were important because, as media analyst Kathleen Hall Jamieson observed, the 'civil rights movement of the 1950s and 1960s was catalyzed not by eloquent words but by eloquent pictures'.[13] Its perverse eloquence was in drawing attention to the ugliness and brutality of racism.

In an abrupt break with the iconography of the civil rights movement, Smith and Carlos are presented as neither victims nor supplicants entreating the white majority for justice, equality, and the alleviation of black poverty. They are demanding those things as their right. Moreover, they are proclaiming the indivisibility of their blackness and their humanity. Smith and Carlos offered the African American community a new kind of black hero: Olympic champions – victors – proffering defiance, dignity, and hope.

Gordon Parks, a colleague of John Dominis at *Life* magazine, understood the power of an iconic image to inspire: 'Having absorbed the message of a memorable photograph, the viewer's sense of compassion and newfound wisdom come together like two lips touching. And it is an extraordinary thing when an unforgettable photograph propels you from an evil interlude to the conviction that there must be a better day.'[14]

In his book *The Sovereignty of Quiet*, Kevin Quashie draws attention to another element of the photograph: the 'compositional similarity between photographs of their 1968 protest and images of lynched bodies. But at its horrible best, the image of the lynched body is one of silence and speaks through the alphabet of violent repression. Smith and Carlos's image, on the other hand, is alive, is articulate in its quiet; though they do not speak, their language is a generous vocabulary of humanity. In this context, Smith and Carlos are a triumphant, beautiful alternative.'[15]

Less visually obvious than the main elements of their performance were their stockinged feet. Visually, this projects vulnerability, which contrasts with the defiance and strength of their upraised fists. They are Olympic winners, being celebrated for their heroics on the track, yet there is no triumph to their pose. Rather, their stockinged feet reveal their empathy with those living in poverty.

Embedded in the photograph of Smith and Carlos are intriguing contrasts: strength and vulnerability; inward reflection and outward assertiveness; quietude and rhetorical energy; solemnity and emotional power. Depending on the audience, it has the ability to either generate empathy or create anxiety, even fear. It is these contrasting elements that aesthetically and intellectually make the image so compelling.

By co-opting the victory ceremony, Smith and Carlos were able to embrace the athletes' 'new double identities as native sons and daughters and as initiated representatives of a wider human community,'[16] according to cultural anthropologist John MacAloon. As Smith and Carlos now had the status of global citizens, they were endowed with the moral status to legitimately address the world.

Their protest was also extraordinarily brave: Smith and Carlos knew that they would be punished. Not only were they expelled from Mexico but their reputations were trashed when they returned home. Smith ran through a number of low-paying jobs, barely able to afford formula for his infant son. The stress ended his marriage to Denise, who left for Paris. It was even worse for Carlos: 'By 1969 and into 1970, my life was beg, beg, borrow, and steal.'[17] The strain was too much for Kim, Carlos's wife, who committed suicide in 1977, four years after they split up.

These misfortunes only added to the potency of the image, as it was now of two men martyred for their principled stand on human rights.

In 2003, *Life* magazine included Dominis's photograph in its anthology of 100 photographs that changed the world: 'Dominis' image turned the somber protest into an iconic emblem of the turbulent 1960s,' noted the caption.[18] The *Washington Post* described it as 'one of the most influential protest images of all time',[19] and it is often associated with youth ferment that was much in evidence in 1968.

The image has also entered popular culture, appearing on T-shirts, posters, wall murals, and graffiti. Andre Gray, a striker for Watford Football Club in the UK, had it tattooed on his back; and in 2000, Rage Against the Machine used the image on the cover of their album *Testify*.

The proliferation of the images of the salute form what Rutger van der Hoeven, foreign editor of *De Groene Amsterdammer*, called the 'global visual memory'. He argued that iconic photographs are '"cultural vehicles", that represent historical narratives that function as "agents of memory"'.[20]

This historical memory has inspired a new generation of activist athletes, the most dramatic recent example being Colin Kaepernick, a quarterback for the San Francisco 49ers. In August 2016 Kaepernick refused to stand during the playing of *The Star-Spangled Banner*. Instead, he knelt, head bowed. On social media, Kaepernick praised Smith and Carlos: 'I have read about them, studied their public protest, admired their courage and, like many others, I have emulated them.'[21] Protests by sportspeople 'taking the knee' have spread in the wake of Black Lives Matter. In 2020 Andy Murray took the knee on the first day of the Battle of the Brits tennis tournament in London, as did Australian players and umpires during round two of the Australian football season. And in Germany, the soccer teams Hertha Berlin and Borussia Dortmund took the knee around the centre circle before a match.

### SOON FORGOTTEN

While the protest by Smith and Carlos has grown in stature over time, other protests and political demonstrations associated with the Mexico Games have been forgotten, in large measure because they are not associated with memorable images or were unable to effectively exploit the global platform provided by the Olympics.

Smith and Carlos's salute was a direct outcome from the failure of the boycott planned by Harry Edwards. In supporting the boycott, Dr Martin Luther King Jr had argued that the absence of African Americans in Mexico City would deal a blow to the Games.[22] He was wrong. Had the boycott succeeded and the US had gone on to field an all-white team, it may have prompted a passing comment during the opening ceremony. However, an all-white team marching into the Estadio Olímpico Universitario would not have created a memorable image that drew attention to the plight of African Americans.

In the case of the exclusion of South African and Rhodesian athletes from the Olympics, there is also no visual memory to mark the success of those campaigns. Newspaper reports of the bans were scant and, of course, it was not possible to photograph the athletes' failure to appear in Mexico. So, once competition started, their absences were forgotten, despite being deeply felt by the athletes themselves, and by the public in South Africa and Rhodesia.

Once the Games commenced, African American Wyomia Tyus protested by wearing black shorts – rather than the white US uniform – when she won gold medals in the 100 metres and the 4 × 100 metres relay. Tyus's protests lacked visual drama, but there is another reason they have been forgotten. After Tyus and her teammates won the relay they attended a press conference and announced they were dedicating their medals to Smith and Carlos. Tyus was upset because she saw no news items that cited their show of solidarity.[23] Why? 'Because I was a woman,' explained Tyus. 'Who cared?'[24]

One other protest that did receive passing media coverage at the time was after the 400 metres for men. When three African American athletes – Lee Evans, Larry James, and Ron Freeman – arrived to receive their medals, they wore black berets. At the time these were associated with the Black Panthers. However, when *The Star-Spangled Banner* was played they removed their berets and stood respectfully at attention, with their arms by their side – in contrast with Smith and Carlos's actions. On 19 October the *New York Times* ran a photograph of the Smith and Carlos protest with the caption 'Black Power Gesture', and it included another image of James, Freeman, and a grinning Evans on the victory podium that described their protest as 'Not Quite the Same Thing'.[25] It should therefore come as no surprise that their diffident protest has been largely forgotten.[26]

One protest that deserves to be remembered was staged by Czechoslovakia's Věra Čáslavská. On two occasions she turned her head away and looked down when the Soviet flag was raised during victory ceremonies. The gesture lacked drama, so it is not surprising that photographers in the auditorium missed it. Čáslavská's protest was much too subtle. There was a video taken of the ceremony, but stills of her protest are blurry, poorly framed, and lack visual impact. And unlike Smith and Carlos, Čáslavská failed to appropriate the ritual power of the victory ceremony or the global space offered by the Olympics to amplify her protest.

Even though her protest had not been emphatic or widely broadcast, Čáslavská knew it would be noticed by Soviet officials watching the gymnastics competition, some of whom would certainly have been KGB agents. She would have also known that other Czechoslovak athletes who had protested in the past had served time for their actions, either in prison or in the uranium mines in Jáchymov.[27] Knowing of these consequences, her protest was truly heroic; but heroic gestures that are not photographed, nor seen by a mass audience, are lost to history.

After the fall of communism in the winter of 1989, censorship was lifted and the public became aware of Čáslavská's Olympic protest.

Figure 12.1  Still image of Věra Čáslavská's protest taken from an ABC sportscast.

However, without an iconic photograph that captured the moment, it never had the impact that the Black Power salute has had.

### SUPPRESSED, BUT NOT FORGOTTEN

Had the Mexican government not acted decisively, another incident would have dominated the historic memory of the 1968 Olympic Games – perhaps even more so than the iconic photograph of Smith and Carlos.

Students had chosen to protest ten days before the opening ceremony because they knew the international media would be out in force in Mexico City. There were at least twenty foreign correspondents and photojournalists in the Plaza de las Tres Culturas in Tlatelolco to cover the protest. In the days that followed, Oriana Fallaci (*L'Europeo*), John Rodda (*The Guardian*), and Uli Schetzer (*Chicago Tribune*), among others, filed stories about the bloodbath,

and they blamed government troops for the large loss of life, estimated to be in the hundreds.

These accounts were in stark contrast to the news stories that
appeared in the Mexican press, which parroted the government's
account: the gunfight was started by student sharpshooters who
were located on the upper floors of high-rise buildings around
the plaza, and regrettably a few students and bystanders had been
caught in the crossfire and killed. Official figures ranged from six
victims to thirty-three.

Photographs on the front pages of the Mexican newspapers supported this account. One photograph in *El Universal* showed soldiers
crouched behind an armoured vehicle, looking apprehensively up,
as the caption explained, at student sharpshooters. In another, soldiers protect a family fleeing gunfire, each parent carrying a small
child and with an older girl between them.[28] On the front page of
*La Prensa* a photograph showed people fleeing 'gunfire from sniper
terrorists, who had attacked the police and, subsequently, the Army,'
according to its caption.[29]

While there was no official censorship of the Mexican press, newspaper proprietors knew that it was unwise to cross the government,
which controlled the distribution of newsprint. Newspapers that did
not toe the official line could easily be put out of business. Telesistema, Mexico's only television station, was publicly owned – and
meekly did the government's bidding.

There was, however, one small sign of discord. On the front
page of the daily newspaper *Excélsior*, a brief item appeared that
informed readers that 'Excélsior's photojournalist Jaime González
was wounded yesterday by a bayonet in to his left hand and his camera destroyed by a rifle butt. Minutes later, another photographer
from this newspaper, Ricardo Escoto, had his camera confiscated
and it too was destroyed.'[30]

As it turned out, harassment of *Excélsior* photojournalists was not
isolated, and other parts of the media were also targeted. The government understood that uncensored photographs of the massacre
would put a lie to its account.

Working through the night, Bernardo Arredondo Aguilar was
developing photographs delivered to the offices of *El Universal* immediately after the rally. In the early hours of the morning, agents
from the Federal Security Directorate burst into the offices: 'The

photos, you bastard, the photos!' one demanded. The head of photography, Daniel Soto, had no choice but to comply. Other agents scrutinized galley proofs, crossing out the number of fatalities, telling the editor: 'just 33 dead, 33, huh? That's the official figure!'

After the raid, Soto phoned around to the other newspapers – *Excélsior, Novedades, El Heraldo, Ovaciones* – and found they had all had similar visits, ordered by President Díaz Ordaz. 'And did they also take your photos?' he asked. 'Yes, *la chingada!*' [the fuckers]. Soto concluded that 'the government was willing to intimidate publishers, loot the newsrooms, and threaten the lives of reporters'.[31] Unsurprisingly, most newspaper articles echoed the government's account.

Frustrated that news of the massacre had been suppressed, student activists employed guerrilla tactics – graffiti, pamphlets, and posters – to express their discontent. One street poster depicted the Olympic rings as five smoking grenades, and in another a policeman holds his club aloft like a flaming Olympic torch. The appropriation of Olympic symbols was clever, pointing to the disconnect between the celebration of a festival of peace and the death of so many in Tlatelolco. Activists hoped such images would draw attention to the massacre. Unfortunately, few in the media reported these graphics. The exception was the dabs of red paint that had been splashed on the doves of peace, which were on banners on all major thoroughfares, which Bob Ottum of *Sports Illustrated* described as 'creating the effect of a bird shot through the heart, blood dripping down'.[32]

Student activist Mariclaire Acosta described the mood after the Olympics ended: 'The world was totally indifferent. ... It's very difficult to overcome that traumatic experience of this terrifying thing that is not happening officially.'[33] Such was the government's success at suppressing evidence of the massacre.

In the decades that followed, a few brave writers, journalists, and filmmakers continued to gather evidence and put it before the Mexican population.

In 1971 Elena Poniatowska published *La noche de Tlatelolco* [The Night of Tlatelolco], a collection of oral histories.[34] Her book also contains photographs that had not been confiscated. One shows debris left on the ground of the plaza. Its caption reads: 'Many discarded shoes and torn clothes, especially those belonging to women, lie on the ground between shredded shrubs: silent witnesses to the disappearance of their owners.' Another shows a young boy, perhaps

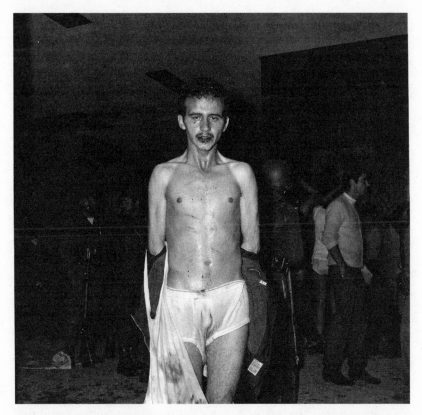

Figure 12.2    Florencio López Osuna arrested after the Tlatelolco massacre.

twelve years old. He is dead, and the caption reads: 'Who ordered this? Who could order this? This is a crime.'[35]

In the 1990s, when the Partido Revolucionario Institucional government was in decline, newspapers, magazines, and documentary makers started to publish more images of the massacre that had previously been hidden by photojournalists.[36]

In December 2001 a package of thirty-five black and white prints was delivered in a black plastic bag to the home of the journalist Sanjuana Martínez. It arrived anonymously.[37] They were published in the Mexican magazine *Proceso*. The front cover shot is a photograph of one of the protesters, Florencio López Osuna. He stands impassively, staring into the camera. He is almost naked, wearing only loose-fitting white underwear, now stained with his blood. His rake-thin body shows abrasions and bruising. There is a cut below his right eye. His arms are tied behind his back. Andrea Noble, Professor of Latin American Studies at Durham University, suggests that the image of Osuna bore a resemblance to St Sebastian 'after the martyrdom – characterized by his youthful body, naked save for a loincloth, his arms tied behind his back, his flesh pierced'.[38] There are photographs from the massacre at Tlatelolco that are much more harrowing, but the simplicity of a young man, standing with quiet dignity despite the obvious attempt to humiliate him, is powerful. Accompanying the *Proceso* article, Luis González de Alba, one of the student leaders, wrote: 'These photos prove once and for all that our version of the truth is the truth. They show the power of images over words.'[39]

This cache of photographs also attracted attention overseas. *The Guardian* claimed that the photographs 'provided the first proof in 33 years that Mexican governments have lied about the role of paramilitaries in a massacre of students just before the 1968 Olympic Games', adding that the violence was provoked by members of the Batallón Olimpia not 'highly dangerous anti-Mexican elements', as the government had alleged.[40] The *New York Times* reported that these photographs 'give new life to the testimonies repeated year after year by students who were there'.[41] The Spanish newspaper *El Mundo* said that the photographs 'prove what was an open secret: that the government of President Gustavo Díaz Ordaz and the Mexican Army were responsible for the killing of hundreds of students in the Plaza de las Tres Culturas, perpetrated on the night of October 2, 1968'.[42]

These photographs, as well as others that emerged in the following years, have gone a long way towards helping Mexicans recover memories of Tlatelolco. However, outside Mexico they came too late to become part of the historical memory of the 1968 Olympic Games.

# Epilogue

The Olympic Games are a theatre – sometimes farce, sometimes tragedy, theatre of the absurd, opera buffa, reality TV, morality play or soap opera – where geopolitical, social and technological dramas are played out.

Tim Olds

### THE GAMES MUST GO ON

The next Olympic Games, held in Munich in 1972, were the first test of what impact the Mexico Olympics – the 'Games of Discontent' – would have on the Olympic movement.

Smith and Carlos's successful demonstration in Mexico City alerted others to the benefits of using the Olympic global space – the 'isle of the blessed' – to protest. The presence of the global media, particularly television, was an important plus.

Television networks scrambled to win the rights to televise the 1972 Munich Games, paying US$18 million (equivalent to US$135 million in 2020).[1] The bidding was fiercest for the North American rights, which ABC won, paying almost three times as much as it had for the Mexico Games.

ABC was upbeat, starting its coverage by playing Burt Bacharach's *What the World Needs Now Is Love Sweet Love*. With so much invested in their success, ABC and other rights holders hoped that these Games would be about sport. Nothing else. No protests. No salutes on the victory podium. No threats of boycotts. No political demonstrations. ABC expected the IOC to ensure that the *Heiteren Spielen* [Cheerful Games], as the Munich organising committee wanted them to be remembered, would be just that: cheerful, a celebration of peace and friendship, an unforgettable spectacle, and a feast of sport that would attract record ratings.

The IOC hoped that the punishment meted out to Smith and Carlos would be sufficient to discourage future protests, although Brundage had his doubts. Following the 1972 Olympics he would re-tire as IOC president, after twenty years in the job. On the eve of the Olympics, when he addressed his Executive one last time, Brundage shared his fears for the future: 'Ironically, the greater the success of the Olympic Movement, the more and greater the commercial and political intrusion.'[2]

Brundage had long opposed opening up the Games to television. He worried that once the IOC became dependent on income from corporate sponsors, its ideals would be compromised. Nevertheless, he reluctantly agreed to sell the rights, surrendering to the inevita-ble because the IOC's financial position was dire.

As for political intrusion, now that the Olympics were broadcast to a global audience, they might again attract protests, as he had seen in Mexico.

Brundage's warning would prove to be prescient in Munich and during the Games that followed, in ways that he could not have imagined.

The IOC did not have to wait long to see whether it had done enough to stop politics intruding into the Olympics. However, ra-ther than coming from athlete activists, the threat came from an unexpected quarter.

On 5 September 1972, at around 4.30 a.m., eight tracksuit-clad members of the Palestinian terrorist group Black September climbed over the chain-linked fence surrounding the Olympic Village. In their duffel bags they had hidden AK-47 assault rifles, Tokarev TT-33 pistols, and hand grenades. They then went to the Is-raeli men's dormitory where they killed two and held nine athletes, officials, and trainers hostage.

Why had they targeted the Olympic Games? According to Abu Daoud, who planned the attack: 'we decided to use their Olym-pics, the most sacred ceremony of this religion, to make the world pay attention to us. We offered up human sacrifices to your gods of sport and television. And they answered our prayers. From Munich onwards, nobody could ignore the Palestinians or their cause.'[3] He was right. The terrorist attack was reported and broad-cast in real time across the globe. It certainly made for morbidly compelling television.

Having reported the unfolding drama for sixteen straight hours, at around 5 a.m. the next day ABC's Jim McKay struggled to keep his emotions under control: 'When I was a boy, my father told me that in life, our greatest ambitions and our worst fears are seldom realized. Tonight, our worst fears have been realized.' He then described the fate of the hostages, ending with a despondent shake of his head: 'They're all gone.'[4]

Just as the image of Smith and Carlos on the victory podium became synonymous with the Mexico Games and the turbulent 1960s – as well as becoming an inspiration to African Americans – there is one photograph for which the Munich Olympics is best remembered. Taken by Kurt Strumpf, it shows one of the members of Black September wearing a homemade knitted balaclava with two circular cut-outs for his eyes and a horizontal slit for his mouth. He stands on a balcony outside the rooms where the Israeli hostages were being held.

The meaning of an image depends on the emotional response it evokes. In the West, the power of this particular photograph lies in the balaclava, which presents the anonymous face of terrorism. He could be anyone among us, hiding in plain sight. The photograph therefore stirs up fear. However, for militant supporters of the Palestinian cause it is perversely inspirational, celebrating the sacrifice of the heroes – not terrorists – martyred in Munich.

The massacre showed the political value of staging incidents at the Olympics. According to a statement issued by Black September afterwards, its raid 'was like painting the name of Palestine on the top of a mountain that can be seen from the four corners of the earth'.[5]

On the day after the hostages were taken, a memorial service was held in the Olympic stadium to honour the fallen. While the Olympic flag hung limply at half mast in the still, humid air, the Olympic flame still burned. At the end of the service, Brundage announced that 'the Games must go on',[6] and they resumed later the same day.

After some rescheduling, on 7 September the 400 metres for men was run. Vince Matthews was first across the line, with Wayne Collett second. Both men are African Americans.

After receiving their medals, Collett broke with custom and joined Matthews on the top step of the podium, where they chatted and joked. When *The Star-Spangled Banner* began to play they stopped talking and turned side on, so they were not facing the flag. Collett stood with his hands on his hips while Matthews stroked his goatee, sighed, and looked restless. The only man looking at the flags and standing to attention was the bronze medallist Julius Sang, from Kenya.

Contrasting this protest with that of Smith and Carlos four years earlier, sociologist Douglas Hartmann observed that the salute was effective because it reshaped the Olympic ritual, 'its symbols and so-ciologics into a meaningful expression of their own racially inflected sense of self and social solidarity'.[7] The iconic image of Smith and Carlos was eloquent and memorable. By contrast, the photograph of Matthews and Collett on the podium is forgettable; if it was a pro-test, it was crude and its meaning was opaque, as neither athlete bothered to provide a plausible explanation for his actions.

To discourage other demonstrations, the IOC immediately ex-pelled Matthews and Collett. As a result, they were not allowed to compete in the 4 × 400 metres relay, in which the Americans had a very good chance of taking gold.

Ominously, Brundage warned that any future repetition would re-sult in medals being 'withheld from the athletes in question'.[8]

It was eight years before the Olympics saw another protest. At the 1980 Olympics in Moscow, Polish pole vaulter Władysław Kozak-iewicz made an obscene gesture after winning the gold medal: he slammed his left hand against his right bicep as he raised his right fist. In cultured circles, this is known as *bras d'honneur*; in down-to-Earth Anglo-Saxon, it means 'screw you'. He was responding to an angry Moscow crowd, upset that he had beaten hometown favour-ite Konstantin Volkov.

Back in Poland there was widespread dissatisfaction with Soviets and their brand of communism. A month before the Olympics there had been strikes across Poland. These led to the creation of *Solidar-ność* [Solidarity], a union that would pave the way for the overthrow of the communist regime in 1989. While Kozakiewicz's gesture was mainly driven by his anger at the unsporting behaviour of Russian spectators, at home it was interpreted as a protest against the So-viets. As a result, Poles in the streets chanted Kozakiewicz's name, shook his hand, and hugged him.

In 2012, at the London Olympics, Australian indigenous boxer Damien Hooper wore a T-shirt featuring the Aboriginal flag during his first fight against America's Marcus Browne, which he won. When he was warned by Olympic officials that he had broken its rules and could be punished, Browne apologised and promised not to wear the T-shirt again.

At the 2014 Sochi Winter Olympics, Russian slopestyle snowboarder Alexey Sobolev rode a snowboard featuring a knife-wielding woman wearing a ski mask. This is what the members of Pussy Riot wore when they performed. A feminist punk-rock band, its members had been jailed for their anti-religious and anti-Putin protests. When asked whether this was a political protest, Sobolev artfully replied: 'Yes, there is some resemblance with Pussy Riot symbols, but I had nothing to do with the design of this picture. Anyway I like this picture. It looks cool.'[9]

Also in Sochi, Dutch Snowboarder Cheryl Maas, who is openly gay, wore a glove displaying a rainbow-and-unicorn motif, which was interpreted as a protest against Russia's anti-gay laws.

Two years later, at the Summer Olympics in Rio de Janeiro, Ethiopian Feyisa Lilesa came second in the marathon. As he crossed the finish line he raised his arms above his head, creating an 'X' by crossing his wrists. This gesture is used by the people of Ethiopia's Oromia region to protest against government persecution. The abuses had been ignored by the world media, but this changed after Lilesa's protest.

One reason for the decline in protests by activist athletes was undoubtedly the threats to take their medals off them, but there were other reasons too.

The protesters who targeted the Mexico Olympics were infected by the spirit of their generation: '68ers, keen to challenge the status quo. By the early 1970s the '68ers were a diminishing force. Some were disillusioned while others looked to less confrontational ways of reforming the system. 'The riptide of The Revolution went out with the same force it had surged in with, the ferocious undertow proportionate to the onetime hopes,' wrote political activist Todd Gitlin.[10]

Politically apathetic and inward-looking, the next generation was not interested in taking up the baton. They made the 1970s the 'Me decade', as described by Tom Wolfe.[11] This was a sobriquet that could equally be applied to young people who came of age during the following decades too.

By the 1980s another factor predicated against activism by athletes. As amateur rules were gradually relaxed and would eventually disappear, elite athletes attracted sponsorships, and after they retired they could become brand ambassadors.

These deals became particularly lucrative as global television audiences made athletes international celebrities, whose names could become valuable brands in their own right.

There is no better example than Michael Phelps, one of the most successful swimmers of all time. The high-water mark of his career was winning a record eight gold medals at the Beijing Olympics in 2008. While still competing he earned US$2 million, and afterwards his earnings went above US$75 million in advertising and sponsorships deals. Phelps is a marketer's dream according to Peter Carlisle, an agent who negotiates deals for elite sportspeople: 'To the extent anyone can be a global icon, Michael is. He's recognizable and relevant in just about every market we want to be working in.'[12]

Unsurprisingly, successful athletes understood that should they protest at the Olympics, such opportunities would be taken off the table.

## ONE WORLD, ONE DREAM

Even though the danger of protests by athletes receded, the Olympic movement faced a new threat in 2008, as activists in nongovernmental organisations targeted hosts and sponsors.[13]

The main vehicle the IOC used to attract sponsors was the TOP (The Olympic Partners) programme, launched in 1986. TOP allowed transnational corporations to use the Olympic five rings logo to promote their brands.

What the Olympic movement had to sell – its five rings logo – was precious. It had become one of the world's most recognisable and valuable logos, not only because it was associated with the premier international sporting festival but because it was associated with noble objectives, like promoting international amity and peace. Transnational corporations were willing to pay handsomely to be associated with these admirable qualities. This is called the 'halo effect', which, according to research conducted by the television network NBC, allows corporations to signal to customers 'that the company is a supporter of good causes and of the Olympic ideals'.[14]

Between 2013 and 2016, the IOC earned US$1.02 billion from TOP companies like Coca-Cola, McDonald's, Panasonic, and Visa.[15] Together with increasing income from selling television rights and other business deals, the IOC, which once eschewed commercial entanglements as corrupting, had found its tryst with the corporate sector highly satisfying: its total income reached US$5.16 billion over that same period.[16]

At the 2008 Olympic Games in Beijing, Human Rights Watch and Amnesty International decided to draw attention to humanitarian abuses committed by the host nation. They knew that protests at summer Olympic events gave them unparalleled access to the global media, which reported all matters Olympic with forensic intensity every four years.

This new strategy created a problem for sponsors, who did not want their brands associated with bad publicity. It was also possible that rather than benefiting from the 'halo effect', they could be shown to be associated with the unprincipled activities of the host.

Abuses of human rights in China, particularly in Tibet, became the main target of protests.

The first shot in this campaign was fired in September 1993 when Beijing first bid to host the 2000 Olympic Games. Four years earlier Chinese protesters had been massacred in Tiananmen Square, and there were unsettling reports coming out of Tibet of violent suppression of dissent by the government.

A month before the IOC vote, Robert Bernstein, founder of Human Rights Watch, wrote to the IOC. He predicted that 'China would put people away and clean up the city like you wouldn't believe'. He went on to argue that giving the Olympics to Beijing would allow the Chinese government 'to say it was well respected by the world community while it was still torturing prisoners'.[17] Pressure from Human Rights Watch may well have been responsible for the outcome: Beijing lost to Sydney by two votes.

Beijing's next bid was not opposed by Human Rights Watch, which decided it would be more effective to use IOC influence over China to bring about reforms. Amnesty International was not entirely comfortable with this approach but reluctantly decided not to oppose the bid. Beijing succeeded in the second round, easily beating Toronto, Paris, and Istanbul.

For the Chinese government, hosting the Olympic Games was politically important. It announced the peaceful rise of China as a superpower, and the government intended to use the Olympic brand to 'propagate a virtuous identity'.[18]

Protesters planned to puncture this virtue signalling by drawing attention to the ugly underbelly of China's human rights record.[19]

The violent suppression of protests throughout Tibet in March 2008 provided impetus for demonstrations. According to Kalaya'an Mendoza, a coordinator for Students for a Free Tibet, disrupting the torch relay was 'a monumental opportunity for Tibetan people to be put in the international spotlight'.[20] Other activist groups joined in.

Billed as the 'Journey of Harmony' by Beijing, the torch relay was a 137,000-kilometre journey through twenty-one countries over 129 days. The length of the relay provided numerous opportunities for activists to disrupt the event.

At Olympia in Greece, where the sacred flame always begins its journey, three members of Reporters sans Frontières unfurled a banner showing the Olympic rings as handcuffs. Afterwards, activists issued a statement: 'If the Olympic flame is sacred, human rights are even more so. We cannot let the Chinese government seize the Olympic flame, a symbol of peace, without denouncing the dramatic situation of human rights in the country.'[21]

When the torch reached France, the eternal flame was extinguished four times by protesters before security guards took it onto a public bus to escape. Eighteen protesters were arrested.

In San Francisco, a banner that read 'One world, One Dream: Free Tibet' was strung across the Golden Gate Bridge, fifty metres above traffic.

In Buenos Aries, protesters decided not to disrupt the official torch relay. Instead, activists organised their own 'Human Rights Torch Relay'. 'The Olympics Games and crimes against humanity cannot coexist in China,' explained Falun Gong member Axel Borgia.[22]

These were just a few of the protests that were widely aired in the international media. What was promoted as a Journey of Harmony turned out to be a public relations disaster for China. The IOC also came under unwelcome scrutiny as it was repeatedly asked about its attitude towards human rights in China. It repeatedly avoided the question.

A major sponsor of the torch relay was Coca-Cola, which paid an estimated US$25 million for the privilege. To get full value out of its investment, Coca-Cola turned this Olympic ritual into a craven marketing exercise. It was a peerless opportunity for the company because the route took the torch through many of the markets in which Coca-Cola already had a presence and wanted to expand.

The relay has important symbolic meaning to the Olympic movement. The torch is carried by ordinary people, who 'represent common humanity in precisely the opposite way than the Olympians do,' according to cultural anthropologist John MacAloon.[23] The demands of commerce, however, made a mockery of this ritual and its symbolism.

Accompanying the torch was a caravan of twenty official vehicles, some displaying Coca-Cola signage. There were cheerleaders – cheerleaders! – who revved up the crowds along the route while pop music blared out of loudspeakers. Men and women dressed in garish Coca-Cola livery handed out flags and trinkets bearing the company's logo.

Torchbearers were escorted by motorcycle security, not only to protect the torch but to ensure that protests did not upset the sponsors. There were also vehicles carrying television cameras and print journalists around the torchbearer. So rather than representing 'common humanity', the 'caged torch procession' – as the BBC sports editor Mihir Bose described the relay[24] – all but blocked the public's view of the flame.

The symbolism of the relay was further debased when it was discovered that rather than representing 'ordinary people', many torchbearers had been selected by Coca-Cola as part of its sponsorship deal.

During the relay, and then at the Beijing Olympics, Coca-Cola's marketing message – according to their vice president of worldwide sports marketing Scott McCune – was 'refreshment, connection, the best of humanity and global unity'.[25] Who would have thought that a company that sold a sugary beverage was committed to such noble objectives?

The final leg of the relay was through China itself, and its route would take it through Tibet and to the summit of Mount Everest.

At Coca-Cola's annual general meeting, held on 16 April 2008, Lobsang Choephel, a member of Students for a Free Tibet, asked Coca-Cola's Chairman and Chief Executive Officer Neville Isdell: 'Will you tell the IOC to stop taking the Olympic Torch Relay into Tibet, because Tibet belongs to Tibetans?' By parading the torch through Tibet, protesters argued that it gave the false picture that the region was at peace. Isdell said that the relay 'has symbolized openness, it has symbolized hopes. I don't believe that stopping the torch run is in any way over the long term going to be the right thing to do.'[26]

Coca-Cola was in a difficult position. The company was happy to enjoy the nebulous morality conferred by its association with the Olympic movement. On the other hand, the company did not want to be seen as criticising the government of its most promising market. It would have been bad for business. Virtue had its limits.

The IOC was also in an awkward position when protesters challenged it to live up to its position in the global moral order. Under pressure, IOC president Jacques Rogge said: 'The IOC is not authorised and has no means to interfere in sovereign matters.' Unable to deny human rights abuses in China, he lamely argued that: 'The Games hold up a mirror and show what is happening. We bring the media to the Games, and I firmly believe the Games have a positive effect.'[27] His statement was carefully worded so it gave the appearance that China had human rights issues that needed to be exposed, but it avoided direct criticism of the host nation.

The stance taken by the IOC was unsurprising. It could ill-afford to upset the Chinese government, as this could adversely affect its major sponsors and the television networks that had paid handsomely for the rights to the Beijing Olympics. As Rogge explained after the Beijing Games: 'Without the support of the business community, without its technology, expertise, people, services, products, telecommunications, its financing – the Olympic Games could not and cannot happen.'[28]

So rather than being a staunch defender of the 'island of the blessed', the IOC showed that it was less than saintly when it came to protecting its income from television and corporate sponsorships by ignoring human rights.

After the Games, when the IOC was no longer in the spotlight, it released a factsheet that had nothing but praise for the Beijing Olympics, describing them as 'a landmark event for the universality of sport'.[29] No mention was made of the universality of human rights, and there was certainly no mention of human rights abuses by China in Tibet and elsewhere. The result was that China was able to project a virtuous image without changing its approach to human rights.

Nevertheless, the IOC was damaged by its stance during 2008, as it had been by the human rights protest by Smith and Carlos. In each instance, the high priests of the 'isle of the blessed', the IOC, repeatedly failed to match their rhetoric about the moral order with moral action.

# Notes

AUTHOR'S NOTE

1   It was not until 1988 that the term 'African American' started to replace 'Black'.
2   Deborah Posel, 'Race as Common Sense: Racial Classification in Twentieth-Century South Africa', *African Studies Review* 44, 2 (2001): 87–113.


INTRODUCTION

1   'Roone at the Top', *The Gazette* (Emporia, KS), 28 October 1968, 4.
2   Miquel de Moragas Spa, Nancy Kay Rivenburgh, and James F. Larson, *Television in the Olympics,* Academic Research Monograph 13 (London: John Libbey, 1995), 213.
3   By 1968, ATS-1 Applications Technology Satellite, Intelsat I F-1 (nicknamed 'Early Bird'), Intelsat II F-2 ('Lani Bird'), and Intelsat II F-3 ('Canary Bird') were in orbit, providing global coverage. On 25 June 1967, to demonstrate the capability of this technology, a multicountry show was televised called 'One World', with feeds to twenty-four countries. The audience was estimated to be around 400 million.
4   Toby Miller, Geoffrey Lawrence, Jim McKay, and David Rowe, *Globalization and Sport: Playing the World* (London: Sage Publications, 2001), back-cover blurb.
5   Roone Arledge, *Roone: A Memoir* (New York: HarperCollins, 2003), 96.
6   During this ceremony, Peter Norman stood to attention, with his arms at his side. By wearing a badge, though, he was also part of the protest, even if most of the media focus was understandably on Smith and Carlos: it was their emphatic and photogenic demonstration that is

remembered. At the time, Norman's role was hardly noticed, which is why he is not mentioned here. His role is covered later in the book.

7   *Official Report of the Organizing Committee of the Games of the XIX Olympiad*, vol. II (Mexico City: Organizing Committee, 1969), 303.

8   Paul Auster, 'The Accidental Rebel', *New York Times*, 23 April 2008, A21.

9   Rod Ackerman, '1968: Das Jahr, als selbst im Sport alles möglich schien', *Neue Zürcher Zeitung*, 8 May 2018, https://www.nzz.ch/sport/1968-das-jahr-als-selbst-im-sport-alles-moeglich-schien-ld.1384014.

10  While its origin is uncertain, it is likely that the term '68ers was first used in West Germany and went on to gain currency in Western Europe. Members of this generation are also known as a *soixante-huitard* in France, a *sessantottino* in Italy, and a *sesentaochero* in Spain or Latin America. Importantly, the activities of the '68ers were not confined to 1968, but spanned the decade. Nor was there a single archetype of a '68er.

11  John S. Saul, 'Liberation Support and Anti-apartheid', in *New World Coming: The Sixties and the Shaping of Global Consciousness*, ed. Karen Dubinsky (Toronto: Between the Lines, 2009), 127–40.

12  Timothy Scott Brown, *West Germany and the Global Sixties: The Anti-authoritarian Revolt, 1962–1978* (Cambridge: Cambridge University Press, 2013), 77.

13  The term 'global village' was coined by Marshall McLuhan in *Understanding Media* (New York: New American Library, 1964), 93.

14  The identification of the period 1870–1914 as the first wave of globalisation is contested, with some scholars arguing it started much earlier. See Robbie Robinson's *The Three Waves of Globalization* (London: Zed Books, 2003) and Nayan Chanda's *Bound Together* (New Haven, CT: Yale University Press, 2007).

15  Maurice Roche, 'Mega-events and Modernity Revisited: Globalization and the Case of the Olympics', *Sociological Review* 54, 2 Supplement (2006): 27–40.

16  Pierre de Coubertin, cited by Charlene Weaving in 'Buns of Gold, Silver, Bronze: The State of Olympic Women's Beach Volleyball', in *The Olympics and Philosophy*, ed. Heather L. Reid and Michael W. Austin (Lexington, KY: University Press of Kentucky, 2012), 228–42.

17  Pierre de Coubertin, cited by Sigmund Loland in 'Coubertin's Ideology of Olympism from the Perspective of the History of Ideas', *OLYMPIKA: International Journal of Olympic Studies* 4 (1995): 49–78.

18 Pierre de Coubertin, 'The Olympic Games of 1896', in *Olympism: Selected Writings*, ed. Norbert Müller (Lausanne: IOC, 2000), 350–60.

19 Clarence Bush, 'An International Sovereignty Created', Avery Brundage Collection, RS 26/20/37, Box 259, Folder USOAC – Bush, Clarence, AOC Publicity Director folder 3 of 3, ca. 1936. Provided courtesy of the University of Illinois Archives.

20 'Address of Mr. Avery Brundage, President of the IOC, at the Opening of the 73rd IOC Session in Munich', *Olympic Review* 59 (1972): 371–80, available from LA84, https://digital.la84.org/.

21 'Wir werden immer erpreßbar sein', *Der Spiegel*, 14 May 1984, 128.

22 de Coubertin, 'The Philosophic Foundation of Modern Olympism', in *Olympism*, 580–3.

23 Liam Stockdale, 'More than Just Games: The Global Politics of the Olympic Movement', *Sport in Society* 15, 6 (2012): 839–54.

24 Anne Koedt, 'Women in the Radical Movement', Speech delivered at a city-wide meeting of radical women's groups at the Free University in New York City on 17 February 1968. It was subsequently published in *Notes from the First Year* (New York: New York Radical Women, June 1968), 26–7, https://dukelibraries.contentdm.oclc.org/digital/collection/p15957coll6/id/650/.

25 de Coubertin, 'Educational Use of Athletic Activity', in *Olympism*, 184–94.

26 de Coubertin, 'The Philosophic Foundation of Modern Olympism'.

27 Marion Stell, 'Women with Altitude: Resisting the Role of the Australian "Chaperone" in Mexico 1968', *International Journal of the History of Sport* 36, 9–10 (2019): 779–95.

## CHAPTER ONE

1 Pierre de Coubertin, 'Olympic Memoirs. XIII: The fifth Olympiad (Stockholm 1912)', *Olympic Review*, issue 119 (September 1977), 562–7.

2 The truce did not stop wars. Instead, some believe that it granted safe passage to competitors and visitors to and from Olympia. Only warfare against Elis, the host city, was forbidden. Other wars could, and did, carry on. For more on this, see Cindy Burleson, 'The Ancient Olympic Truce in Modern-Day Peacekeeping: Revisiting Ekecheiria', *Sport in Society* 15, 6 (2012): 798–813.

3 John Underwood, 'The Tokyo Games', *Sports Illustrated*, 5 October 1964, 34–41.

4 Bernd Walter Raeke, 'German–German Relations in the Fields of Sport, With Particular Reference to the Olympic Games 1952–1972' (PhD dissertation, Plymouth University, UK, 2014), 72.

5 Justus Johannes Meyer, 'Politische Spiele – Die deutsch-deutschen Auseinandersetzungen auf dem Weg zu den XX. Olympischen Sommerspielen 1972 und bei den Spielen in München' (PhD dissertation, Hamburg University, Germany, 2010), 171.

6 While East Germany had not formally broken ties, in July and August 1961, before the Wall was erected, it cancelled more than a hundred sporting events in West Germany.

7 Letter from Heinz Schöbel to Avery Brundage, dated 21 August 1961, cited by Manfred Lämmer in *Deutschland in der Olympischen Bewegung: eine Zwischenbilanz* (Frankfurt: Nationales Olympisches Komitee für Deutschland, 1999), 245.

8 Letter from Willi Daume to Avery Brundage, dated 10 November 1961, cited by Erin Elizabeth Redihan in *The Olympics and the Cold War, 1948–1968* (Jefferson, NC: McFarland & Company, 2017), 177.

9 Willy Brandt, *Ordeal of Conscience* (Cambridge, MA: Harvard University Press, 1963), 78.

10 Letter from Avery Brundage to Otto Mayer, dated 6 April 1963, cited by Kay Schiller and Christopher Young in *The 1972 Munich Olympics and the Making of Modern Germany* (Berkeley, CA: University of California Press, 2010), 161.

11 At the time, Brandt was in the middle of an election campaign, which he won handsomely on 17 February 1968. In a secret session, Berlin's Senate formally approved the joint bid on 19 March 1963.

12 Letter form Willy Brandt to Otto Mayer, dated 27 March 1963, cited by Karsten Lippmann in 'Verhilft Olympia zur Einheit? Deutsch-deutsche (Nicht-)Bemühungen um die Spiele 1968 für Berlin', *Bundeszentrale für politische Bildung*, 5 April 2018, https://www.bpb.de/geschichte/ zeitgeschichte/deutschlandarchiv/267428/verhilft-olympia-zur-einheit-deutsch-deutsche-nicht-bemuehungen-um-die-spiele-1968-fuer-berlin.

13 Oskar (Hans Bierbrauer), *Berliner Morgenpost*, 30 May 1963, cited by Noel D. Cary in 'Olympics in Divided Berlin? Popular Culture and Political Imagination at the Cold War Frontier', *Cold War History* 11, 3 (2011): 291–316.

14 Peter Bender, 'Olympiade in Berlin?', *Die Zeit*, 31 May 1963.

15 Associated Press, 'Berlin a Candidate to Stage 1968 Olympics if East German Officials Agree. Brundage gives strong support', *New York Times*, 22 May 1963, 68.

16 'Woche zu Woche', *Das Ostpreussenblatt*, 15 June 1963, 24.

17 *Deutsches Sportecho*, 11 June 1963, cited by Noel D. Cary in 'Olympics in Divided Berlin? Popular Culture and Political Imagination at the Cold War Frontier', *Cold War History* 11, 3 (2011): 291–316.

18 Paul Zimmerman, 'LA Gets New Chance for Olympic Bid', *Los Angeles Times*, 13 February 1963, III, 1.

19 'Battle in Baden-Baden', *Sports Illustrated*, 15 September 1963, 6.

20 'Lyon Confident on Olympic Bid', *New York Times*, 16 October 1963, 57.

21 'Open Occupancy Pot Still Bubbles Bitterly', *Detroit Free Press*, 8 October 1963, 6.

22 Photos of the protest and placards are available at https://www.joestevensphotos.com/Detroit-Black-History-Photos/i-MFfSS8P/M.

23 David Goldberg, 'Detroit's Radical', *Jacobin*, May 2014, https://www.jacobinmag.com/2014/05/detroit-s-radical-general-baker/.

24 Frank Beckman, 'Mayor Blasts Booing Pickets', *Detroit Free Press*, 12 October 1963, 3.

25 '"*México México*", Dice la Mayoría', *El Nacional*, 17 October 1963, cited by Keith Brewster and Claire Brewster in 'The Rank Outsider: Mexico City's Bid for the 1968 Olympic Games', *International Journal of the History of Sport* 26, 6 (2009): 748–63.

26 David Maraniss, *Once in a Great City: A Detroit Story* (New York: Simon and Schuster, 2015), 265.

27 David Briggs, 'Detroit Came Close to Holding Olympics', *The Blade* (Toledo), 25 June 2012, https://www.toledoblade.com/news/nation/2012/06/24/Detroit-came-close-to-holding-Olympics/stories/201206240053.

28 Maraniss, *Once in a Great City*, 267.

29 'Romney Consoles Crowd at Airport on Olympic Loss', *Detroit Free Press*, 20 October 1963, 8.

30 UPI, 'Mexico City Picked Over Detroit, Lyon and Buenos Aires for '68 Olympics', *New York Time*, 19 October 1963, 42.

31 Miguel Rodriguez, 'Mexico 1968: "Todo es posible en la paz"', *Outre-Terre* 3, 8 (2004), 319–30, https://www.cairn.info/revue-outre-terre1-2004-3-page-319.htm.

## CHAPTER TWO

1 Dennis Brutus, 'Sports Test for South Africa', *Africa South* 3, 4 (July–September 1959), 35–9.

2 Dennis Brutus, *Poetry & Protest: A Dennis Brutus Reader* (Chicago, IL: Haymarket Books, 2006), 38.

3 Dennis Brutus, *The Dennis Brutus Tapes: Essays at Autobiography*,
   ed. Bernth Lindfors (London: James Curry, 2011), 137.

4 At the time, negotiations to create an independent country were
   underway, and the Union of South Africa was formally declared on
   31 May 1910. The Union consisted of four former colonies: Cape,
   Transvaal, and Natal, as well as the Orange Free State republic. The
   Union became a sovereign nation in 1931. Nevertheless, for the
   Olympic Games, Great Britain allowed the colonies to be represented
   as 'South Africa', while marching under the Union Jack. Four years
   earlier, at the 1904 St Louis Olympics, three South Africans competed
   in the marathon. Bertie Harris, who was white, dropped out at the
   halfway point. The other two competitors were black, and they'd
   been brought to the St Louis Exhibition for a Boer War reenactment.
   Both had been Tswana dispatch runners during the war, on the Boer
   side. They were Len Taunyane and Jan Mashiane: they came ninth
   and twelfth. Taunyane would have done better but he was chased off
   course by a pack of vicious dogs. The 1904 Olympics was an informal
   affair, where anyone who happened to be in St Louis could compete.
   There was no official South African team. For more, see https://
   mg.co.za/article/2016-07-07-00-story-of-south-africas-first-black-
   olympians-keeps-us-guessing.

5 There was earlier legislation that introduced apartheid measures,
   so 1948 did not mark a sudden change. For example, the Natives
   Land Act of 1913 banned the sale of land between black and white
   landowners. Later, in 1936, the Representation of Natives Act
   effectively disenfranchised black voters.

6 Cosmo Pieterse, 'Dennis Brutus', in *African Writers Talking*,
   ed. Cosmo Pieterse and Dennis Duerden (London: Heinemann,
   1972), 53–61.

7 Connie Field, *Fair Play, Have You Heard from Johannesburg?*, part 4
   (Berkeley, CA: Clarity Films, 2010).

8 Dr Dönges's statement in *Die Burger*, dated 26 June 1956, was cited by
   John Nauright in *Sport, Cultures, and Identities in South Africa* (London:
   A&C Black, 1997), 127.

9 Chris Bolsmann, 'White Football in South Africa: Empire, Apartheid
   and Change, 1892–1977', *Soccer & Society* 11, 1–2 (2010): 29–45.

10 Over the course of the events covered in this chapter, the South Africa
   national Olympic committee would change its name. First it was the
   South African Olympic and Commonwealth Games Association, then
   the South African Olympic Games Association, and finally the South

African Olympic and National Games Committee. They were all basically the South Africa National Olympic Committee (SANOC), so that formulation is used throughout.

11 Extract of the minutes of the 55th session of the International Olympic Committee, in Munich (Haus des Sportes), 25–28 May 1959, https://digital.la84.org/digital/collection/p17103coll1/id/26893/rec/1.

12 Extract of the minutes of the 59th session of the International Olympic Committee, in Moscow (Hotel Sovetskaia), 5–8 June 1962, https://digital.la84.org/digital/collection/p17103coll1/id/27746/rec/1.

13 The organisation that it grew out of was the South Africa Sports Association. An in-principle decision to create SAN-ROC was made on 7 October 1962; it was formally approved three months later.

14 The report turned in by Balsiger was not a critical examination of whether non-white sportspeople suffered discrimination, but rather a ringing endorsement of apartheid. He states that the homelands are necessary to help the 'peaceful and systematic development of Whites and Bantus', which he explained needed to be 'led and assisted by Whites'. Cited by Douglas Booth in *The Race Game: Sport and Politics in South Africa* (Abingdon, UK: Frank Cass Publishers, 1998), 86.

15 Field, *Fair Play*.

16 Brutus, *The Dennis Brutus Tapes*, 76.

17 *Ibid.*, 83.

18 Brutus, *Poetry & Protest*, 69.

19 Brutus, *The Dennis Brutus Tapes*, 93.

20 'South Africa Stands Fast', *New York Times*, 27 June 1964, 5.

21 Richard Edward Lapchick, *The Politics of Race and International Sport: The Case of South Africa* (Westport, CT: Greenwood Press, 1975), 64.

22 Dennis Brutus, 'The Sportsman's Choice', in *Apartheid: A Collection of Writings on South African Racism by South Africans*, ed. Alex LaGuma (Chadwell Heath, UK: Lawrence and Wishart, 1972), 149–60.

23 The Supreme Council for Sport in Africa served as a specialised agency of the Organization of African Unity for the coordination of the African Sports Movement.

24 Brutus, *Poetry & Protest*, 133.

25 'South Africa: "We quit Olympics if …"', *The Sunday Times* (London), 18 February 1968.

26 William F. Fry, 'No Springboks', *The Sunday Times* (London), 24 March 1968, 16.

27 Brutus, *Poetry & Protest*, 134.

28 'About the South African Team', IOC *Newsletter* 5 (February 1968): 66–9, https://digital.la84.org/digital/collection/p17103coll1/ id/28395/rec/1.

29 Field, *Fair Play*.

30 Lloyd Garrison, 'African Shock Waves: Olympic Boycott Raises Doubts that Sports Can Be Freed from Politics', *New York Times*, 28 February 1968, 57.

31 Tex Maule, 'A Flare in the Dark', *Sports Illustrated*, 3 June 1968, 60–73.

32 'Mexico without the South Africans', IOC *Newsletter* 8 (May 1968): 147–50, https://digital.la84.org/digital/collection/p17103coll1/ id/28114/rec/90.

33 John Hennessy, 'South Africa Expelled from Olympics', *The Times* (London), 26 April 1968, 1.

34 Brutus, 'Sports Test for South Africa', 35–9.

35 The first South African Games were held in 1964 and were trials for the Tokyo Olympic Games, even though some overseas competitors participated. The Olympic rings were displayed, which did not create a problem as the Games were under the aegis of SANOC and the purpose was to prepare for the official Olympic Games.

36 The choice of Bloemfontein was significant as it was in the heart of Afrikanerdom and had once been the capital of the Boer Orange Free State.

37 The original location for the non-white Games was in Umlazi, a black township south-west of Durban, and they were finally held in the Orlando Stadium in Johannesburg.

38 'South African Games Prove to Be a Flop', *Los Angeles Times*, 24 March 1969, part III, 10.

39 Derek Du Plessis, 'Symbol of White Supremacy', *The Times* (London), 2 April 1969, 12.

40 'Deplorable Apartheid and Sport', *The Times of India*, 7 March 1969, 10 (italics in the original).

CHAPTER THREE

1 Transcript of Salisbury Radio broadcast, 13 July 1968 (FCO 25/549).

2 Transcript of Salisbury Radio broadcast, 13 January 1968 (PRO 36/317).

3 The IOC finally expelled the South Africa National Olympic Committee from the movement in 1970.

4   The team of the Federation of Rhodesia and Nyasaland was composed of modern-day Malawi, Zambia, and Zimbabwe.

5   The Federation of Rhodesia and Nyasaland dissolved in 1963, and Nyasaland became Malawi in 1964. A team from Southern Rhodesia competed under the Union Jack. Northern Rhodesia competed as a separate team and became Zambia during the Games. At the closing ceremony its athletes marched under its new flag.

6   Bernard Dzoma, telephone interview with the author, 1 November 2018.

7   John Cheffers, *A Wilderness of Spite: Rhodesia Denied* (New York: Vantage Press, 1972), 34.

8   Eddy Norris, 'Rhodesian Sport Profiles: Bernard Dzoma', 12 November 2012, http://rhodesiansportprofiles.blogspot.com/2012/11/bernard-dzoma.html.

9   A circular issued by Joseph Alfred Curtis Houlton, the Secretary for Education, refers to 'unpleasant incidents' having prompted the new rules, without explaining or giving any specifics. The circular stated: 'It has now therefore been ruled that schools may arrange no further fixtures of this nature (including with private schools which admit races other than Europeans) unless the School Advisory Council and/or the Parents–Teachers Association has been specifically consulted and has expressed a wish for such fixtures to continue.'

10  Bernard Dzoma, telephone interview with the author, 1 November 2018.

11  Cheffers, *A Wilderness of Spite*, 73.

12  Myra Fowler, telephone interview with the author, 28 November 2018.

13  Memorandum from C.M. Le Quesne to E. Michael Rose, 'Visit of French Rugby Team to Rhodesia', 7 July 1967, 7 (PRO 25/549).

14  George Thomas, 'Oldham AFC (Rhodesia Visit)', Written Answers (Commons), Hansard 1803–2005, 23 June 1967.

15  Daniel Chapman (writing under the byline 'Moscowhite'), 'Positive Action Movement: When Ken Bates Took Over His Homeland in 1968, Noel Lloyd Led the Fight to Take it Back', *The City Talking*, 6 June 2012, http://www.thecitytalking.com/noel-lloyd-ken-bates-leeds-united/.

16  Simon Demissie, 'Cricket Controversy: Yorkshire, Sobers and Touring Rhodesia', National Archives Blog, 4 September 2013, https://blog.nationalarchives.gov.uk/blog/cricket-controversy-yorkshire-sobers-and-touring-rhodesia/.

17  *Daily Telegraph,* 13 September 1967, cited by Charles Little in 'Rebellion, Race and Rhodesia: International Cricketing Relations with Rhodesia During UDI', *Sport in Society* 12, 4 (2009), 523–36.

18  *Ibid.*

19  *Yorkshire Post,* 13 September 1967, cited by Little, 'Rebellion, Race and Rhodesia'.

20  'No Rhodesia Tour for Yorkshire', *The Times* (London), 19 September 1967, 3.

21  Dennis Howell's correct title was Parliamentary Undersecretary with Special Responsibility for Sport, but in effect he was a junior minister responsible for sport.

22  'British Lions Say: Rhodesia Tour is On', *Daily Mail,* 10 October 1967.

23  Douglas Ian Smith, *Bitter Harvest: Zimbabwe and the Aftermath of Its Independence* (London: John Blake Publishing, 2008), 140.

24  Cypher from the Secretary of State for Foreign and Commonwealth Affairs (SOSFA) to the British Embassy in Mexico, 9 May 1968 (FRO 25/549).

25  James Bottomley to George Thomas, Secretary of State for the Commonwealth Relations Office, 29 November 1967 (PRO FCO 36/316).

26  Minutes of a meeting held between Denis Howell, the Marquis of Exeter, and Lord Luke, 12 January 1968 (FRO 25/549); memorandum from J.R.A. Bottomley to Sir Leslie Monson, 22 January 1968 (PRO 36/317); note of a meeting at the Department of Education and Science, 12 January 1968 (PRO 36/317).

27  Cypher from R. Michael Hadow, Ambassador to Israel, to the Foreign Office, 1 March 1968 (PRO 36/317).

28  Handwritten note from Eric Young to Richard Faber, 5 March 1968 (PRO 36/317).

29  Note for the Record written by James Bottomley to Richard Faber, 'Rhodesia: Olympic Games. Meeting Held in the Secretary of State's Room at 3 p.m. on Monday, 12 February', 13 February 1968 (FCO 36/317).

30  Security Council Resolution 253, 1968 [Southern Rhodesia].

31  Cypher from Ambassador Hope to Foreign Office, 12 June 1968 (FRO 25/549).

32  Cypher from the Secretary of State for Foreign and Commonwealth Affairs (SOSFA) to the UK Mexican Embassy, 24 June 1968 (FRO 25/549).

33  'Olympic Bombshell for Rhodesia', *Rhodesian Herald,* 8 June 1968, 1.

34 Minutes, 'Rhodesian Participation in the Olympic Games', 30 July 1968 (PRO 36/318).

35 Transcript of a Salisbury Radio broadcast, 28 May 1968 (FCO 25/549).

36 Cypher from Ambassador Hope to the Foreign Office, 17 August 1968 (FCO 25/549).

37 'Rhodesia out of Games', *Kansas City Times*, 31 August 1968, 45.

38 Cheffers, *A Wilderness of Spite*, 16.

39 *Ibid.*, 17.

40 'Rhodesians out of the Olympics', *The Times* (London), 31 August 1968.

41 Bernard Dzoma, email exchange with the author, 20 December 2018.

42 Bernard Dzoma, interview with the author, 15 March 2019.

43 Cheffers, *A Wilderness of Spite*, 16.

44 The black population was severely disadvantaged. Land was divided inequitably, with the whites getting the best farming land. The black majority were denied political, social, and economic rights. The education system was largely segregated, and the government spent twelve times as much on schooling for each white child as it did for each African child. The list goes on. For a snapshot of black disadvantage, see 'Rhodesian Alphabet', *Africa Today* 13, 6 (1966), 9–11.

45 Cheffers, *A Wilderness of Spite*, 159

46 *Ibid.*, 151.

47 Andrew Novak, 'Rhodesia's "rebel and racist" Olympic Team: Athletic Glory, National Legitimacy and the Clash of Politics and Sport', *International Journal of the History of Sport* 23, 8 (2006): 1369–88.

## CHAPTER FOUR

1 Harry Edwards, *The Revolt of the Black Athlete* (New York: The Free Press, 1969), 42.

2 Philip Fradkin, 'Tommie Smith Tells Negro Threat to Boycott Olympics', *Los Angeles Times*, 23 September 1967, A1.

3 Harry Edwards, *The Struggle that Must Be: An Autobiography* (New York: MacMillan, 1980), 27.

4 Edwards, *The Struggle that Must Be*, 74.

5 Harry Edwards, 'Harry Edwards: An Oral History', interview by Nadine Wilmot in 2005, Oral History Center, Bancroft Library, University of California, Berkeley, 2010, https://digitalassets.lib.berkeley.edu/roho/ucb/text/edwards_harry.pdf.

6 Edwards, *The Struggle that Must Be*, 87, italics in the original.

7 Robert Lipsyte, 'Striking Nerves', *New York Times*, 16 December 1967, 63.

8 Edwards, *The Revolt of the Black Athlete*, 43.

9 Al Stump, 'The Man Who'd Like to Wreck Our Olympic Team', *True, The Man's Magazine*, April 1968, 44–6, 70–3.

10 Edwards, *The Struggle that Must Be*, 165.

11 Lipsyte, 'Striking Nerves'.

12 Philip Fradkin, 'Negro Gain May Set US Pattern: San Jose State Negro Gains May Set Pattern', *Los Angeles Times*, 24 September 1967, 3.

13 Edwards, *The Revolt of the Black Athlete*, 38.

14 Johnathan Rodgers, 'A Step to an Olympic Boycott', *Sports Illustrated*, 4 December 1968, 30–1.

15 Al Stump, 'The Man Who'd Like to Wreck Our Olympic Team'.

16 Rodgers, 'A Step to an Olympic Boycott'.

17 *Ibid.*

18 'Cracks Are Seen in Boycott Plans', *The Evening Sun* (Hanover, PA), 25 November 1967, 10.

19 'Should Negroes Boycott the Olympics?', *Ebony*, March 1968, 110–16.

20 Jim Murray, 'Life Goes on Whether Tommie Runs or Not', *Los Angeles Times*, 26 September 1967, part III, 1, 6.

21 Charles Mayer, 'Boycott Would Bring More Grief than Good', *Los Angeles Times*, 25 November 1967, 21.

22 By 1968, 'black power' would become closely associated with the Black Panther Party and black separatists, but it was a broad movement and for many ordinary African Americans it was a statement of black pride and an assertion that they would take what was rightly theirs regardless of what the white majority thought. For more, see Jeffrey O.G. Ogbar, *Black Power: Radical Politics and African American Identity* (Baltimore, MD: Johns Hopkins University Press, 2019).

23 Associated Press, 'One Group Suggests 1968 Boycott – American Negro Athletes Divided on Olympics Ban', *Indiana Gazette*, 25 November 1967, 8. There are two other accounts in which Brundage is quoted using similar language in September 1968. Both were written many years later, but they may relate to the same episode. Those accounts appear in George Wright's *Stan Wright – Track Coach* (San Francisco, CA: Pacifica Sports Research Publications, 2005), 188–9; and Melvin Pender and Debbie Pender's *Expressions of Hope* (Meadville, PA: Christian Faith Publishing, 2017), 102.

24 On 29 April 1967 boxing authorities stripped Muhammad Ali of his world heavyweight championship title after he refused the draft: an emphatic statement about the separation of sport and politics.

25 Qqara, 'Dr. King: Boycott Olympic Games', YouTube video, 3:31, 3 April 2008, https://www.youtube.com/watch?v=L7QJmpEGvdE.

26 Lipsyte, 'Striking Nerves'.

27 Elaine Brown, *A Taste of Power: A Black Woman's Story* (New York: Doubleday, 1992), 357.

28 Dexter L. Blackman, 'Stand Up and Be Counted: The Black Athlete, Black Power and the 1968 Olympic Project for Human Rights' (PhD dissertation, Georgia State University, 2009), 236.

29 Kenny Moore, 'The Eye of a Storm', *Sports Illustrated*, 12 August 1991, 60–73.

30 Will Grimsley, 'US Blacks, Whites Remain Segregated', *Moline Daily Dispatch* (Illinois), 15 October 1968, 15.

31 Cecilia Gutierrez Venable, 'Jarvis Lavonne Scott (1947–2017)', *BlackPast*, 13 September 2013, https://www.blackpast.org/african-american-history/people-african-american-history/scott-jarvis-lavonne-1947/.

32 Edwards, *The Struggle that Must Be*, 168–9.

33 *Ibid.*, 169.

34 Homer Higart, 'Militants Lose 7th Ave. Scuffle', *New York Times*, 17 February 1968, 19.

35 Harry Edwards, 'Why Negroes Should Boycott Whitey's Olympics', *Saturday Evening Post*, 9 March 1968, 6–10.

36 Tommie Smith, 'Why Negroes Should Boycott', *Sport*, March 1968, 40–1, 68.

37 Edwards, *The Struggle that Must Be*, 186.

38 Arnold Hano, 'The Black Rebel Who "Whitelists" the Olympics', *New York Times Magazine*, 12 May 1968, 32–4, 39–50.

39 *Ibid.* Note that 'crackers' is slang for white trash.

40 Bob Burns, 'A Tranquil Setting in Turbulent Times', *San Francisco Examiner*, 14 July 2000, D1.

41 Wyomia Tyus and Elizabeth Terzakis, *Tigerbelle: The Wyomia Tyus Story* (New York: Edge of Sport, 2018), 152.

42 Fraser C. Gerald, 'Negroes Call Off Boycott, Reshape Olympic Protest', *New York Times*, 1 September 1968, 1.

43 Kenny Moore, 'A Courageous Stand', *Sports Illustrated*, 5 August 1991, 60–72.

CHAPTER FIVE

1 The correct name of this area is the Nonoalco-Tlatelolco housing unit, but when describing the events around the plaza it is simply referred to as Tlatelolco.

2 There are many accounts of what happened in Tlatelolco on 2 October 1968, not all of them consistent. This chapter is largely based on a tape recording that Oriana Fallaci made from her hospital bed soon after she had been shot. It was originally published in *L'Europeo*, no. 42, as 'Oriana Fallaci da Città del Messico: La notte di sangue in cui sono stata ferita', and it was republished on her website at http://www.oriana-fallaci.com/numero-42-1968/articolo.html. Fallaci also wrote of her experiences in at article titled 'The Shooting of Oriana Fallaci', which appeared in *Look* magazine on 12 November 1968. Other sources are: Oriana Fallaci, *1968. Dal Vietnam al Messico: Diario di un anno cruciale* (Milan: Rizzoli, 2017); Cristina De Stefano, *Oriana Fallaci: The Journalist, the Agitator, the Legend*, trans. Marina Harss (New York: Other Press, 2017). For accounts of the events in Tlatelolco see the newspaper accounts written by John Rodda in *The Guardian*; Elena Poniatowska, *Massacre in Mexico*, trans. Helen R. Lane (Columbia, MO: University of Missouri Press, 1991); José Carlos Melesio Nolasco, 'Una crónica personal, 2 de octubre de 1968', 2 October 2013, http://mundonuestro.e-consulta.com/index.php/cronica/item/una-cronica-personal-2-de-octubre-de-1968; Heinrich Jaenecke, 'Parole: Batallón Olímpico', *Der Zeit*, 11 October 1968; Sergio Aguayo, *De Tlatelolco a Ayotzinapa: Las Violencias del Estado* (Mexico City: Proceso), Kindle edition; Keith Brewster and Claire Brewster, 'The Mexican Student Movement of 1968: An Olympic Perspective', *International Journal of the History of Sport* 26, 6 (2009): 814–39; Luis González de Alba, 'Tlatelolco aquella tarde', *Nexos*, 1 November 2016, https://www.nexos.com.mx/?p=30019; Elaine Carey, *Plaza of Sacrifices: Gender, Power, and Terror in 1968 Mexico* (Albuquerque, NM: University of New Mexico Press, 2005); Uli Schmetzer, 'At Long Last, Truth but not Justice', *Chicago Tribune*, 19 October 2003; Claude Kiejman and Jean-Francis Held, *Mexico, le pain et les jeux* (Paris: Éditions du Seuil, 1969); Paco Ignacio Taibo II, *'68: The Mexican Autumn of the Tlatelolco Massacre*, trans. Donald Nicholson Smith (New York: Seven Stories Press, 2019).

3 Francisco Ortiz Pinchetti, 'González de Alba y los mitos del 68', *SinEmbargo.mx*, 14 October 2016, http://www.sinembargo.mx/14-10-2016/3103633.

4  Speech by President Díaz Ordaz, delivered on 1 September 1968.
   Legislatura XLVII, Año II, Período Ordinario, Fecha 19680901,
   Número de Diario 3, http://cronica.diputados.gob.mx/
   DDebates/47/2do/Ord/19680901-I.html.
5  Jaenecke, 'Parole: Batallón Olímpico'.
6  De Stefano, *Oriana Fallaci: The Journalist, the Agitator, the Legend*,
   151.
7  Poniatowska, *Massacre in Mexico*, 310.
8  Julio Scherer García and Carlos Monsiváis, *Parte de guerra, Tlatelolco
   1968: documentos del general Marcelino García Barragán: los hechos y la
   historia* (Mexico City: Nuevo Siglo Aguilar, 1999), 120.
9  This is not the only difference in accounts of that night. Most
   witnesses believed that the flares were thrown out of one of the
   helicopters, but we now know that they were in fact shot out of an
   upper-storey window of the Foreign Affairs building. These differences
   and others in the accounts of eyewitnesses can be explained by the
   confusion caused by the traumatic events that would take place over
   the next twenty-four hours.
10 Poniatowska, *Massacre in Mexico*, 203.
11 *Ibid.*, 274.
12 Aguayo, *De Tlatelolco a Ayotzinapa: Las Violencias del Estado*, ePub
   location 1586.
13 García and Monsiváis, *Parte de guerra, Tlatelolco 1968*, 49.
14 de Alba, 'Tlatelolco aquella tarde'.
15 José Gil Olmos, 'Vivieron para contarlo', *Proceso*, 16 December 2001,
   8–15.
16 Elia Baltazar, 'La desconocida historia del cantante de ópera que
   le salvó la vida a Oriana Fallaci en México y que ella siempre creyó
   un traidor', *Infobae*, 24 December 2017, https://www.infobae.com/
   america/mexico/2017/12/24/la-desconocida-historia-del-cantante-de-
   opera-que-le-salvo-la-vida-a-oriana-fallaci-en-mexico-y-que-ella-siempre-
   creyo-un-traidor/.
17 Fallaci, *1968*, ePub location 309.
18 Luis González de Alba, 'El terrorismo en México', *Letras Libres*,
   September 2002, 108–11.
19 'Historias del 68: La Nacha Rodríguez, un privilegio seguir viva',
   *Proceso*, 2 October 2008, https://www.proceso.com.mx/202172/
   historias-del-68-la-nacha-rodriguez-un-privilegio-seguir-viva.
20 Mireya Cuellar, 'Una boda teñida de sangre', *La Jornada*, 2 October
   2001, http://www.jornada.com.mx/2001/10/02/044n1con.html.
21 Elena Poniatowska, 'Regina', *La Jornada*, 11 February 1993, 1, 24.

22  Alejandro Toledo, 'Regina Teuscher, entre ka mitification y lo real', *El Universal*, 23 March 2003, https://archivo.eluniversal.com.mx/cultura/27180.html.

23  Ernesto Gomez Tagle, 'Tlatelolco 68, Batallón Olimpia. Testimonio inédito de su comandante', *Proceso*, 3 October 2004, 11.

24  Rodriguez Ignacio Reyna, 'Los meurtos de Tlatelolco', *El Universal*, 11 February 2002, https://archivo.eluniversal.com.mx/nacion/79161.html.

25  Fallaci, *1968*, ePub location 309.

26  Olmos, 'Vivieron para contarlo'.

27  Fallaci, *1968*, ePub location 319.

28  'Oriana Fallaci da Città del Messico'.

29  Editorial, 'Los caídos en Tlatelolco', *Proceso*, 1 March 2009, http://www.proceso.com.mx/86140/los-caidos-en-tlatelolco.

30  'Ottoz esplicito "Se sparano io non gareggio"', *L'Unità*, 9 October 1968.

31  'Historias del 68'.

32  Belatedly, La Tita published her account in Roberta Avendaño Martínez, *De la libertad y el encierro* (Mexico City: La Idea Dorada, 1998). The book is out of print and difficult to find. In the historiography of the Tlatelolco massacre, it is the many accounts by male participants that dominate.

33  Lessie Jo Frazier and Deborah Cohen, 'Defining the Space of Mexico '68: Heroic Masculinity in the Prison and "Women" in the Streets', *Hispanic American Historical Review* 83, 4 (2003): 617–60.

34  Scherer and Monsiváis, *Parte de guerra, Tlatelolco 1968*, 53.

35  Mireya Cuellar, 'Callé por miedo y porque amo la vida', *La Jornada*, 18 February 2002, https://www.jornada.com.mx/2002/02/18/044n1con.php.

36  Olmos, 'Vivieron para contarlo'.

37  'Former Mexican President Sheds Light on 1968 Massacre', *CNN*, 4 February 1998, http://edition.cnn.com/WORLD/9802/04/mexico.massacre/.

38  Alfredo Mendez, 'Arraigan a Echeverría por la matanza de 1968', *La Jornada*, 1 July 2006, http://www.jornada.unam.mx/2006/07/01/index.php?section=politica&article=014n1pol.

39  Luis Gutiérrez Oropeza, *Díaz Ordaz. El Hombre. El Gobernante* (Mexico City: Gustavo de Anda, 1988), 26.

40  John Rodda, '"Prensa, Prensa": A Journalist's Reflections on Mexico '68', *Bulletin of Latin American Research* 29, 1 (March 2010), 11–22. In

this paper, Rodda reveals that the message was delivered by Artur Takač, technical director of the IOC, a member of the Organizing Committee of the 1968 Olympic Games in Mexico City, and confidante of Avery Brundage.

41  Brian Glanville, 'A Memory of Mexico', *Commentary*, 1 March 1969, 77–8.

42  'Veinte Muertos, 75 Heridos y 400 Presos', *Excélsior*, 3 October 1968, http://www.mit.edu/course/other/modulos/www/tlatelolco/ excelsior3.html.

43  Schmetzer, 'At Long Last, Truth but not Justice', part 2, 1.

44 Jaenecke, 'Parole: Batallón Olímpico'.

45 John Rodda, 'Trapped at Gunpoint in Middle of Fighting', *The Guardian* (UK), 4 October 1968, 1, 2. The reference to the 'secret service' refers to the Batallón Olimpia.

46  Paul L. Montgomery, 'Deaths Put at 49 in Mexican Clash', *New York Times*, 4 October 1968, 1, 3.

47  Bob Ottum, 'Grim Countdown to the Games', *Sports Illustrated*, 14 October 1968, 36–43.

48  '¿Qué van a hacer con su Olimpiada?', *Proceso*, 2 October 2005, https://www.proceso.com.mx/195463/que-van-a-hacer-con-su- olimpiada.

49  Neil Allen, 'Olympics Definitely Go On', *The Times* (London), 4 October 1968, 1.

50  Dave Hemery, telephone interview with the author, 2 May 2020.

51  Dick Beddoes, 'French Count Beaten in Bid to Govern IOC', *Globe and Mail*, 11 October 1968, 27.

52  Fallaci, *1968*, ePub location 325.

## CHAPTER SIX

1  Pan Dodd Eimon, 'Olympic-Sized Fiesta', *The American City*, August 1968, 4.

2  'Sport: The Scene a la Mexicana', *Time*, 18 October 1968, 37.

3  Rubin Salázar, 'Wonderland of Color Welcomes Olympics', *Los Angeles Times*, 13 October 1968, 8.

4  'Should the Show Go On?', *Los Angeles Times*, 5 October 1968, 8.

5  de Coubertin, 'The Modern Olympic Games', in *Olympism*, 308–11.

6  de Coubertin, 'The Neo-Olympism: Appeal to the People of Athens (16 November). Lecture Given to the Parnassus Literary Society at Athens', in *Olympism*, 533–41.

7 Pierre de Coubertin, *Mémoires olympiques* (Paris: Bureau International de Pédagogie Sportive, 1931), 102.

8 John J. MacAloon, 'Double Visions: Olympic Games and American Culture', *The Kenyon Review* 4, 1 (1982): 98–112.

9 François Carrard, 'The Olympic Message in Ceremonies: The Vision of the IOC', in *Olympic Ceremonies: Historical Continuity and Cultural Exchange*, ed. Miquel de Moragas Spà, John MacAloon, and Montserrat Llinés (Lausanne: International Olympic Committee, 1996), 23–8.

10 Frank Zarnowski, 'A Look at Olympic Costs', *International Journal of Olympic History* 1, 2 (1993): 16–32.

11 Brian R. Hamnett, *A Concise History of Mexico* (Cambridge: Cambridge University Press, 2006), 282.

12 Paul Gillingham and Benjamin T. Smith, eds, *Dictablanda: Politics, Work, and Culture in Mexico, 1938–1968* (Durham, NC: Duke University Press, 2014).

13 Karl Lennartz, 'The Story of the Rings', *Journal of Olympic History* 10 (2001/12): 29–61.

14 John J. MacAloon, *This Great Symbol: Pierre de Coubertin and the Origins of the Modern Olympic Games* (Chicago, IL: University of Chicago Press, 1981), 265–6.

15 *Ibid.*, 266.

16 de Coubertin, 'Why I Revived the Olympic Games', in *Olympism*, 542–6.

17 MacAloon, 'Double Visions'.

18 Ron Devlin, 'Olympic Memories: The 1968 Games in Mexico City Were a Lesson in Camaraderie for Allentown Man on Weightlifting Team', *The Morning Call* (Philadelphia), 20 February 2002, https://www.mcall.com/news/mc-xpm-2002-02-20-3394030-story.html.

19 Francie Kraker Goodridge, phone interview with author, 25 March 2020.

20 de Coubertin, 'Olympic Letter III: Olympism and Education', in *Olympism*, 548.

21 de Coubertin, 'The Athletes' Oath (Letter to Charles Simon)', in *Olympism*, 598–9.

22 Roland Renson, *The Games Reborn: The VII Olympiad, Antwerp 1920* (Antwerp: Pandora, 1996), 33.

23 John J. MacAloon, 'Hyperstructure, Hierarchy and Humanitas in Olympic Ritual', *Anthropology Today* 35, 3 (2019): 7–10.

24 Paul Hoffman, phone interview with the author, 4 March 2020.

25  Frederick W. Rubien, 'Ninth Olympiad: Report of the Secretary', in *American Olympic Committee Report: Ninth Olympic Games, Amsterdam, Holland, 1928* (New York: American Olympic Committee, 1928), 29.

26  J.C. Vargas, 'Queta Basilio, la musa de México 68', *Adrenalina-Excélsior*, 27 August 2018, https://www.excelsior.com.mx/adrenalina/queta-basilio-la-musa-de-mexico-68/1261053.

27  Ronald Austin Smith, *Play-by-Play: Radio, Television, and Big-Time College Sport* (Baltimore, MD: John Hopkins University Press, 2001), 104–5.

28  Avery Brundage, 'The Fumbled Ball', *Vital Speeches of the Day*, 15 April 1967, 411–16.

29  'The Olympics Live', *Sports Illustrated*, 4 November 1968, 9.

30  Edith Turner, *Communitas: The Anthropology of Collective Joy* (New York: Palgrave Macmillan, 2012), 1.

CHAPTER SEVEN

1   In his autobiography, *The Struggle that Must Be*, 200–3, Harry Edwards explains why he did not go to Mexico City. He claimed that on 7 October 1968 his good friend Louis Lomax warned him not to travel to Mexico City because he had received credible information that he could be killed if he went there. To put himself out of harm's way, Edwards attended the Black Writers Congress, held at McGill University in Montreal between 11 and 14 October 1968. Edwards was not on the programme, but when he arrived the organisers found a spot for him to speak. His speech oddly made no mention of the Olympic Project for Human Rights or the Olympic Games.

2   Tommie Smith as told to Bruce Henderson, 'Why I Raised My Fist at Uncle Sam', *Sepia*, July 1973, 28–32.

3   Robert Philip, 'Gloved Fist Is Raised in Defiance', *Daily Telegraph*, 11 October 1993, 38.

4   *Ibid.*

5   Moore, 'A Courageous Stand'.

6   Tommie Smith and David Steele, *Silent Gesture: The Autobiography of Tommie Smith* (Philadelphia, PA: Temple University Press, 2007), 62.

7   Stump, 'The Man Who'd Like to Wreck Our Olympic Team'.

8   John Carlos and Dave Zirin, *The John Carlos Story: The Sports Moment that Changed the World* (Chicago, IL: Haymarket Books, 2011), 9.

9   Steve Redgrave, 'John Carlos Reveals the Personal Pain that Inspired his Famous Black Power Salute', *The Telegraph* (UK), 18 May 2012.

10 Carlos and Zirin, *The John Carlos Story*, 11.

11 David P. Cline, 'John Carlos Oral History Interview: 2013', *Journal of Pan African Studies (Online)* 10, 1 (2017): 337.

12 *Ibid.*

13 *Ibid.*

14 Pete Axthelm, 'The Angry Black Athlete', *Newsweek*, 15 July 1968, 56–60.

15 Skip Myslenski, 'I Do What I Think Is Right', *Sports Illustrated*, 9 June 1969, 56–62.

16 Gary Holdsworth, phone interview with the author, 13 June 2018.

17 Damian Johnstone and Matt Norman, *A Race to Remember: The Peter Norman Story* (Melbourne: JoJo Publishing, 2008), 41.

18 *Ibid.*, 25.

19 Carlos and Zirin, *The John Carlos Story*, 117.

20 Institute of the University of the Bahamas, 2017, 'The Truth Behind the Salute Begins!', *Oral & Public History*, 24 April 2017, https://www.facebook.com/fdt242/videos/.

21 Johnstone and Norman, *A Race to Remember*, 19.

22 'Spell of the Olympics', *Newsweek*, 22 October 1968, 64–5.

23 Associated Press, 'America's Blacks Don't Share Winner's Circle with Brundage', *New York Times*, 16 October 1968, 52.

24 Johnstone and Norman, *A Race to Remember*, 31.

25 Mike Wise, 'SYDNEY 2000: The Third Man In Mexico City', *New York Times*, 17 September 2000, Section 8, 1.

26 John Carlos also took credit for suggesting the gloved salute. It is unlikely it was his suggestion, though, as he did not pack the gloves his wife bought him.

27 Peter Norman, face-to-face interview with Stewart Russell and Kate Daw, 13 July 2006.

28 In accounts of the genesis of the salute, both Tommie Smith and John Carlos take full credit for the idea, each contradicting the other. A discussion of the differences in their accounts is presented by Douglas Hartmann in *Race, Culture, and the Revolt of the Black Athlete* (Chicago, IL: University of Chicago Press, 2003), 23–4, crediting Smith with taking the initiative. I would differ with his account in pointing out that Brundage did not present the medals in the 100 metres because he had been warned that the winners might wear gloves when shaking his hand. It was his absence in Acapulco, to avoid such a snub, that caused Smith and Carlos to rethink their protest. According to Linda Evans, she, Denise Smith, and Kim Carlos decided

to buy the black paraphernalia, including the gloves, in the hope of encouraging their husbands to protest. Most of the evidence, other than from Carlos himself, points to there being no premeditation, but the idea of the salute was raised by Smith in the locker room, an hour or so before the medal ceremony. A taped interview with Peter Norman was an invaluable resource on what happened in the Athletes' Lounge and during the medal ceremony. However, as accounts from participants differ, the truth is unlikely to ever be known for certain.

29  Wise, 'SYDNEY 2000'.

30  Paul Hoffman, interview with the author, 16 June 2018.

31  Jim Clash, 'Interview: Sprinter John Carlos on his 1968 Black-Glove Olympic Protest', *Forbes*, 1 April 2016, https://www.forbes.com/sites/jimclash/2016/04/01/interview-sprinter-john-carlos-on-his-1968-black-glove-olympic-protest/#67f3c6b4b8eb.

32  David Wharton, '1968: Medals Stand Protest Became Model for Sports Activism; It Just Took a While', *Los Angeles Times*, 20 July 2018, D1, D8.

33  de Coubertin, 'The Philosophic Foundation of Modern Olympism'.

34  de Coubertin, *Mémoires olympiques*, 201.

35  de Coubertin, 'The Neo-Olympism'.

36  MacAloon, 'Hyperstructure, Hierarchy and Humanitas in Olympic Ritual'.

37  Carrard, 'The Olympic Message in Ceremonies', 23–4.

38  Johnstone and Norman, *A Race to Remember*, ii.

39  Hartmann, *Race, Culture, and the Revolt of the Black Athlete*, 20.

40  Kathryn McClymond, *Ritual Gone Wrong: What We Learn from Ritual Disruption* (Oxford: Oxford Scholarship Online, 2016), 128–9.

41  Wise, 'SYDNEY 2000'.

42  Bert Bonanno, phone interview with author, 30 November 2019. He was sitting about fifty metres from the victory podium.

43  Pete Hamill, 'Report from Olympic Village', *Ramparts*, 30 November 1968, 21–8.

44  Associated Press, 'Other Athletes Respond with Mixed Feelings', *The Times* (San Mateo, CA), 17 October 1968, 19.

45  Alan Trengrove, 'A White Lift for Colour on the Dais', *Courier Mail* (Brisbane), 18 October 1968, 1.

46  Smith and Steele, *Silent Gesture*, 173.

47  Tommie Smith's autobiography *Silent Gesture*, 139, and John Carlos's autobiography *Why?* (Los Angeles, CA: Milligan Books, 2000), 196, suggest that the shopping expedition by their wives was at the men's

behest. In fact, it was the women's idea to buy props in the hope that their husbands would use them to protest.

48 Carole Boyce-Davies, 'Writing Black Women into Political Leadership: Reflections, Trends, and Contradictions', in *Black Women and International Law: Deliberate Interactions, Movements, and Actions*, ed. Jeremy I. Levitt (Cambridge: Cambridge University Press, 2015), 23–36.

49 Linda Evans, phone interview with the author, 8 March 2019.

50 Richard Majors and Janet Mancini Billson, *Cool Pose: The Dilemma of Black Manhood in America* (New York: Touchstone Books, 1992), 1.

51 David Miller, *The Official History of the Olympic Games and the IOC: Athens to Beijing, 1894–2008* (Edinburgh and London: Mainstream Publishing, 2008), 144.

52 William Oscar Johnson, 'Avery Brundage: The Man Behind the Mask', *Sports Illustrated*, 4 August 1980, 48–63.

53 'The Olympics' Extra Heat', *Newsweek*, 28 October 1968, 74–80.

54 Peter Norman, face-to-face interview with Stewart Russell and Kate Daw, 13 July 2006.

55 Joseph M. Sheehan, '2 Black Power Advocates Ousted from Olympics', *New York Times*, 19 October 1968, 1.

56 Hamill, 'Report from Olympic Village', 21–7.

57 Paul Hoffman, email exchange with the author, 21 March 2020.

58 Paul Hoffman interviewed by Desiree Harguess on 5 March 2013. 1968 US Olympic Team Oral History Project, H.J. Lutcher Stark, Center for Physical Culture and Sports, https://archives.starkcenter.org/1968ohp/histories/histories.html#hoffman_p.

59 Johnstone and Norman, *A Race to Remember*, 55–6.

60 Paul Hoffman, email exchange with the author, 20 March 2020.

61 Wright, *Stan Wright – Track Coach*, 210.

62 Ira Berkow, *Red: A Biography of Red Smith* (Lincoln, NE: University of Nebraska Press, 2007), 189.

63 Pete Waldmeir, '2 Black Sprinters Go All Out to Act Childishly at Olympics', *The Detroit News*, 17 October 1968, C1.

64 Editorial, 'Stunting at the Olympics', *Chicago Sunday American*, section 6, 1.

65 Editorial, 'The Natural Right of Being a Slob', *Chicago Tribune*, 19 October 1968, 10.

66 Editorial, 'Racial Display at the Olympics', *Los Angeles Times*, 24 October 1968, C6.

67 John Hall, 'Foreman's Fan Club', *Los Angeles Times*, 6 November 1968, H3.

68 Associated Press, 'Black Power Outdoes Gold Medal', *The Norwalk Hour* (Connecticut), 17 October 1968, 1, 16.

69 Brent Musburger, 'Bizarre Protest by Smith, Carlos Tarnishes Medals', *Chicago American*, 17 October 1968, 43.

70 Jim Murray, 'The Olympic Games – No Place for a Sportswriter', *Los Angeles Times*, 20 October 1968, H1.

71 Bob Rose, 'Expelled Pair Blast Anthem', *Chicago Daily News*, 22 October 1968.

## CHAPTER EIGHT

1 Joseph M. Turrini, *The End of Amateurism in American Track and Field* (Champaign, IL: University of Illinois Press, 2010), 87. Smith refers to the shoes in the plural, although he only brought one shoe with him for his demonstration.

2 David Davis, 'A Courageous Man: An Interview with John Carlos', *Los Angeles Review of Books*, 16 October 2015, https://lareviewofbooks. org/article/a-courageous-man-an-interview-with-john-carlos/#!. While Carlos suggests that they both had two shoes, this is incorrect and he should have spoken about the shoes in the singular.

3 From interviews with athletes, I found that there were African American athletes who received payments from Adidas. However, anecdotally, it appears that white athletes were offered more. This may be true or it may be that African American athletes were less open about the amounts of money they received.

4 Henderson, 'Why I Raised My Fist at Uncle Sam', 24–32.

5 *Ibid.*

6 Davis, 'A Courageous Man'.

7 Public statements like this were at odds with what happened behind the scenes, and there are numerous exceptions to strictures on commercial sponsorship. De Coubertin's magazine, *Olympic Review*, featured advertisements for a Parisian sporting goods manufacturer and Benedictine brandy, and at the 1924 Paris Olympics the stadium had advertising hoardings for Ovomaltine, Dubonnet, and Cinzano. Coca-Cola's association with the Olympic movement started in 1928, when it provided free drinks to athletes. For more on this, see Robert Knight Barney, Scott G. Martyn, and Stephen R. Wenn, *Selling the*

*Five Rings: The International Olympic Committee and the Rise of Olympic Commercialism* (Salt Lake City, UT: University of Utah Press, 2004). The difference here was that the IOC was the beneficiary, and was presumably incorruptible, while athletes were more vulnerable to commercial enticements.

8 Vyv Simson and Andrew Jennings, *Dishonored Games: Corruption, Money & Greed at the Olympics* (Toronto: S.P.I. Books, 1992), 28.

9 John Underwood, 'No Goody Two-Shoes', *Sports Illustrated*, 10 March 1969, 14–23.

10 *Ibid.*

11 Conventional spikes were designed for the loose cinder, gravel, and grass tracks. The legal number of spikes during that time was six per shoe, but it was debatable whether the brushes were spikes or not.

12 'The Forbidden Shoe', *Puma Archive*, 24 September 2014, https://www.puma-catchup.com/the-forbidden-shoe/.

13 Puma stuck to the deal and produced the TS#200. According to a marketing poster: 'Puma makes the shoe for runners who make the records'. The shoe was not a commercial success, although Tommy Smith earned US$7,500 out of the deal.

14 Horst Dassler had come to an exclusive arrangement with the Mexican government to import shoes in return for handing a local company, called Canada, a license to manufacture Adidas shoes in Mexico. Canada eventually sold 10,000 pairs of shoes in the Olympic Village, and once its supplies were exhausted Adidas was allowed to import German-made shoes into Mexico, duty free.

15 Underwood, 'No Goody Two-Shoes'.

16 This account is based on a telephone interview with Art Simburg by the author on 5 October 2018, and it differs from another account given by Barbara Smit in *Pitch Invasion* (London: Allen Lane/Penguin Books, 2006), 95. In the other account, Art Simburg was picked up with a bag of shoes and arrested for doing business on a tourist visa. At this point in time, Puma did not have access to its shoes, which were in Customs, making this account improbable. It also notes that he was engaged to Wyomia Tyus. This did not occur until some time after the Olympic Games.

17 Tom Farrell, telephone interview with the author, 6 July 2018.

18 Ross Newhan, 'She Plays With a Full Deck: Martha Watson Is Now a Card Dealer', *Los Angeles Times*, 3 February 1988, 11.

19 Joseph M. Turrini, 'Running for Dollars: An Economic and Social History of Track and Field in the United States, 1820–2000' (PhD dissertation, Wayne State University, Detroit, MI, 2004), 325.

20 Chad Dundas, 'Montana Olympian Larry Questad: Breaking Stride. Forty Years Later, Montana Sprinter Reflects on Glory, Turmoil of '68 Olympics', *Missoulian*, 3 August 2008, http://missoulian.com/sports/montana-olympian-larry-questad-breaking-stride-forty-years-later-montana/article_9ae6e23c-4c8f-59f2-b417-074819ob5c9d.html.

21 Jack Olsen, 'In an Alien World', *Sports Illustrated*, 15 July 1968, 29–43.

22 Ron Reid, 'Rival Made a Large Contribution to Beamon's Feat', *The Philadelphia Inquirer*, 18 June 1988, D10.

23 'Streifen gewechselt', *Der Spiegel*, 15 July 1964.

24 Arthur Daley, 'The Incident', *New York Times*, 20 October 1968, S2.

## CHAPTER NINE

1 Mel Pender cited by Richard Hoffer in *Something in the Air: The Story of American Passion and Defiance in the 1968 Mexico City Olympics* (New York: Free Press, 2009), 149–50. After the Olympics Mel Pender was sent back for another tour of duty.

2 'US Apologizes for Black Protest', *The Washington Post*, 18 October 1968, D1.

3 John G. Griffin, 'Reaction to Black Glove among Olympians – Good', *Daily Freeman* (Kingston), 18 October 1968, 20. This UPI report was widely syndicated in the US.

4 Tom Waddell and Dick Schaap, *Gay Olympian: The Life and Death of Dr. Tom Waddell* (New York: Knopf, 1996), 107.

5 Paul Hoffman, telephone interview with the author, 16 June 2018.

6 Others on the committee included Bob Mathias, Rafer Johnson, Dr Nell Jackson, John Sayre, and Billy Mills, all former Olympic stars. The committee included three African Americans, one Native American, and two white former athletes.

7 David Zirin, *A People's History of Sports in the United States: 250 Years of Politics, Protest, People, and Play* (New York: The New Press, 2008), 170.

8 'Statement – United States Olympic Committee – Re. Suspension – John Carlos and Tommy Smith – Oct. 18th, 1968', Smith and Carlos incident folder, box 5, Douglas F. Roby papers, Bentley Historical Library, University of Michigan.

9 Linda Evans, telephone interview with author, 8 March 2018.

10 Jeremy Larner and David Wolf, 'Amid Gold Medals, Raised Black Fists', *Life*, 1 November 1968, 64C–64D.

11 *Ibid.*

12 Moore, 'The Eye of the Storm'.

13 Larner and Wolf, 'Amid Gold Medals, Raised Black Fists'.

14 'The Olympics' Extra Heat'.

15 Wright, *Stan Wright – Track Coach*, 217. There are different accounts of this encounter. See Hoffer, *Something in the Air*, 191–2. Hoffer's version is based on an interview with Lee Evans. Douglas Roby gives essentially the same story, although he does not mention an attack on him, in Robert Lipsyte, 'Ringing Up Roby', *New York Times*, 23 December 1968, 57. The account in Vincent Matthews, *My Race Be Won* (New York: Charterhouse, 1974), 198, is essentially very similar to the one given here.

16 Axthelm, 'The Angry Black Athlete'.

17 Moore, 'The Eye of the Storm'.

18 *Ibid.*

19 'Evans Puts Aside Racial Problems', *New York Times*, 19 October 1968, 44.

20 'Evans Won His Medal for Blacks and Others', *Washington Post*, 19 October 1968, C1.

21 'The Olympics' Extra Heat'.

22 Martin Jellinghaus, email exchange with author, 21 July 2018.

23 Matthews and Amdur, *My Race Be Won*, 205.

24 Edwards, *The Revolt of the Black Athlete*, 105.

25 Sheehan, '2 Black Power Advocates Ousted from Olympics', 1.

26 *Ibid.*

27 Lipsyte, 'Ringing Up Roby'.

28 Steve Cady, 'US Boxers Spurn Racial Fights', *New York Times*, 23 October 1968, 51.

29 George Foreman and Joel Engel, *By George: The Autobiography of George Foreman* (New York: Villard Books, 1995), 56.

30 *Ibid.*, 18, 37, 217.

31 Ed McCoyd, *To Live and Dream: The Incredible Story of George Foreman* (New York: New Street Publishing, 1997), 20

32 John Hall, 'Foreman's Fan Club', *Los Angeles Times*, 6 November 1968, H3.

33 George Foreman interviewed by Desiree Harguess on 16 January 2013. 1968 US Olympic Team Oral History Project, H.J. Lutcher Stark, Center for Physical Culture and Sports. Transcript available at https://archives.starkcenter.org/1968ohp/Transcripts/68OHP_Foreman_George_BOX_Final_Transcript.pdf.

34 *Ibid.*

35 Smith and Steele, *Silent Gesture*, 181.

36 Davis, 'A Courageous Man'.

37  Foreman and Engel, *By George*, 62.

## CHAPTER TEN

1   Martin Moravec, 'V bratrově smrti má prsty StB, říká Věra Čáslavská', *iDNES.cz*, 21 August 2008, https://zpravy.idnes.cz/v-bratrove-smrti-ma-prsty-stb-rika-Věra-caslavska-f7k-/domaci.aspx?c=A080820_073135_domaci_lpo.

2   Even before Dubček was elected, other segments of Czechoslovak society were restive for change. At the end of June 1967 members of the Fourth Congress of the Writers' Union revolted against 'doctrine and dogma' and called for political and literary censorship to be lifted, while on 31 October 1967 students marched on Prague Castle.

3   Jaromir Navrátil, *The Prague Spring '68: A National Security Archive Documents Reader* (New York: Central European University Press, 1998), 92–5.

4   *Věra 68*, directed by Jaromir Sommerová (Prague: Evolution Films and Česká Televize, 2012).

5   'Naše slovo, zvláštní vydání týdeníku ONV v Šumperku', 24 August 1968, republished at https://sumpersky.denik.cz/zpravy_region/srpen-1968-sumperk-obsadili-polaci-20150820.html.

6   Pavel Kosatík, *Věra Čáslavská: život na Olympu* (Prague: Mladá fronta, 2016), 80.

7   Only František Kriegel refused to sign the agreement.

8   Tomáš Macek, 'Příběh Věry Čáslavské: život na sinusoidě propastných rozdílů', *iDNES.cz*, 3 September 2016, https://www.idnes.cz/sport/ostatni/Věra-caslavska-vzpominka.A160831_213538_sporty_ten.

9   Karel Tejkal, 'Věra Čáslavská – Život na vrtkavé kladrýně', *Vital*, 31 August 2016, https://vitalplus.org/Věra-caslavska-zivot-na-vrtkave-kladryne/.

10  Věra Čáslavská-Odložilová, *Cesta Na Olymp* (Prague: Mladá fronta, 1972), 143.

11  'Radziecka gimnastyczka Natalia Kuchinsky: biografia, osiągnięcia i ciekawe fakty', *stuklopechat.com*, undated, https://pl.stuklopechat.com/novosti-i-obschestvo/72511-sovetskaya-gimnastka-kuchinskaya-natalya-aleksandrovna-biografiya-dostizheniya-i-interesnye-fakty.html.

12  'Un échec aujourd'hui peut être une réussite demain écrit M. Dubcek aux membres de l'équipe olympique', *Le Monde*, 12 October 1968.

13  *Věra 68*.

14  Moravec, 'V bratrově smrti má prsty StB, říká Věra Čáslavská'.

15 Petr Volf, 'Věra Čáslavská: Jak mě Brežněv pustil do Mexika', *Reflex*, 31 August 2016, https://www.reflex.cz/clanek/rozhovory/74446/Věra-caslavska-jak-me-breznev-pustil-do-mexika.html.

16 Veronika Boušová, 'Věra Čáslavská – Portrét samuraje', *CzechFolks.com PLUS*, 19 September 2012, http://czechfolks.com/plus/2012/09/19/veronika-bousova-Věra-caslavska-portret-samuraje/.

17 'Věra Caslavska: idool van Mexico', *Trouw*, 28 October 1968, 9.

18 Mary Prestidge, telephone interview with author, 19 June 2018.

19 Christopher Brasher, *Mexico 1968: A Diary of the XIXth Olympiad* (London: Stanley Paul, 1968), 105.

20 Transcribed from the video of Věra Čáslavská's induction into the International Gymnastics Hall of Fame, https://www.youtube.com/watch?v=KlqUIB5LAiI.

21 Allen Guttmann, *The Games Must Go On: Avery Brundage and the Olympic Movement* (New York: Columbia University Press, 1984), 145.

22 František Kolář, 'Development of the Olympic Movement in the Czech Republic', Český olympijský výbor, http://www.olympic.cz/docs/osmus/vyvoj_olympijskeho_hnuti_v_cesku.pdf.

23 Kosatík, *Věra Čáslavská*, 85.

24 *Věra 68*.

25 Věra Čáslavská-Odložilová, *Československý sport*, 23 January 1969, 1, cited by Lenka Kodoňová in 'Sportovec jako mediální celebrita v proměnách času' (PhD dissertation, Univerzita Karlova v Praze, 2013), 83.

26 Steve Cady, 'A Citizen of Prague Speaks Her Mind', *New York Times*, 1 February 1969, 36.

27 Paul Hoffman, 'Czech Party Ousts Champion Runner', *New York Times*, 25 October 1969, 15.

28 *Věra 68*.

29 Kosatík, *Věra Čáslavská*, 116.

30 Moravec, 'V bratrově smrti má prsty StB, říká Věra Čáslavská'.

31 *Věra 68*.

32 It was rumoured that the Mexican government had threatened to suspend oil exports to Czechoslovakia if they released Věra Čáslavská to coach their Olympic team.

CHAPTER ELEVEN

1 Bruce Howard, *15 Days in '56* (Sydney: Angus & Robertson, 1995), 193.

2 Daryl Adair, 'Olympic Ceremonial, Protocol and Symbolism', in *Managing the Olympics* (London: Palgrave Macmillan, 2013), 182–205.

3 Associated Press, 'IOC Opposed Intervention', *Sunday Sun* (Baltimore), 10 October 1965, A10.

4 Christopher Brasher, 'Why It's the End of a Love Affair', *The Observer* (UK), 27 October 1968, 24.

5 John Rodda, 'Colourless Ceremony in Offing', *The Guardian* (UK), 25 October 1968, 23.

6 'March is Cut Sharply for Closing of Games', *Philadelphia Inquirer*, 25 October 1968, 36.

7 'US Stars Angered by "Rule 59"', *Washington Post*, 27 October 1968, C5.

8 Madeline Manning Mims interviewed by Brennan Berg on 4 April 2011. 1968 US Olympic Team Oral History Project, H.J. Lutcher Stark, Center for Physical Culture and Sports, https://archives.starkcenter.org/1968ohp/audio/68OHP_Manning_Madeline_Mims_ATH.mp3.

9 Dave Hemery, telephone interview with the author, 2 May 2020.

10 Brasher, *Mexico 1968*, 123.

11 Al Cartwright, 'Olympics End on Gay Note', *The News Journal* (Delaware), 28 October 1968, 32.

12 Arthur Daley, 'The True Olympic Spirit', *New York Times*, 29 October 1968, 57.

13 John G. Griffin, 'Olympians Bid Good-bye to Mexico', *Dixon Evening Telegraph* (Illinois), 28 October 1968, 10.

14 Editorial, 'Olympics' Finale was Grand', *Decatur Daily Review* (Illinois), 31 October 1968, 8.

## CHAPTER TWELVE

1 The US rights to telecast the Mexico Olympics had been sold to ABC, but this was only to cover sporting events, so nothing stopped Margolies interviewing athletes.

2 Marjorie Margolies-Mezvinsky, telephone interview with the author, 29 August 2019. Interviews with other athletes and a statistician who witnessed the salute revealed that they were underwhelmed by the protest at the time, echoing the reaction of Marjorie Margolies. Most of them viewed the protest from the athletes' stand, which was about 200 metres away.

3 The Associated Press photograph appeared in most newspaper reports immediately after the protest. Neil Leifer first appeared on page 25 of

*Sports Illustrated* on 28 October 1968. It was in colour, and the half-page photograph cropped Peter Norman out of the frame. It was taken from the front, with the Olympic rings visible on the victory podium and the athletes in profile. By not showing the faces of the athletes from the front, it lacks the impact of the other photographs, which capture the faces of the protesters. John Dominis's black and white photograph appeared in *Life* magazine on 1 November 1968 on page 64C. It was small and the athletes' feet were cropped. It was only when it was syndicated and not crudely cropped that the power of the photograph was fully realised. Like the Associated Press photograph, it was taken from the front. The difference was that Dominis shot the scene from a lower angle, giving the figures a greater presence. The photograph by Angelo Cozzi was taken from some way away, and is therefore inferior to the others.

4   Through interviews, autobiographies, and speeches, Smith and Carlos have articulated their intentions, but such is the prevalence of the photograph that most viewers are not privy to these explanations and respond to the image on emotional and intellectual levels. Smith and Carlos used small details and different props – Black scarfs, beads, black socks, and Olympic Project for Human Rights badges; Carlos's open jacket – to convey various messages, but most of these did not come across in the photograph. Tommie Smith, in particular, has taken exception to his protest being referred to as a 'Black Power salute'. As he explained in his autobiography, it is about 'human rights, not civil rights, nothing to do with the Panthers or Black Power': see Smith and Steele, *Silent Gesture*, 161. He described it as a 'silent gesture'. Despite trying to correct the record, the protest by him and Carlos is almost universally known as the 'Black Power salute'.

5   Smith and Steele, *Silent Gesture*, 170.

6   Mike O'Mahony, *Olympic Visions: Images of the Games through History* (London: Reaktion Books, 2012), 116.

7   Philip, 'Gloved Fist Is Raised in Defiance'.

8   Jack Olsen, 'The Black Athlete – A Shameful Story', *Sports Illustrated*, 1 July 1968, 12–27.

9   Sarah L. Trembanis, *The Set-Up Men: Race, Culture and Resistance in Black Baseball* (Jefferson, NC: McFarland, 2014), 57.

10  Patricia Hill Collins, *Black Sexual Politics: African Americans, Gender, and the New Racism* (New York: Routledge, 2004), 152.

11  Jeremy D. Mayer, 'Nixon Rides the Backlash to Victory: Racial Politics in the 1968 Presidential Campaign', *The Historian* 64, 2 (2002): 351–66.

12 Gertrude Wilson, 'UFT Egos – And Black Athletes', *New York Amsterdam News*, 2 November 1968, 19.

13 Kathleen Hall Jamieson, *Eloquence in an Electronic Age: The Transformation of Political Speechmaking* (New York: Oxford University Press, 1988), 57–8.

14 Gordon Parks, 'This Rare Collection', *Life: 100 Photographs that Changed the World* (New York: Life Books, 2003), 7–9.

15 Kevin Quashie, *The Sovereignty of Quiet: Beyond Resistance in Black Culture* (New Brunswick, NJ: Rutgers University Press, 2012), 23.

16 MacAloon, 'Double Visions'.

17 Carlos and Zirin, *The John Carlos Story*, 136.

18 *100 Photographs: The Most Influential Images of all Time* (New York: Time Warner, 2003), 68.

19 DeNeen L. Brown, '"A Cry for Freedom": The Black Power Salute that Rocked the World 50 Years Ago', *Washington Post*, 16 October 2018.

20 Rutger van der Hoeven, 'The Global Visual Memory: A Study of the Recognition and Interpretation of Iconic and Historical Photographs' (PhD dissertation, University of Utrecht, 2019), 206.

21 Colin Kaepernick, Instagram post, 15 November 2017, https://www.instagram.com/p/BbiH6bhlgkc/.

22 La Risa Lynch, 'Olympic Medalist John Carlos Reflects on '68 Black Power Salute', *Chicago Defender*, 10–16 March 2010, 45.

23 There is at least one mention of their support of Smith and Carlos. It appeared in the *San Francisco Examiner* on 27 October 1968 (in the 'World' section, page 8). However, Tyus is correct. Most other newspapers ignored the expression of solidarity by the women's relay team.

24 Shana Renee, 'Track Legend Wyomia Tyus Protested at the '68 Olympics and Hardly Anyone Noticed', *ESPNW.com*, 11 November 2018, http://www.espn.com/espnw/voices/article/25211468/track-legend-wyomia-tyus-protested-68-olympics-hardly-anyone-noticed.

25 'Some Negro Athletes Threaten to "Go Home" along with Smith and Carlos', *New York Times*, 19 October 1968, 1, 45.

26 After the 4 × 400 metres relay, berets and smiles were once again in evidence. However, the media largely ignored their performance during the medal ceremony.

27 In 1950 members of the Czechoslovak ice hockey team were due to play in the IIHF World Championship in London. When members of the team expressed unhappiness about the tour being cancelled by a government fearful that some members of the team might defect,

six were arrested. Bohumil Modrý would spend thirteen years in jail, including time working in the uranium mines in Jáchymov.

28 Jorge Randolph Aviles, 'Tlatelolco, Campo de Batalla', *El Universal*, 3 October 1968, 1.

29 'Balacera del Ejército con Estudiantes', *La Prensa*, 3 October 1968, 1.

30 'Atropello a Excélsior', *Excélsior*, 3 October 1968, 1.

31 Alejandro Almazán, 'Se Querían Robar la Historia', *El Universal*, 13 February 2002, https://archivo.eluniversal.com.mx/nacion/79315.html.

32 Ottum, 'Grim Countdown to the Games'.

33 Interview with Mariclaire Acosta on 3 December 1993, cited by Margaret E. Keck and Kathryn Sikkink in *Activists Beyond Borders: Advocacy Networks in International Politics* (Ithaca, NY: Cornell University Press, 2014), ix.

34 Elena Poniatowska, *La noche de Tlatelolco* (Mexico City: Ediciones ERA, 1971). While this book is the best known account of the massacre, other accounts were also published soon after the event: Ramón Ramírez and Ramón Ramírez Gómez, *El movimiento estudiantil de México* (Austin, TX: University of Texas Press, 1969); Carlos Monsiváis *Días de guardar* (Mexico City: Ediciones ERA 1970); Luis González de Alba, *Los días y los años* (Mexico City: Ediciones ERA, 1971).

35 Poniatowska, *La noche de Tlatelolco*.

36 Examples include documentary maker Carlos Mendoza; historians Nuevo Siglo Aguilar, Carlos Monsiváis, and Sergio Aguayo Quezada; and journalist Jacinto Rodríguez. They have reviewed various collections and domestic and foreign declassified archives and published their findings in a range of articles and books.

37 Sanjuana Martínez, '2 de octubre: imágenes de un fotógrafo del gobierno', *Proceso*, 9 December 2001, 8. Another cache of photos was published in *Proceso* on 16 December 2001: 'Las Fotos del '68ers'. The account of the anonymous donation is disputed, and the photos may have come from the estate of Manuel Gutiérrez Paredes, which was sold to the Universidad Nacional Autonomous de Mexico (National Autonomous University of Mexico) in December 2000 but not officially released when they were published in *Proceso*. The photos are available at https://ahunam.wordpress.com/2008/. It was later revealed that these photographs were taken by Manuel Gutiérrez Paredes, who was a government photographer. As a result, none of the images had been censored and they therefore provided some of the most stunning images.

38 Andrea Noble, 'Recognizing Historical Injustice through Photography: Mexico 1968', *Theory, Culture & Society* 27, 7–8 (2010): 184–213.

39 Olmos, 'Vivieron para contarlo'.

40 Giles Tremlett and Jo Tuckman, 'Mexican Police Exposed as Killers', *The Guardian* (UK), 11 December 2001, 11.

41 Ginger Thompson, 'Flashback to Deadly Clash of '68 Shakes Mexico: Photographs Show Abuse of Students', *New York Times*, 13 December 2001, A3.

42 *El Mundo*, 9 December 2001, cited in 'Prensa extranjera: reacciones e impresiones', *Proceso*, 16 December 2001, 12.

## EPILOGUE

1 International Olympic Committee, *Olympic Marketing Fact File 2020 Edition*, updated January 2020, https://stillmed.olympic.org/media/Document%20Library/OlympicOrg/Documents/IOC-Marketing-and-Broadcasting-General-Files/Olympic-Marketing-Fact-File.pdf.

2 'Address of Mr. Avery Brundage, President of the IOC, at the Opening of the 73rd IOC Session in Munich'.

3 Christopher Dobson and Ronald Payne, *The Carlos Complex: A Pattern of Violence* (London: Hodder and Stoughton), 1977, 16.

4 Jim McKay, *The Real McKay: My Wide World of Sports* (New York: Dutton, 1998), 16.

5 David Hirst, *The Gun and the Olive Branch: The Roots of Violence in the Middle East* (London: Faber & Faber, 1977), 311.

6 Guttmann, *The Games Must Go On*, 254.

7 Hartmann, *Race, Culture, and the Black Athlete*, 19.

8 Neil Amdur, 'Matthews and Collett Banned From Olympics', *New York Times*, 9 September 1972, 17.

9 Dmitriy Rogovitskiy, 'Sochi Games Protest? Russian Snowboarder not Saying', *Reuters*, 7 February 2014, https://www.reuters.com/article/us-olympics-snowboarder-pussyriot/sochi-games-protest-russian-snowboarder-not-saying-idUSBREA1516V20140206.

10 Todd Gitlin, *The Sixties: Years of Hope, Days of Rage* (New York: Bantam Books, 1993), 420.

11 Tom Wolfe, 'The Me Decade and the Third Great Awakening', *New York Magazine* 23, 8 (1976): 26–40.

12 Tim Nudd, 'Brand Phelps', *Adweek* 57, 41 (12 December 2016): 14–17.

13 External protesters were at the 1976 Montreal Games. Ukrainian activists protested outside Olympic venues, insisting that Ukrainian athletes compete under their flag rather than that of the Soviet Union. While 2006 marked the first large-scale protests targeting sponsors, there had been earlier protests. At the Calgary Winter Olympics in 1998, members and supporters of the Lubicon Cree First Nation staged protests against oil mining in their ancestral lands during the 18,000-kilometre torch relay around Canada. At the 1988 Seoul Games, anti-China demonstrators lobbed stones at the torch bearers before the police intervened. The first major protest specifically targeted at an Olympic sponsor occurred at the Beijing Olympic Games.

14 Horst Stipp and Nicholas P. Schiavone, 'Modeling the Impact of Olympic Sponsorship on Corporate Image', *Journal of Advertising Research* 36, 4 (1996): 22–8.

15 Nela Șteliac, 'An Economic Approach to the Olympic Games: The Olympic Marketing Revenues', *EcoForum*, 6, 3 (2017).

16 International Olympic Committee, *Olympic Marketing Fact File 2020*.

17 Filip Bondy, 'IOC Pressured to Make Beijing a Forbidden City', *New York Times*, 21 April 1993, B18.

18 Liam Stockdale, 'More Than Just Games: The Global Politics of the Olympic Movement', *Sport in Society* 15, 6 (2012): 839–54.

19 There were also protests about China's role in selling arms to belligerents in Sudan, and blaming it for contributing to the ethnic cleansing in Darfur. Although not wishing to downplay these protests, I have narrowed the focus of this chapter to the protests over Tibet.

20 Stephanie Clifford, 'Tibet Backers Show China Value of PR', *New York Times*, 14 April 2008, C1.

21 Nicholas Paphitis, 'Protests Mar Olympic Ceremony', *The Post-Star* (Glens-Falls, NY), 25 March 2008, A3.

22 'Sound Bites', *San Francisco Examiner*, 11 April 2008, A19.

23 John J. MacAloon, 'Introduction: The Olympic Flame Relay. Local Knowledges of a Global Ritual Form', in *Bearing Light: Flame Relays and the Struggle for the Olympic Movement*, ed. John J. MacAloon (Abingdon, UK: Routledge, 2013).

24 John Horne and Garry Whannel, 'The "Caged Torch Procession": Celebrities, Protesters and the 2008 Olympic Torch Relay in London, Paris and San Francisco', *Sport in Society* 13, 5 (2010): 760–70.

25  Carol Emert, 'Olympic Seal of Approval: Advertisers Spend Millions to Bask in the Glow of the Games', *SFGate*, 2 September 2000, https://www.sfgate.com/business/article/OLYMPIC-SEAL-OF-APPROVAL-Advertisers-spend-2741013.php.

26  Stephanie Clifford, 'Coca-Cola Faces Critics of Its Olympics Support: Activism over China's Treatment of Tibet', *New York Times*, 17 April 2008, C3.

27  Jacquelin Magnay, 'Olympic Movement Provides a Mirror on China: Rogge', *The Age* (Australia), 28 July 2008, Sport 17.

28  International Olympic Committee, *IOC Marketing Media Guide: Beijing 2008* (Lausanne: IOC Marketing Department, 2008), 8.

29  International Olympic Committee, *Factsheet: Beijing Facts & Figures*, August 2009 update, https://www.olympic.org/olympic-legacy/~/media/A8264DD681D34B459B026CBD6FFD4D78.ashx.

# Index